Harry Potter's
Bookshelf

Harry Potter's Bookshelf

The Great Books Behind the Hogwarts Adventures

John Granger

BERKLEY BOOKS, NEW YORK

THE BERKLEY PUBLISHING GROUP
Published by the Penguin Group
Penguin Group (USA) Inc.
375 Hudson Street, New York, New York 10014, USA
Penguin Group (Canada), 90 Eglinton Avenue East, Suite 700, Toronto, Ontario M4P 2Y3, Canada
(a division of Pearson Penguin Canada Inc.)
Penguin Books Ltd., 80 Strand, London WC2R 0RL, England
Penguin Group Ireland, 25 St. Stephen's Green, Dublin 2, Ireland (a division of Penguin Books Ltd.)
Penguin Group (Australia), 250 Camberwell Road, Camberwell, Victoria 3124, Australia
(a division of Pearson Australia Group Pty. Ltd.)
Penguin Books India Pvt. Ltd., 11 Community Centre, Panchsheel Park, New Delhi—110 017, India
Penguin Group (NZ), 67 Apollo Drive, Rosedale, North Shore 0632, New Zealand
(a division of Pearson New Zealand Ltd.)
Penguin Books (South Africa) (Pty.) Ltd., 24 Sturdee Avenue, Rosebank, Johannesburg 2196,
South Africa

Penguin Books Ltd., Registered Offices: 80 Strand, London WC2R 0RL, England

This book is an original publication of The Berkley Publishing Group.

This book is not authorized, prepared, approved, licensed, or endorsed by J. K. Rowling, Warner Bros., or any other individual or entity associated with the HARRY POTTER books or movies. HARRY POTTER® is a registered trademark of Time Warner Entertainment Company, L.P. HARRY POTTER® is a registered trademark of Warner Bros.

The publisher does not have any control over and does not assume any responsibility for author or third-party websites or their content.

PRINTING HISTORY
Berkley trade paperback edition / July 2009

Library of Congress Cataloging-in-Publication Data

Granger, John, 1961–
  Harry Potter's bookshelf : the great books behind the Hogwarts adventures /
John Granger. — Berkley trade pbk. ed.
    p. cm.
  Includes bibliographical references.
  ISBN 978-0-425-22979-8
  1. Rowling, J. K.—Knowledge—Literature.   2. Rowling, J. K.—Sources.
3. Rowling, J. K.—Themes, motives.   4. Potter, Harry (Fictitious character)   I. Title.

  PR6068.O93Z676 2009
  823'.914—dc22

                                                          2009011708

PRINTED IN THE UNITED STATES OF AMERICA

10 9 8 7 6 5 4 3 2 1

Most Berkley Books are available at special quantity discounts for bulk purchases for sales promotions, premiums, fund-raising, or educational use. Special books, or book excerpts, can also be created to fit specific needs.

For details, write: Special Markets, The Berkley Publishing Group, 375 Hudson Street, New York, New York 10014.

Contents

Part Two: The Moral Meaning

Part Three: The Allegorical Meaning

Part Four: The Mythic or Anagogical Meaning

Harry Potter's Bookshelf

What This Book Tries to Do and How
You Can Get the Most Out of It

This is the fourth book I've written on *Harry Potter*, believe it or not, and, as in all the others, my e-mail address is at the end of the introduction with an invitation asking you to write to me with your comments and corrections. The only real compensation for being a Potter Pundit is conversation with serious readers like you about books you love and the ideas you have—and I have been richly compensated with conversation and far-flung friendships. I hope very much that you will write to me to share your thoughts as you read and when you finish reading this book.

The most common request I get in my in-box is for "further

reading." A common ambition of the books I have written is answering the question, "Why are the *Harry Potter* books so popular?" and my response is always a variation on "It's the literary artistry that engages and transforms readers that is the real magic of the books." That answer involves discussing the usual English literature topics like narratological voice and setting, as well as the more bizarre and less well-known devices and story scaffolding that Ms. Rowling uses, like literary alchemy and vision symbolism.

Take alchemy as an example. The requests I get for "further reading" are for books that use literary alchemy as Ms. Rowling does (Shakespeare's *Romeo and Juliet*, *Perelandra* by C. S. Lewis, Dickens's *A Tale of Two Cities*) and for books about literary alchemy per se (*Darke Hieroglyphicks* by Stanton Linden, Lyndy Abraham's *A Dictionary of Alchemical Imagery*). These requests, which I get from serious readers, as well as from teachers, students, and librarians, usually come with one note of delight about understanding and experiencing an unexpected dimension of storytelling and another note of disappointment that their studies hadn't ever mentioned something that spans English literature from *Canterbury Tales* to *Harry Potter*.

I taught a *Harry Potter* online course from 2003 to 2005 and started writing this book then because of the interest expressed in learning more about *Harry Potter* as English literature. My hope at that time was to write a fun and inviting text that would simultaneously open up the meaning and magic of Ms. Rowling's novels while revealing how much of her artistry has its roots in the traditions of great writing. That hope continues to be the heart of what *Harry Potter's Bookshelf* tries to do.

Writing *Bookshelf* has been, to risk a cliché, a labor of love. It has also been more than a little frustrating over the years it has taken to put it together, with stops and starts to work on other projects. The big problems I ran into were selection and organization. I knew, for instance, that the book would have ten chapters from the first time I outlined it. There are ten genres that the author "rowls" together seamlessly from hero's journey and alchemical drama, to satire and Christian fantasy. But how was I to select what specific authors and works to choose and leave out? Certainly I'd be obliged to include the five or six authors and books Ms. Rowling has mentioned in ten years of interviews as important influences on her work, but what about those subjects she rarely if ever mentioned?

Taking alchemy again for illustration, Ms. Rowling said in 1998 that she read a boatload of books on alchemy before she started writing *Harry Potter* and that it sets the magical parameters and logic of the books. She hasn't been asked or said a word about it since, so your guess is almost as good as mine about what books she read and which alchemical authors she found helpful and meaningful. Shakespeare? Dickens?

Charles Williams? Blake? Yeats? The Metaphysical Poets? That's quite a range.

And Ms. Rowling has mentioned quite a few authors and books that she loves that I don't think influenced her writing of the *Harry Potter* adventure stories as much as others she hasn't mentioned or downplays when asked. She has said more than once that her "big three" favorites are "Nabokov, Collette, and Austen"; that her favorite living writer is Rodney Doyle;[1] and that she loved Noel Streatfield's *Ballet Shoes*, Paul Gallico's *Manxmouse*,[2] Clement Freud's *Grimble*,[3] and Roald Dahl's books. Jane Austen overshadows much of Ms. Rowling's work certainly (see chapter two), but Lewis and Tolkien, with whom Ms. Rowling has a bizarre love-hate relationship, are obvious influences in a way Nabokov and Collette are not, and Jonathan Swift, whom Ms. Rowling hasn't mentioned, is a bigger part of *Harry* than Doyle or Clement Freud, acknowledged or not.

It may strike you as a bit snooty and bizarre not to focus just on the authors Ms. Rowling has mentioned in interviews (Nabakov, Collette, etc.), but *Harry Potter's Bookshelf* is not *Joanne Rowling's Library*—and the author herself has made it clear that she is skeptical about tracking point-to-point influences from her reading list and history. It isn't a mechanical one-way process, in which the writer reads a book, enjoys it, and writes a book very much like the first. As she says, it's a more organic, human thing than that.

Speaking with *Writer's Digest* in February 2000, she listed several authors she admired but added quickly, "But as for being influenced by them . . . I think it [may be] more accurate to say that they represent untouchable ideals to me. It is impossible for me to say what my influences are; I don't analyze my own writing in that way."[4] In an interview with Amazon in 1999, though, she explained that "it is always hard to tell what your influences are. Everything you've seen, experienced, read, or heard gets broken down like compost in your head and then your own ideas grow out of that compost."[5] Writers read books, and the best writers, like Ms. Rowling, have read voraciously, profoundly, and widely. These books, as she says, don't mechanically become models for the writers' stories. They become the soil out of which the seeds of the author's talent and ideas can grow. The richer and more fertile the soil, the more the talent and ideas will flourish and blossom. The greater the talent and ideas, the more nutrients will be drawn from the rich soil and the more delicious and refreshing will be the fruits from this tree and vine.

My job in selection, consequently, has meant less sifting through the historical record to find things Ms. Rowling has admitted reading and liking and more exploring the various streams of the English literary tradition in which she lives and writes. That meant, inevitably, making controversial inclusions and omissions; I look forward to reading your thoughts on my biggest blunders and better catches. (Before you write to share your disappointment, yes, I wish I could have included Tennyson, Chesterton, and more Dante and Shakespeare!) The selection argument is one of the more powerful engines of the "Potter as literature" conversation, and I'm not offering my choices as anything but a fresh beginning to that discussion.

Organization of the choices I have made, as I mentioned, fell naturally into ten genre and story element divisions based on those Ms. Rowling uses. I decided fairly late in the assembly of the book, though, not to write this up as simply "Here are the choices Ms. Rowling makes for setting (or voice or allegory, etc.) with the most important historical giants that are echoed in her books." Not only would that be a boring book to write, it wouldn't challenge readers who want to gain a larger perspective on what literature is and what reading does to them. I decided, consequently, in addition to producing a book that simultaneously opens up both *Harry Potter* and English literature, using one as key to the other, to try to provide a model for thinking about great books and to provoke you with a controversial thesis about the intention of a large part of better literature. I'm confident that most readers will find the model and thesis helpful, if only because they will define the field of battle for spirited disagreement.

There are books available online and at your local bookstore that offer to help you learn *How to Read Literature Like a Professor* or *How Fiction Works*, and I don't doubt that there is great value in these guides. I suggest, though, that such introductions do more to take us *out of* our reading experience for objective knowledge rather than *deeper into* that experience for our transformation. I wonder, too, if books like this do more than confirm the prejudices and blind spots of our age, i.e., how we think already.

The thousands of *Harry Potter* readers I have met and spoken or corresponded with during the last nine years love the books because of the way the meaning resonates within them. They want to learn more about Ms. Rowling's artistry, not for credits toward a general studies or English degree but to understand and amp up that experience. Postmodern aesthetic surveys or deconstruction exercises throw a wet blanket on the fire driving their transformation. Yeats is supposed to have said that education is lighting a fire not filling a bucket; the model and thesis of *Bookshelf* are kindling for the fire rather than just more information for your cranial data files.

The model I've chosen is what Northrop Frye called the iconological school of literary criticism. In a nutshell, we'll be looking at *Harry Potter* as a text like all great art with four layers of meaning: the surface, the moral, the allegorical, and the anagogical or spiritual. *Bookshelf*'s chapters are divided into four sections corresponding to these layers. Voice, drive, and setting, for example, are the subjects of the surface meaning section in the first few chapters and in which I discuss the important influence of Jane Austen, Dorothy Sayers, and Enid Blyton on Ms. Rowling's surface meanings.

The controversial aspect of iconological layered reading, and the reason it has largely disappeared from the modern academy, for instance, despite being the default model until the twentieth century, is that it assumes writers are writing for the readers' edifying transformation rather than for pure, mindless entertainment. That books work to "baptize the imagination"—to overturn our mistaken view of reality—is the heart of iconological criticism.

Which brings me to the thesis I offer for your consideration and our continuing conversation. What I found when reading the authors featured in this book was that they were writing on multiple levels, certainly, and that they had a larger purpose in writing than storytelling for storytelling's sake. I think this diverse group of writers, from Austen to Lewis, from E. Nesbit to Elizabeth Goudge, were writing with a shared, subversive purpose that Ms. Rowling has picked up and run with. In brief, beginning with Swift's Ancients versus Moderns "Battle of the Books," and defined largely by the natural theology of Samuel Taylor Coleridge and the Romantic vision, great writers seem to believe that materialism and reductive thinking are dehumanizing, and thus are arguing against and undermining by parable the modern materialist worldview. Austen is dueling David Hume, Gothic writers like Shelley and Stoker the amorality of science, and Goudge and Lewis with their unicorns and lions campaign as Platonic idealists and Christians against the empiricists and Marxists of our age. The better poets, playwrights, and novelists, in brief, of the last few centuries have been waging an under-the-radar war to "baptize the imagination" and overturn our mistaken view of reality.

So, how then can you get the most out of this book? First, take a look at the table of contents to see how the four sections correspond with the four layers of meaning in iconological criticism and how I've divided up the ten genres and tools Ms. Rowling weaves into the Hogwarts adventures. You can start anywhere you want, of course, though the book was written to be read front to back as the argument builds to the finish in chapter ten.

Next, I hope you'll take notes while you're reading of examples you think are better than the ones I chose or which contradict my thesis. I make the case that Ms. Rowling is only the most recent warrior in the centuries-old subversive resistance to Dursley-an "normalcy" and conventional materialism and scientism. I do not believe for a minute that my argument is in any way final or demonstrative. It is meant to be only engaging, perhaps even goading, to stimulate you to think about what reading does to us and what layered meanings writers are sharing with readers who are willing to do the "slow mining" and meditative reflection to get at the subversive, spiritual heart of better books. That mining and meditation may draw you out of the story occasionally, but we won't, as Wordsworth says in his poem *The Tables Turned*, "murder to dissect" or deconstruct. The step back will only be to enter the books again and, as Lewis's heroes in *The Last Battle* chant as they enter paradise, to rush "further up and further in." I'm hopeful that both the iconological model I provide and the thesis I use to provoke your thinking will help you have a more profound and rewarding experience of Harry's adventures and apotheosis.

I hope, too, as I said, that you'll write and tell me what you think or just join in the conversation serious readers like you have already been enjoying online at HogwartsProfessor. com. Thank you for purchasing and reading this book, and, in advance, for your correspondence, comments, corrections, and questions.

Gratefully,

John Granger
John@HogwartsProfessor.com

PART ONE

The Surface Meaning

CHAPTER ONE

Narrative Drive and Genre: Why We Keep Turning the Pages

Harry Potter as a Dickens Orphan and the Hero in a Sayers Mystery

In this literary companion to Harry Potter I'm attempting Olympian multitasking, as we descend layer by layer from the surface meaning down to the more profound depths of *Harry Potter*. Starting at the surface, we're obliged to be clear about what specific tools Ms. Rowling chose to tell her story because her decisions about how to move the plot along, the voice in which to tell the story, as well as the stage setting for the drama determine in large part how much any reader will be engaged enough to read the book. As counterpoint to that discussion, I'll talk about other authors and the books in which they made similar decisions, immersing us in English literature via *Harry Potter*.

To begin, let's talk about what genre the *Potter* novels fall into. It turns out they don't have one. Believe it or not, there are at least ten different types of stories being told in the *Harry Potter* novels. If it hadn't been confirmed by reporters and biographers, I would suspect Ms. Rowling's surname was a cryptonym, as are so many of her characters' names. Her books are a gathering together of schoolboy stories, hero's journey epics, alchemical drama, manners-and-morals fiction, satire, gothic romance, detective mysteries, adventure tales, coming-of-age novels, and Christian fantasy.

So how do we know where to start? Well, one easy way is to figure out what keeps you turning the pages. Literature professors call this the *narrative drive*, but you can think of it as the novel's conveyor belt. When we think about Harry and his adventures, what is it that moves us along from page to page to learn how the story turns out?

Despite our fascination with Hermione's love choices (Ron or Harry?), the Potter epic is not the boy-meets-girl, boy-loses-girl, lovers-unite romance formula. It's also not a hero's epic: We are not caught up in mythic history, as we are in the *Aeneid* and *The Lord of the Rings*, in which we travel along to learn Aeneas's and Frodo's fates and their ultimate destinations.

We have some idea of what Ms. Rowling thinks about the stories she has written because of the following comments made in an interview with two very young fan-website leaders in 2005:

> *There's a theory—this applies to detective novels, and then Harry, which is not really a detective novel, but it feels like one sometimes—that you should not have romantic intrigue in a detective book. Dorothy L. Sayers, who is queen of the genre, said—and then broke her own rule, but said—that there is no place for romance in a detective story except that it can be useful to camouflage other people's motives. That's true; it is a very useful trick. I've used that on Percy and I've used that to a degree on Tonks in this book, as a red herring. But having said that, I disagree inasmuch as mine are very character-driven books, and it's so important, therefore, that we see these characters fall in love, which is a necessary part of life.[1]*

Ms. Rowling says her *Harry Potter* epic is "not really a detective novel, but it feels like one sometimes." With respect to how the story works and what keeps us turning pages, however, it certainly is a detective mystery. Exploring how Harry's years at Hogwarts are and are not formula mysteries will introduce us to a wonderful (and currently neglected) writer of detective fiction and point us to the second power driving the conveyor belt of Ms. Rowling's stories.

Hercule Poirot, Meet Harry Potter

There is a simple formula for detective fiction and accepted rules by which most writers abide. Tess Gerritsen tells us the crime novel detective formula: "A crime is committed. An investigator seeks out the truth. The truth is revealed."[2] In the classic formula from the Golden Age of Detective Fiction, essentially the first fifty years of the twentieth century, this involves an English country estate, characters from the Edwardian minor gentry, a murder, a brilliant detective, stumbling policemen, and a drawing room finale in which the whodunit is resolved with an explanation of the hows and whys, not to mention a confrontation with and the confession of the guilty party ("Colonel Mustard in the library with the revolver!"). *The Mysterious Affair at Stiles* and *The Murder at the Vicarage*, the mysteries in which Agatha Christie introduced Hercule Poirot and Miss Marple, respectively, are mysteries of this type.

Harry Potter is clearly not a mystery according to this Country Estate murder formula, but it does hold to the narrative drive elements of a good mystery well told. Those elements are reader mystification, the detection of cause, and restoration of order.[3]

From Poe to Chandler

From Poe to Chandler, the characters and action of mysteries are largely the same. We are given a disturbing, seemingly insoluble situation, usually involving a murder, preferably in a closed room in which the murderer could not have entered or exited. The essential players are the detective, the individual who needs his help (often but not always the one accused of the crime or not satisfied with the official explanation of it), the victim, and the criminal, with a supporting cast of Dr. Watsons and incompetent, empiricist gendarmes. The insoluble problem is set, the narrator presents the clues, the detective resolves the mystery, the criminal is confronted in a dramatic denouement, and the moral order returns to one degree or another.[4]

The essential part of this formula with respect to its ability to keep us turning pages, however, doesn't involve the players or the murder. It is our confusion. We are engaged first and foremost by the *mystery* involved, the insoluble puzzle confronting us. Our desire to learn what we don't understand, how what couldn't have happened did in fact actually happen, not to mention why it happened, all but drags us headlong into and through the story—from beginning to resolution.

Harry Potter's adventures do not feature a private detective like Sam Spade, Sherlock Holmes, or Poe's Auguste Dupin. Every year at Hogwarts, though, a puzzle or mystery unfolds that Harry, Ron, and Hermione team up to solve. One by one:

* In *Sorcerer's Stone*, the U.S. title, the trio are desperate to learn about what Hagrid picked up at Gringott's bank and brought to Hogwarts. Most of the story turns on their search for the Stone and the identity of Nicolas Flamel.

* In *Chamber of Secrets*, Harry is all but accused of being the Heir of Slytherin responsible for the mysterious attacks on Hogwarts students. The gang teams up again to discover who really is the Heir and the location of the Chamber.

* *Prisoner of Azkaban*'s mystery is the identity, location, and "crime" of Sirius Black.

* Harry's agonies in *Goblet of Fire* during the three tasks of the Triwizard Tournament are all consequent to his mystification about who put his name into the Goblet and why they would have done it.

* *Order of the Phoenix* turns on both the dementor attack on Harry and Dudley in Little Whinging and the visions Harry has of a corridor ending in a door that fascinate him sufficiently that he does not shield his mind from them—with tragic consequences.

*   The mystery of *Half-Blood Prince* is the question of who the "Half-Blood Prince" is or was.

*   And the series finale's puzzle, besides the question of what sort of man Albus Dumbledore really was, is how the trio understands the "triangular eye" Hallows symbol correctly and why Dumbledore left them this puzzle to solve.

Harry, as we'll see in chapter two, is anything but the razor-sharp incarnation of deduction and induction that we look for in heroic detectives or even sad sacks like Columbo. For the most part, as earnest as he is in the search for clues and answers with Ron and Hermione, our boy hero is at least as clueless as the mystery formula's affable sidekick-narrator and as often as not is the suspect of the crime or the aggrieved party seeking relief—hence Ms. Rowling's assertion that *Harry* is "not really a detective novel, but it feels like one sometimes," as well as her mention of Dorothy Sayers and her belief that her stories differ from detective novels in being character driven. The detective fiction of Dorothy Sayers is the mystery model for Ms. Rowling's work precisely because of the depth of the development of her characters.

Dorothy Sayers: Rule Maker, Rule Breaker

Dorothy Sayers's mysteries featuring Lord Peter Wimsey have fallen out of popular taste today, but during her lifetime she was famous for her detective fiction. Her Peter Wimsey work includes fourteen volumes of novels and short stories, but Sayers was also known for her work with the Detection Club. The detective writers' equivalent of the more celebrated Inklings, the Detection Club had members who were the brighter lights of the age, including G. K. Chesterton, the club's first president, and Agatha Christie, president for nearly twenty years. Sayers was a founding member and a club president, too, from 1949 to 1958, and it was in this role that Ms. Rowling probably thinks of her as a detection rule maker.

The Detection Club's rules are the definition of the classical formula. They prohibit any concealing of essential clues, any servant murderers, or unimaginative mystery clichés like an unknown evil twin, the dog who does not bark, and "the bogus spiritualistic séance to frighten the culprit into giving himself away."[5]

The Detection Club's idea of the detective fiction puzzle is essentially that it must be a fair puzzle and just about the puzzle. Hence:

A detective novel should contain no long descriptive passages, no literary dallying with side-issues, no subtly worked-out charac-

ter analyses, no "atmospheric" preoccupations. Such matters have no vital place in a record of crime and deduction. They hold up the action, and introduce issues irrelevant to the main purpose, which is to state a problem, analyze it, and bring it to a successful conclusion. To be sure, there must be a sufficient descriptiveness and character delineation to give the novel verisimilitude.[6]

Sayers, however, thinks there can be more to good mystery writing and that the formula as proposed by the Detection Club is ultimately limiting.

We also took occasion to preach at every opportunity that if the detective story was to live and develop it must get back to where it began in the hands of [Wilkie] Collins and [Sheridan] Le Fanu, and become once more a novel of manners instead of a pure cross-word puzzle. My voice was raised very loudly to proclaim this doctrine, because I still meant my books to develop along those lines at all costs and it does no harm to let one's theory act as a herald to one's practice.[7]

Which, of course, means "no romance." As Wright requires in Rule #3:

There must be no love interest. The business in hand is to bring a criminal to the bar of justice, not to bring a lovelorn couple to the hymeneal altar.[8]

Sayers, however, thinks that Collins is the model for good mystery writing and that the formula as proposed by Wright is ultimately "a literature without bowels"[9] and the last thing she wanted to be writing. She prefaced her Wimsey play, *Busman's Honeymoon*, consequently, with this apology for its romantic interest:

> It has been said, by myself and others, that a love interest is only an intrusion upon a detective story. But to the characters involved, the detective intrusion might well seem an irritating intrusion upon their love-story. This book deals with such a situation.[10]

Ms. Rowling is correct in saying that Dorothy Sayers breaks the "no romance in detective fiction" rule but not in saying that she "broke her own rule"; it was Wright's rule and the Detection Club's, not hers. And this is no small thing because J. K. Rowling breaks the strict rules of mystery fiction for precisely the same reason as Sayers did: for the sake of full-blooded characters rather than cardboard cutouts or Clue board game figurines. Sayers is known, in fact, as a "character-driven" mystery writer and this is what distinguishes her from the more formulaic whodunit writers of the Golden Age, like Agatha Christie and John Dickson Carr.

J. K. Rowling shares the outlook and much of the experience of Sayers. For starters, both had a classical education with modern language studies at university, a spell of single motherhood, and remarkable if not proselytizing Christian faith. To that mix add, as I'll argue in later chapters for Rowling, a taste for Dante, hermetic writing, and a penchant for delivering layers of meaning in stories that on the surface are light reads for diversion. At least half the narrative drive in the *Harry Potter* novels comes from the mystery Harry, Ron, and Hermione are trying to solve. Ms. Rowling follows Ms. Sayers's lead in using the genre and its formulas only until such obedience to literary convention makes it harder to deliver the story's intended meaning.

* * *

What sort of meaning was Sayers smuggling into her stories? A sacramental worldview, certainly, from her upbringing and education as an Oxford Platonist and "an existence on a totally different plane," a non-local eternity within mundane reality but invisible to Muggles:

> One must remember that though in one sense the Other World was a definite place, somewhere beyond the Atlantic Ocean, yet in another the kingdom of gods was within one. Earth and fairy-land coexist upon the same foot of ground. *It was all a matter of the seeing eye* . . . The dweller in this world can become aware of an existence on a totally different plane. To go from Earth to faery is like passing from this time to eternity; it is not a journey in space, but a change in mental outlook.[11] (Emphasis added.)

Remember "the seeing eye" and the Oxford Platonists; we'll be running into them repeatedly as we work through Rowling's greater influences to get to the many "seeing eyes" in *Deathly Hallows*. It is the heart of the subversive attack of Romantic writers in English literature on the soulless scientism of the modern era.

As mentioned above, the mystery element is "at least half" of the narrative drive of the *Harry Potter* novels. Ms. Rowling gives us the clue we need to find the missing half that powers her literary conveyor belt. She points to it in her claim that Harry's adventures are less mystery than "character-driven books." What is it about the lead character that keeps us reading through books that are up to eight hundred pages long? It cannot be romance; Harry's romantic life doesn't begin in earnest until *Phoenix*, the fifth book, and *Half-Blood Prince*, the sixth book.

It's not anything Harry says, has, or does; it's what Harry *is*. An orphan.

Loveable Underdog

When I first got out of college, I taught Latin at a small prep school in western North Carolina called the Asheville School. I think it was there I first heard a teacher say, "They won't care how much you know 'til they know how much you care." It's true in the classroom and on the playing field with high-school age students, certainly, but it also is something of a guideline for writers. Until the reader cares about the characters in the story, really identifies with them, drops the disbelief, and experiences the story as if he or she had passed through the looking glass into Wonderland, nothing else matters.

Write majestic prose like Philip Pullman or J. R. R. Tolkien. Baptize the imagination like Bunyan, Spencer, and Lewis. Create locked-door and chilling mysteries like John Dickson Carr and Edgar Allan Poe. If the reader doesn't care for the character involved like he or she would for a dear family member in need (assuming the reader isn't at war with his or her family . . .), it won't matter. No one will read the book to its finish.

Beyond believability, then, an author has to do whatever is possible to get the reader on board with the characters. There are tricks that can be done with narratological voice. As we'll see in the next chapter, choosing to tell the story in the "third person limited omniscient" view—sitting on a character's shoulder and sharing his or her perspective—fosters sympathy. Another way to grab the reader by the heart is to trigger the trip wire tied to the reader's sense of fairness or justice. This is the "gotcha" of mystery writing, truth be told. When presented with a crime and a messy set of clues, not to mention the stray corpse or two, our conscience flashes a red light, especially if there is someone unjustly accused or a murderer escaping without punishment. I don't know if we are hard-wired this way (I suspect we are) or if this is a conditioned response from childhood training. Whatever the cause, it's a rare reader who doesn't want to have the pieces to the puzzle assembled and justice served for the innocent and the guilty. Who won't read to the very end to learn the solution and hear the confession of the bad guy?

Take this one step further and you have Rocky (the boxer, not the squirrel). Readers love the underdog, the nobody who fights all odds and comes out on top. The traction of this kind of story is in our immediate sympathy for the little guy, the disadvantaged person, the poor, the minority, and the disenfranchised. Unless the marginalized protagonist is a real loser, just the fact that he or she lives on the periphery, outside of an in crowd, means the reader will wave pom-poms on the sidelines of the playing field.

No one gets this better than Ms. Rowling: All of her good guys are misfits. Hermione is a Mudblood. Ron and the Weasleys are dirt poor and blood traitors. Hagrid is a half-giant. Sirius is an escaped prisoner and convicted murderer looking at a Dementor's Kiss first thing if he is caught. Remus? Werewolf. Tonks? Metamorphmagus. Firenze is a friendly centaur who might as well have a red shiny nose like Rudolph. Mad-Eye has gone round the twist with "constant vigilance." Mundungus is a thief and coward. Severus . . . well, where do you start with the Potions Master? Dumbledore seemed the only Boy Scout in his army but we learn in *Deathly Hallows* he has a Machiavellian streak as big as the Room of Requirement.

You get the picture. All the bad guys are pureblood psychopaths, too, or over the top in pursuit of power. But they are *normal* in terms of fitting in with every accepted convention. Like the Dursleys, they take conformity steroids and are on constant watch for folks who are different just in order to despise them. Why do we hate their guts? And I mean really despise them, however hypocritical, for their despising our misfit heroes?

One of the core beliefs of our times is that "prejudice is evil," the flip side of which is that "tolerance is good." I'll come back to this in chapter six but, for now, just remember that Ms. Rowling, by celebrating the underdog, is playing what politicians call the "identity card."

The Ultimate Underdog:
The Dickensian Orphan

Ms. Rowling, though, doesn't just make Harry a sympathetic character or underdog to win your sympathy and enlist you in his cause. She pulls the ultimate empathy-winning card in English literature and plays it to the hilt. Harry Potter is an orphan, and, not only does he not have loving parents, he is saddled with relations who are almost unbelievably cruel to him. Game. Set. Match. Every reader not on heavy medication for psychoactive disorders is on Harry's side and wants the Dursleys locked up in the room under the stairs.

Quite simply, there is no one to care for the orphan. The reader can step right in, at least imaginatively, and do the human, caring, right thing—namely, adopt and embrace him as one of our own. He has no one, so we identify him as one of us.

If you struggle to see this and imagine I'm overstating the importance of Harry being an orphan in our engagement with his story and this fascination carrying us through his oversized adventures, I plead "Dickens." A finalist in any "greatest novelist of all time competition"—not one of whose books has ever gone out of print—Charles Dickens changed the English novel almost single-handedly from gentry diversion to popular entertainment, agency for social change and personal transformation, and vehicle of profound meaning.

And he did all that with orphan novels.

✳ ✳ ✳

From *Oliver Twist* (1837) to *David Copperfield* (1849) to Pip in *Great Expectations* (1860), Dickens created orphans who won readers' hearts. In fact, if you survey Dickens's complete portfolio, you find sixteen leading-role characters in the fifteen novels without surviving parents or parents known to them, two novels featuring title characters with only one parent, and only Dickens's first book, *The Pickwick Papers,* an ad hoc collection of stories, does not feature an orphan or a neglected and estranged child.

I want to come back to Dickens and his influence on Rowling in chapter nine, where we'll cover Shakespeare, Dickens, and alchemical drama with a close look at *A Tale of Two Cities.* Here, though, we need only note the importance and impact of Ms. Rowling's choice to follow Dickens's lead and write an orphan novel. It is so much a part of Harry—the first thing other than "boy wizard" we remember about Harry—that the meaning and effect of his being an orphan is neglected. Harry's orphan status, like the meaning of his remarkable name (see chapter nine), is overlooked for being hidden in plain sight.

Harry's helplessness as an orphan left on the Privet Drive doorstep of the Dursleys and their borderline sadistic treatment of him lock in our sympathy and our curiosity about how he will turn out. In this fashion, Ms. Rowling has fixed a ring in our noses and can lead us anywhere she likes. She wants to give us the experience of watching Harry grow up with all the attendant changes of adolescence and young adulthood. As she said in a 2001 interview about the differences between Harry's adventures and other children's literature:

> *A problem you run into with a series is how the characters grow up . . . whether they're allowed to grow up.*

I want Harry Potter and his friends to grow up as well as older, though I'll keep it all humorous, well within the tone of the books. I want them eventually to be truly seventeen and discover girlfriends and boyfriends and have sexual feelings—nothing too gritty. Why not allow them to have those feelings?[12]

And we do see changes in Harry. In each book, as I'll explain in chapter nine, Harry goes through an alchemical transformation and the reader does, too, because of our identification with him. Ms. Rowling also delivers on her promise to show us the changes Harry, Ron, and Hermione experience as they grow older beyond their few snogging episodes. The depth of their studies, their growing awareness of the world and their responsibilities, and their heightened sense of injustice is handled masterfully so it is both believably realistic and light enough to be welcome change.

Story Type, Story Drive

I doubt very much that anyone would care much about Harry's growing pains from story to story, though, if the narrative drive didn't own our attention the way Class 5 rapids grab a canoe or kayak. This is why Ms. Rowling's decision about what sort of story she was going to write was as important as in what voice she would tell it. The story type sets the drive, which determines our engagement.

It's no accident that the most popular stories in English literature—the classic mystery, the orphan novels of Charles Dickens, and, now, the hybrid orphan-mystery of the *Harry Potter* adventures—use the most engaging drives. Drive is what gets us hooked and keeps those pages turning. The insoluble mystery that awakens our desire for revelation and resolution as well as our sense of injustice, combined with the ease and surety that an orphan novel uses to win our identification with and interest in a sympathetic character, is a story that acts as a conveyor belt in overdrive.

By understanding the importance of story drive—the first aspect of a story's surface meaning that draws us out of our ego concerns and into what Coleridge called the "primary imagination"[13] in which we can experience more profound meanings—we can begin to appreciate the difference the right choice of voice can make. Ms. Rowling's voice is taken from her favorite book and favorite author, it turns out. I hope you're sufficiently engaged by that mystery to go on to the next page.

CHAPTER TWO

Pride and Prejudice with Wands

*How Jane Austen Haunts the Heart
and Soul of Rowling's Artistry*

J. K. Rowling has said in many interviews that the single writer she admires most is Hollywood's hot property, a woman who never published a book in her own name, who died at forty-one, unmarried and childless, and whose books are anything but magical fantasy. This woman is Jane Austen, the parson's daughter and anonymous author of the world's favorite manners-and-morals novels.

Ms. Rowling has said she read Austen's *Emma* "at least twenty times" and that she "rereads Austen's novels in rotation."[1] If we didn't have Ms. Rowling's testimony in her interviews, the direct allusions in the text might be sufficient to bring us to the same conclusions about the importance of Jane Austen in understanding Harry Potter. The caretaker of Hogwarts Castle, Mr. Filch, has a cat named "Mrs. Norris," the name of a busybody aunt in Austen's *Mansfield Park*; Percy Weasley's letter to his brother Ron in *Order of the Phoenix*, in which he advises him to break off relations with Harry Potter (*Order of the Phoenix*, chapter fourteen), is almost dictated from Mr. Collins's letter to Mr. Bennet in *Pride and Prejudice*, in which Mr. Bennet is advised to "throw off your unworthy child from your affection forever" (*Pride*, chapter forty-eight). Mr. Knightley's comic change of heart about the villainous Frank Churchill as he learns that Emma will consider and accept Mr. Knightley's proposal of marriage (*Emma*, chapter forty-nine) is mirrored in Harry's change of heart about Cedric Diggory in *Goblet of Fire* (*Goblet of Fire*, chapter twenty-two).

Jane Austen is remembered for her style and for her message. Her style is an unaffected lightness that penetrates the surface and reveals the heart. Her message is a middle-class critique of the upper classes and the pride and prejudices that characterized this group. Though considered light satire, Austen's novels are an indictment of snobbery and affectation—and a celebration of right manners and morals—that can be both cutting and inspiring.

As different as Harry's magical education and Jane Austen's English countryside may be on the surface, Austen does reveal two big secrets in understanding Harry Potter, namely, narrative misdirection and the theme of "pride and prejudice." Rowling herself has said that Jane Austen's *Emma* ends with "the best twist ever in literature."[2]

Let's look at the "twist" Ms. Rowling employs and especially the choice in voice she makes that tricks the reader. This "twist" is what we recognize as the Rowling signature surprise ending—and she pulls it on us, as you might have guessed, exactly as did her mentor in *Emma*.

It's All a Matter of Perspective

The first five Harry Potter novels end in almost identical fashion. Before the trip to King's Cross Station on the Hogwarts Express, Harry does battle underground with an agent of the Dark Lord Voldemort himself, dies a figurative death, is saved by a symbol of Christ, and learns from Albus Dumbledore what really happened in that year's adventure. This denouement is usually a forehead-slapping experience.

"How did I miss that?" It is in this conversation between headmaster and disciple at story's end each year except the last that we learn alongside Harry about the good guy we'd thought was a bad guy and the bad guy (or gal) we'd thought was on the good guy's side (at least nominally). Every single year, it seems, we are suckered into believing what Harry believes—and find out how foolish we have been by book's end.

How we are hoodwinked or caught in Ms. Rowling's annual story twist is a plotting finesse that the author picked up from Jane Austen. The fundamental and most practical point of influence between Rowling and Austen is the perspective in which the *Harry Potter* novels are told and how this perspective lulls the passive reader into traveling down the erring path (and far away from the solution of the mystery).

Writers have choices. One of the first choices they have to make when beginning a story is the "voice" they will use when writing: Who will be telling the story? These are the two big options an author has when writing a novel: "Do I tell it from a narrator's experience of the tale à la Dr. Watson in the Sherlock Holmes cases? Or do I tell it as God sees it unfolding in time?" Open up any anthology of detective fiction and quickly check to see whether a story is told by a fictional narrator in the "I saw this" and "then we did that" perspective or if the story comes from the author in the role of an all-seeing God.

There are a few variants on these two options, of course, and the one relevant to our getting beneath the narrative surface of Harry Potter is the perspective in which Jane Austen wrote *Emma*. This particular "narratological voice" is called "third person *limited* omniscient view" and telling the story this way allows Ms. Rowling to pull off her stunning end-of-story surprises.

Think for a minute about how the *Potter* novels are told or flip open any of the books. With very few exceptions (most notably, the first chapter of the first book and the opening chapters of *Goblet of Fire*, *Half-Blood Prince*, and *Deathly Hallows*), the stories are told not from Harry's perspective talking like Dr. Watson: "Ron and Hermione and I then pushed our way through the door and saw a wild three-headed dog!" The stories aren't told by God floating above the Astronomy Tower, seeing and telling all: "Then Draco went back into the Room of Requirement to pick up where he left off on Vanishing Cabinet repair."

* * *

The perspective of these books splits the difference between the first person and third person omniscient perspectives. What this split means in practical terms is that we see all the action in the books as if there were a house-elf sitting on Harry's shoulder with a minicam. This obliging elf can also tell us everything Harry is thinking and feeling in addition to showing us what he sees around him. We don't see any more than Harry sees (hence the "limited" in limited omniscient), but because we're not restricted to Harry's narration, it *seems* as if we're seeing a larger bit of the story than if Harry just told it himself.

Emma is told from the same perspective, if we less obviously identify with Emma. The house-elf in this story is always in the room or on the grounds with Emma but isn't necessarily looking over her shoulder. (Sometimes we get to view the drama or conversation from the ceiling, for instance.) We do get to peer in her ear, however, and know her mind, so the effect on us is much the same, only even stronger than in Harry Potter. We think we're seeing everything because Emma isn't telling us the story, but what we're not seeing— namely, what is happening outside of Emma's view or of her understanding—is, alas, where the *real* story is happening.

This last bit of *seeming* is critical because it is our confusion on this point that allows for what literary geeks call "narrative misdirection." All "narrative misdirection" amounts to really is our being suckered into believing—because the story is not being told by Harry himself—that we are seeing the story as God (or as the omniscient, plotting writer) sees it. Of course this isn't the case, but over the course of the tale as we look down on Harry and friends (and enemies) from "on high"— even if "on high" means only from a few feet over Harry's head—we begin to think we have a larger perspective than we do.

* * *

This trick works because we like Harry and sympathize with him and his struggles. In short, we begin to identify with how Harry thinks and feels, and, because Harry is not telling the story, we think we have arrived at this position of sympathy and identification with the hero because of our unprejudiced view.

When you've arrived at this position—and, we all do—Rowling has you wrapped up. She can take you anywhere she wants to take you and make you think almost anything she wants about any character because, by and large, what Harry thinks is at this point what we believe.

Did you think Professor Snape was a servant of the Dark Lord in *Sorcerer's Stone*? I did. I swallowed Harry's conviction that Snape was evil and made it my own belief. I had all the information that pointed to Professor Quirrell as the black hat—Ms. Rowling plays by the rules—but I shelved that information as I rushed through the underground obstacles with Ron and Hermione in support of Harry to get to the Mirror of Erised and Snape. Severus, of course, wasn't there; and he turned out, in the world-turned-upside-down denouement (when Dumbledore tells us how God sees it . . .), to have been a white hat, despite appearances.

This was possible because of our identification with the orphan boy living under the stairs who was horribly mistreated by his aunt and uncle. We sympathized with him and took his view as our own, though it wasn't his view or an all-knowing one. Pretty embarrassing, but Ms. Rowling uses this same trick in every book—and nowhere more brilliantly than in *Half-Blood Prince*, which we will come back to shortly.

Reading *Emma*, the "best twist ever in literature," we're snookered the same way. Unless you're much better than I am at this sort of thing, you believed that Frank Churchill was very much in pursuit of Emma and that Mr. Knightley had some kind of interest in Harriet Smith. When we learn about Frank and Jane's secret wedding, because we've been wrapped in Emma's musing while thinking we are seeing the scene as it really is, we're floored.

Rowling uses this misdirection trick most brilliantly in her sixth novel because by the time *Half-Blood Prince* opens we've been fooled five times. How she did it is fascinating. First, she turned off the voice we'd become used to hearing. Instead of a house-elf with minicam on Harry's shoulder, we had an elf on the Muggle Prime Minister's shoulder reading his mind in chapter one and another on Bellatrix's shoulder in chapter two. By the time we got to Harry in chapter three, we were ready to resume our comfortable position on our friend's shoulder—a perspective from someone we like.

But for you hard-core readers determined not to identify with Harry, Ms. Rowling had another hook to suck you into delusion with the rest of us. For twenty-eight of the thirty chapters, everyone thought Harry a nutcase for believing Draco was the Death Eater and that Snape was helping him with his mission from the Dark Lord. If we were resistant to believing Harry to be right in these beliefs, we were in good company: Ron, Hermione, Remus Lupin, Nymphadora Tonks, Mr. and Mrs. Weasley, even Albus Dumbledore also thought Harry just as determined to believe the worst of Malfoy and Snape.

But then, of course, events confirm everything Harry thought since the book's beginning! Malfoy was on a suicide mission from the Dark Lord! Snape was his willing comrade and a man capable of killing the beloved headmaster who appears more than a little Christlike! And everyone in a wave in the infirmary conclave around Bill's broken body ends up apologizing to Harry for doubting him and for believing the best of others like Dumbledore when they should have been hating Snape and Malfoy. Harry is a prophet!

You're a better reader than I am if the traction of this current didn't pull you off your feet and send you downstream. This isn't just "narrative misdirection." This is literary judo, and Ms. Rowling has a black belt, third dan, in this martial art, I think.

The Judo Throw at the Finish of *Half-Blood Prince*

If you don't know anything about judo or its cousin aikido, let me explain what I mean. The point of these martial arts is to use the force or direction of the opponent to subdue him or her. If someone tries to punch or kick you, the judo response is to "encourage" him to continue in his unbalanced direction and lock him up. Ms. Rowling's judo move is to get us leaning exactly the way we want and then push us over in that direction.

We began the sixth story as careful readers who had been duped by and large five times. We'd all taken oaths, publicly and privately, not to be fooled a sixth time. Everyone else in the book was on our side. "Sure, Harry," pat on head, shared glance with Dumbledore and Hermione, "we know. Draco's the youngest Death Eater ever and you know best about Snape—like all the other times you've been right about Snape. Which would be 'never, ever, right about Snape.'" As much as we love Harry, we were not going to kick ourselves again at book's end for buying into Harry's jaundiced view. We leaned way back from Harry.

But he was right! And everybody that was with us in leaning away from Harry was on the floor apologizing for not trusting in his discernment. This is the crucial difference between the ending of *Half-Blood Prince* and every previous Harry Potter book. In every other book's finale we swore we wouldn't identify with Harry's view again. We took solemn oaths that *next time* we'd be more like Hermione and we'd see this as one of Harry's mistakes, his "saving people thing."

At the end of *Half-Blood Prince*, though, we weren't saying, "I was suckered again! Doggone it!" We were saying, "Wow. Harry was right. Snape killed Dumbledore as part of the plan that the Dark Lord had for Malfoy to do in the headmaster. Time to line up behind Harry and go Horcrux and Snape hunting on our white hippogriff and in our white cowboy hats."

Ms. Rowling spun us around again. The funny thing, of

course, is that after bruising our foreheads five times previously, we should have expected that the big twist would be coming in the seventh and last book. Dumbledore died, alas, and wasn't available at the end of *Prince* to explain how stupid we were to believe Harry again.

To get to the stunning "twist" at the end of *Deathly Hallows*, though, we need to grasp what the surprise ending means.

The Romance Formula
That Is Philosophical

The Austen books have a formula with which you may be familiar: Boy meets girl, adversity separates boy and girl (parents and family, differences in station, etc.), and boy and girl overcome adversity for storybook ending. The engines of the triumph over the obstacles put before love are devotion, emotion, and passion, more or less. Austen plays with the formula, mocks it really, by showing the disastrous results of these passionate first encounters and mistaken first impressions. Again and again, they lead to unhappy marriages and failed relationships. Just consider:

* Edward Ferrars and Lucy Steele in *Sense and Sensibility*

* Willoughby and Colonel Brandon's foster daughter in *Sense and Sensibility*

* Marianne's feelings for Willoughby in *Sense and Sensibility*

* Elizabeth's feelings for Mr. Wickham in *Pride and Prejudice*

* Wickham's usage of Lydia Bennet in *Pride and Prejudice*

* Emma Woodhouse's fascination with Frank Churchill in *Emma*

All the "happy endings" and positive courtships, in contrast, are the fruit of hard work to overcome the mistakes made on first sight and the characters' deeply held prejudices or convictions.

* Emma Woodhouse and George Knightley in *Emma*

* Harriet and Robert Martin in *Emma*

* Edward Ferrars and Elinor in *Sense and Sensibility*

* Colonel Brandon and Marianne in *Sense and Sensibility*

* Elizabeth Bennet and Fitzwilliam Darcy in *Pride and Prejudice*

* Jane Bennet and Bingley in *Pride and Prejudice*

Austen, in this consistent depiction of hurried judgment from first impressions as bad and of penetrating understanding born of reflection and experience as good, is writing a philosophical argument against David Hume's empiricist position within her comic novels (and Rowling, in the tradition of English letters, is doing the same thing). Let's take a look at what Hume said and how Austen's *Pride and Prejudice* is a response.

Hume's position was, ultimately, that nothing could be known certainly (except, of course, the fact that "nothing could be known certainly," which was certain). The first principle and consequence of what is even on the surface a contradiction is that only sensorial knowledge is even dependable because all of our ideas Hume assumed to be derived from sense impressions. The distance between this belief and the materialism of our times, in which only quantities of matter and energy are thought of as real, is a short walk; the breach made thereby with the Romantic and Platonic vision predominant in literature is correspondingly vast. Not very surprisingly, Austen and Rowling side with Coleridge and Wordsworth against Hume.

Jane Austen, the very widely read Parson's daughter, takes aim at Hume's dependence on sense impressions in the language and meaning of her *Pride and Prejudice*, the first title of which was *First Impressions*.[3] *Pride and Prejudice*, as an example, is an argument against trusting cold and sensorial "first impressions" versus sympathetic judgment based on experience and character. The former, as the story unfolds, are relatively worthless because first impressions are so malleable to the ideas we have from our personal pride and prejudice.

Darcy *seems* the worst of self-important snobs to Elizabeth Bennet, and the Bennets *seem* to Darcy to be beneath his attention. Wickham *seems* the long-suffering innocent to Elizabeth—and Darcy to be Wickham's persecutor. His pride and her prejudice combine to blind them to their real characters, which, of course, circumstances and their ability both to rise above their sensorial impressions and trust their greater judgment beyond pride and prejudice reveal in time. Their nuptials (and sister Jane's with Bingley) are a testament of love's greater perception of truth and goodness than sense, subject as perceived ephemera are to human failings like conceit, class, and inherited beliefs.

"Pride and Prejudice" in Harry Potter

Austen showed the cathartic transformation of her principal players (and thereby her readers) from proud, prejudiced figures wholly subject to first impressions into loving couples who have seen the greater truth about others beyond sensorial knowledge. Ms. Rowling's *Harry Potter* novels, too, turn on this theme.

There are at least four principal themes running through these novels: prejudice, choice, change, and love's victory over death—and prejudice may be the pivotal theme of the four.

Every book is loaded with reminders of how everyone but the long-suffering, brilliant, and saintly (Lupin, Hermione, and Dumbledore, respectively) is captive to their preconceptions about others and usually almost brutal in their unkindness to the objects of their prejudice.

We have, of course, the constant of "proper wizard pride" by which all nonmagical people, indeed, even magical brethren that are not "pure-blood" witches and wizards, are held in disdain. The Muggles we meet, too, hate the abnormality of the people living in Harry's world. The poor, the clumsy, the awkward, the stupid, the ugly, and the unpopular at Hogwarts are also shown to have a hard time. Even the "Nearly Headless" ghost is a second-class citizen among the properly "Headless" ghosts and prevented from participating in the annual Headless hunt.

Magical folk seem preoccupied, like Jane Austen's characters, with the birth condition or circumstances of others over which they had no choice or control rather than on the quality of their characters. Ron learns Hagrid is a half-giant in *Goblet of Fire*, and, though he has been Hagrid's friend for three years, learning this news really disturbs him because of the wizard prejudice against giants. We see the same or similar responses with respect to noble centaurs, house-elves, and even werewolves. Hagrid even has a few unkind words for foreigners in *Goblet of Fire* to show he has his own prejudices to get over.

And this prejudice is institutional as well. The Ministry of Magic refuses to promote Arthur Weasley, in the opinion of his wife, because he lacks proper wizard pride, and though the Ministry opposes the Death Eaters' attacks on Muggles, they certainly share Voldemort's contempt for them. Magical media, too, especially the *Daily Prophet*, transmits and reinforces the prejudices of witches and wizards in almost every story we read. The coverage of news is so biased and irresponsible that when they do report a story correctly Dumbledore notes that "even the *Daily Prophet*" gets one right on occasion.

The ubiquity of prejudice in the magical and Muggle worlds isn't what makes the prejudice theme the pivotal one in the series. The obstacles to the successful resolution of the other themes—love's defeat of death, freewill choice, and personal transformation or change—are essentially prejudice. You simply cannot be loving, capable of unjaundiced decision making, or capable of change when bound by personal prejudice and pride. The big twist at which the books aim, too, turns on the revelation of Harry's foundational misconception and the change in him if he realizes and transcends this misunderstanding.

You'll recall that Ms. Rowling believes that the surprise ending of *Emma* is "the best twist ever in literature." She has said that this finish is "the target of perfection" at which she is aiming with her plot construction. Just as the key to

Darcy and Elizabeth's engagement in *Pride and Prejudice* was his seeing past his pride and her overcoming her prejudice, a victory repeated with Emma Woodhouse in the later novel, Harry's victory over Lord Voldemort must come through love and after the revelation of an unexpected "back" to a revered or reviled "front." Harry, like Emma, Fitzwilliam Darcy, and Elizabeth, however, had to transcend his pride as a Gryffindor and free himself of his "old prejudice" against Slytherins. He also had to come to terms with the Machiavellian aspect and clay feet of his hero Dumbledore.

What Lupin calls Harry's "old prejudice" against Severus (*Half-Blood Prince*, chapter sixteen) is resolved suddenly and forever in his experience of his sworn enemy's memories of his mother. More difficult was coming to terms with the "back" to Dumbledore's "front," recognizing the secretiveness and failings of Harry's beloved mentor. Unquestioning admiration can blind us, Harry learns, as much as inherited prejudice. Most of *Deathly Hallows* turns on Harry's finally choosing to believe in Dumbledore while digging Dobby's grave on Easter morning. Rowling's astonishing final twist was that Snape was a sacrificial hero and Dumbledore a man with a history; Harry's victory over his preconceptions, represented in naming his look-alike son "Albus Severus," is the interior triumph that led to his eventual triumph over Lord Voldemort in the Great Hall (about which see chapters eight and nine).

Conclusion

The perspective that Ms. Rowling borrows from *Emma* to such wonderful effect is more than just a mechanical trick of the trade. The third person limited omniscient view is not just another way of telling a story; it is the view we too-human readers have of the world, as unconscious as we are of our own pride and prejudices. Certainly we are "first person narrators," but, except in times of extreme self-consciousness, we experience the world as if we are seeing it as God sees it, ignorant as Harry is until story's end of everything else that is going on outside our vision.

Because we can only know what we see, confronting and overcoming our pride and prejudices that shape and distort our perceptions is essential work. Until we become more penetrating and sympathetic "readers" of reality before us, we are doomed to be mistaken, trapped, and enslaved by the conventions, blind spots, and misplaced priorities of our historical period. We'll see in coming chapters why and how Austen's premodern view and subversive arguments against empirical scientism help and fascinate us postmoderns as much as it does and how much it informs Ms. Rowling's books.

CHAPTER THREE

Setting: The Familiar Stage and Scenery Props of the Drama

Harry Potter *as a Boarding School Story in the Tradition of* Tom Brown's Schooldays

Here is a cute quiz that I expect to find stuck in my e-mail spam filter someday. Subject line: "Name the famous British woman author I'm describing!"

* She is a bestselling author of children's stories who has sold over 400 million books (some say as many as 600 million books).

* Children, when polled as recently as 2008, chose her as their favorite author (Costas Book Awards).

* Though famous for writing boarding school stories, she was never a boarding or public school student herself. But she was chosen as "Head Girl" of the school she did attend.

* After school, she was a teacher, had a failed marriage, but remarried with custody of the first marriage's offspring.

* Her best books are about the adventures a group of children have, involving a mystery, boarding school life, or a magical event or ability. All of them have a firm moral or Christian message.

* She had a problematic relationship with her father; her mother was no longer part of her life after she left home.

* She developed a unique way of communicating with her readers without newspaper or media intermediaries.

* Despite the Christian element in stories, implicit or explicit, she was not religious in a devotional way, but remained a member of the Church of England.

* Her books set records for number of translations (more than 90 foreign languages) and are famous and beloved by children and adults around the world, especially in India, Japan, and Germany.

* The girl hero in her bestselling adventures is a swotty tomboy the author admitted was modeled after herself.[1]

J. K. Rowling, right? Well, as you probably guessed, that answer is too obvious, even if everything on the list is a spot-on match for Ms. Rowling except that she belongs to the Episcopal Church of Scotland rather than the Church of England.

The correct answer is Enid Blyton (1897–1968), the author of more than 700 children's books, from kindergarten reading primers to the *Famous Five* adventures and a retelling of *Pilgrim's Progress*. What is most remarkable about Blyton, a ubiquitous presence in the lives of children around the world in books and assorted media, is how few American children and adults know anything about her or her stories. She is anything but commonplace in American schools and libraries, and, to my knowledge, her work has never been adapted for television or film in the United States.

But Blyton's work is the backdrop that every U.K. reader and English literature wonk sees first in Harry Potter because it is the most evident literary echo sounding in Rowling's work. Blyton's stories feature a group of young adventurers solving a mystery (*Famous Five* series), often with a magical backdrop (*The Far-Away Tree Stories*), are set in boarding schools (the series *Malory Towers, St. Clare's,* and *Naughtiest Girl*), and have a strong Christian moral (*The Land of Far-Beyond*).

Tom Brown as Harry's Forgotten Father

That her *Harry Potter* books are just a mush of Blyton standards and formulas, i.e., the Famous Five go to boarding school to climb the magical Far-Away Tree and save their souls, is a tempting easy dismissal critics like A. S. Byatt have made of Harry's near universal popularity.[2] But the true critical point of reference and influence worth exploring at length is not Enid Blyton per se, but specifically the tradition of boarding school novels of which Blyton's series are just a small part. Literally *thousands* of boarding school books like Blyton's have been written in the U.K., based on the pattern of Thomas Hughes's *Tom Brown's Schooldays* (1857). It is into this genre, more than any other, that the *Potter* books can be placed.

But American readers, if they're like me, are not familiar with boarding school novels. Our childhood reading of serial literature makes us think of Harry, Ron, and Hermione as the Hardy Boys going to wizard prep school with an enchanting Nancy Drew.

Given Ms. Rowling's evident debt to schoolboy adventure stories and our benign ignorance of the setting British readers recognize as commonplace or even clichéd, it's worth a chapter to explore the tradition of boarding school fiction and the ways Ms. Rowling conforms to and departs from the norm.

The Public School Novel Formula: Tom Brown Visits Hogwarts

Boarding school novels as a rule—to which there are recent exceptions—are set in what Brits call "public schools."[3] The phrase "public school," however, means something very different in Great Britain than in the United States. In the U.K., the "public" part of "public school" means that the school is open to any child the school accepts and whose parents can pay the costs—making it the equivalent of an American private school. The restricted or exclusive "private" contrary to this "public" openness is tutorial instruction that only the truly wealthy can afford. U.K. government schools, the equivalent of U.S. public schools, are called "comprehensives." Though anything but hard and fast, English class lines can still be drawn between those who received public school educations and those who went to comprehensives.

Ms. Rowling comes from a lower-middle-class British family and received her tax-supported education at a comprehensive rather than as a boarder at an expensive public school. She is more than a little put off by the suggestion that she is a supporter or survivor of the elite public schools in the U.K. In an interview with *The Guardian*, Rowling spoke about her reaction upon first meeting someone at university who had been to a boarding school: "I thought it sounded horrible. Not because I was so attached to home—I couldn't wait to leave home—just that the culture was not one I'd enjoy. It staggers me to meet people who want to send their kids away." [4] In fact, she claims to have "never been inside a boarding school." [5] How does a writer this far removed from the playing fields of Eton come to write a boarding school novel with clear ties to the formula story arc and details of the boarding school novel tradition? Simple. The story formula and its clichéd elements are so familiar to British readers and writers that non–boarding school students, like Blyton and Rowling, have no more trouble imagining a fictional public school than law-abiding novelists who are not police officers or private detectives (or killers) have in writing a whodunit with multiple murders.

Every public school novel, of course, be it a boys' or girls' school, has a hero or heroine that goes to school, grows up there, and departs at graduation a much-transformed person. The details of the formula are not so complicated that they, too, aren't easily summarized:

> *[A] boy enters a school in some fear and trepidation, but usually with ambitions and schemes; suffers mildly or severely at first from loneliness, the exactions of fag–masters, the discipline of masters, and the regimentation of games; then makes a few friends and leads for a year or so a joyful, irresponsible, and sometimes rebel-*

lious life; eventually learns duty, self-reliance, responsibility, and loyalty as a prefect, qualities usually used to put down bullying or over-emphasis on athletic prowess; and finally leaves school, with regret, for the wider world, stamped with the seal of the institution which he has left and devoted to its welfare.[6]

A charted comparison of Hughes's *Tom Brown's Schooldays* and Rowling's *Harry Potter and the Sorcerer's Stone* reveals the strong conformity of the latter to the archetype of the school novel genre.[7]

	Tom Brown's Schooldays	*Sorcerer's Stone*
Setting the Scene	Introductory chapters about ten-year-old Tom Brown, son of landowner, why he is sent to Rugby School	Introductory chapters about ten-year-old Harry Potter turning eleven and his invitation to Hogwarts School
Journey to School	Exciting trip across country with flavor of landscape and beginning of adventure	Wonderful trip on Hogwarts Express and discovery of a new world and belonging
Making Friends	Harry East, all boy, and George Arthur, brilliant, effeminate, and pious	Ron Weasley, all boy, and Hermione Granger, girl genius and rule-keeper
Antagonist	Flashman: older boy, bully, braggart, moneyed elitist	Draco Malfoy: age peer, Pure Blood, moneyed elitist

	Tom Brown's Schooldays	*Sorcerer's Stone*
Teachers	Comic, natural adversaries	Comic, natural adversaries
Headmaster	Dr. Howard: wise, benevolent steward of souls	Albus Dumbledore: wise, benevolent steward of souls
Sports	Football, cricket: the keys to individual student popularity and house success	Quidditch: wizard sporting obsession and the key to Harry's popularity and Gryffindor's success
Rule-breaking	Natural part of younger boys' life at school, to get better of Flashman	To answer Malfoy challenge, to deliver dragon, and to defeat Voldemort
Praeposters/ Prefects	Older students with responsibilities and privileges	Older students with responsibilities and privileges
School	Beloved place of wonder for new student to explore	Beloved place of wonder for new student to explore

Note that many of the features in Ms. Rowling's stories, rather than evidence of a singular creative genius, are just delightful, new renderings of Hughes's staples and necessary characters and devices from the school story. If a book is a boarding school novel, there *has to be* a school and it *has to be* a boarding school (so the students can have nighttime adventures free of parental controls). And it needs to be a very special place, different from common experience. Hogwarts, as a school of witchcraft and wizardry, of course, meets this requirement in spectacular fashion.

The school story also *has to be* told on a time line with two story arcs that complement one another: the course of the individual year—fall to spring with holidays—and the set number of years between the hero or heroine's becoming a student and graduating. Ms. Rowling makes her series seven volumes, corresponding to the seven years of a Hogwarts education in contrast to the six years of most school series and conventional public school forms (for reasons to be discussed in chapter seven); each book in the series, conforming to convention, follows Harry from his home to school and back again on an annual cycle.

The "terrible trio" of Harry, Ron, and Hermione only differs from the public school formula by including a female character as the agent of civilization and intelligence:

> *Traditional school stories feature the hero (or heroine) and his (or her) best friend. A third companion commonly joins them, corresponding to the "rule of three" policy that historically operated in many boarding schools. . . . In* Tom Brown's Schooldays, *Tom Brown first makes friends with Harry East, and the two become inseparable. Later, they adopt the frail and saintly newcomer, George Arthur, who then helps, through his example, to transform the two prankish boys into Christian gentlemen.*[8]

Even Fred and George, the comic Weasley twin brothers, turn out to be refreshed clichés of boarding school book stock players: "Frequently found among the hero's friends in classic school stories is a pair of identical twins, often practical jokers whose activities provide both comic relief and confusion that gets sorted out at the end."[9]

A public school in fiction, too, is obliged, naturally, to come with the stock characters every public school is staffed with; we need a headmaster, teachers, and student leaders in the form of team captains or prefects acting as rule monitors. A sadist teacher is commonplace, hence Severus Snape; "every French mistress in the entire girl's school story genre" is "risible,"[10] thus Sybil Trelawney; and a self-important prefect is a must (if only as a foil for resolutions when the hero or heroine assumes that post, also a near certainty), and Perfect Percy, the "Bighead Boy" fills that role.

Some characters in *Harry Potter*, though, are not only necessary representatives to satisfy a formula but pointers to famous characters in the genre U.K. readers will recognize immediately. Harry's cousin Dudley Dursley, for instance, in his outrageous Smeltings school uniform, complete with sadist's shillelagh, is a pointer to Billy Bunter, "the sly, overweight, idle, lying, cowardly, snobbish, conceited, and greedy boy antihero" of Frank Richards's Greyfriars boarding school books.[11]

The funeral of Albus Dumbledore in *Half-Blood Prince* is as much a tribute to Thomas Arnold, the headmaster of Tom

Brown's Rugby, and to the place of the headmaster as guide and guardian in every schoolboy book, as it is to Harry's mentor and the "greatest wizard of his age." Certainly Arnold and Dumbledore have much in common.

As David Steege writes in his wonderful essay comparing Harry Potter with Tom Brown and the typical English boarding school experience:

> *Both Hughes and Rowling . . . stress the important ties between the hero and headmaster, an adult mentor who helps the hero develop into a functioning, useful young man of good character. Tom, Harry, and their friends find themselves often working around their teachers . . . But both the doctor and Albus Dumbledore are adults our heroes come to trust and value, and who in turn support, protect, and guide the boys.[12]*

I'd go even further here. The link between Arnold and Dumbledore is more meaningful than just their both being thoughtful heads of school and mentors to Tom Brown and Harry Potter respectively. Both headmasters inspire a nearly religious devotion in their students. The last chapter of *Tom Brown's Schooldays*, "Finis," ends with Brown weeping at the grave of his "old master." Hughes describes Brown feeling "love and reverence" for Arnold, that his soul was "fuller of the tomb and him who lies there, than of the altar of Him of whom it speaks." As he grieves, Brown vows to "follow his

[Arnold's] steps in life and death."[13] Thomas Hughes is hardly subtle here in making the late Rugby headmaster in his sacred tomb as stand-in for Christ in the heart of Tom Brown.

This scene is echoed in *Half-Blood Prince*. Not only does Harry weep at Dumbledore's grave, he sees a smoke phoenix shape "fly joyfully into the blue" as the white marble tomb appears encasing the headmaster's corpse. Dumbledore's Patronus takes the shape of a phoenix, also known as "the resurrection bird," which is a traditional symbol of Christ. The chapter closes with Harry testifying to the Minister of Magic that he is "Dumbledore's man through and through" (chapter thirty); he is determined to dedicate the rest of his life to pursuing the Horcruxes and the Dark Lord in conformity with Dumbledore's example and instruction.

Dumbledore's sacrificial death in *Half-Blood Prince*, his being the person in whom Harry must "choose to believe in" over the course of *Deathly Hallow*, and his greeting Harry at the place-not-a-place called "King's Cross" with its suggestion of an afterlife all suggest that Ms. Rowling's headmaster is the magical equivalent of Hughes's Rugby headmaster.

Hero as Bully Beater and Protector of the Weak, Strange, and Despised

Beyond the formula elements every boarding school novel has and their echoes from the tradition in specific characters, Rowling is a conformist both to the thematic conventions of the school novel genre and to the core morality of such books. What is this morality? In two words, "friendship" and "character." "Building friendships, proving a good friend, separating from those who hold the wrong values and thus showing one's true character are all central to public school novels."[14] We can see celebrations of "the virtues of chivalry, decency, honor, sportsmanship, and loyalty" in this list of the typical plot devices of schoolboy and -girl stories taken from Karen Manners Smith's essay "Harry Potter's Schooldays":[15]

* [The stories feature] competitive team sports in general (called "games" in England), and intramural—that is, inter-dorm, inter-house, and inter-school-rivalry in athletics and other things in which points can be accumulated toward an annual championship.

The Hogwarts obsession with Quidditch and the importance to every student of winning and losing "house points" in the intramural competition for the House Cup are Ms. Rowling's twists on this standard.

* All the books centralize the schoolboys' (or schoolgirls') code of honor: sticking together with one's peers and never telling tales.

Harry's refusal to go to Dumbledore when tortured by Dolores Umbridge is the heroic version of this code of honor in not telling tales but keeping a stiff upper lip. His telling Cedric about the dragons before the first Triwizard trial and Cedric's revealing how to hear the clue in the magical egg, not to mention his refusal to take the Triwizard Cup in the center of the maze, are other examples of schoolboy honor.

* The books explore relationships between pupils and schoolmasters and schoolmistresses and frequently deal with the isolation experienced by the student who does not "fit in."

Can you say "Luna Lovegood" and "Neville Longbottom?" It's no accident that these square pegs in round holes are redeemed by membership in Dumbledore's Army. But more on Neville in a moment.

* School stories abound with moral dilemmas involving cheating, tattling, smoking, drinking, gambling, rule breaking, and unauthorized absences from school.

It isn't a schoolboy novel unless the students break rules early on and come to terms with the moral implications of this choice as they mature. Remember Lupin's restrained rebuke to Harry in *Prisoner of Azkaban* for going to Hogsmeade—

and Harry's profound shame? That is only possible consequent to poor choices and an implicit moral standard.

* Heroes and heroines and friends often find themselves unjustly accused of misdemeanors and subjected to unjust punishments; often children have to deal detective-fashion with thefts or vandalism of school property or personal possessions.

As we saw in chapter one, the mystery unwound by our trio of detectives is the narrative drive of every book in the series. Harry is accused and punished, too, in every book, often for doing the right thing (smuggling a dragon to the Astronomy Tower, confronting Umbridge publicly with the truth of Voldemort's return, saving Dudley from a dementor, etc.).

* The protagonists typically find themselves promoted— willingly or reluctantly—to authority at some point, such as being made prefect, Head Boy or Girl, or games captain.

Part of the agony of *Order of the Phoenix* is that Harry is passed over for prefect and his best friends are chosen instead. Of course, Ron and Hermione's enthusiasm and discomfort in these positions are clichés of the genre. Harry, the born leader, in contrast to his friends' appointments and relative lack of authority with students, becomes the leader of Dumbledore's Army by acclamation. That he is selected as captain of the Gryffindor Quidditch team in *Half-Blood Prince* and struggles with the selection of teammates is another necessary piece of the schoolboy's development.

* In many of the narratives, the gradual reform of a hitherto unpleasant or incorrigible character takes place; often he or she is reformed by the main character.

There are three "unpleasant or incorrigible" players in the *Potter* dramas: Dudley Dursley, Severus Snape, and Draco Malfoy. Dudley, after Harry saves his life in the opening of *Order of the Phoenix*, is transformed from a spoiled selfish brat to a young man who, if still socially retarded, feels and tries to express his real concern for cousin Harry when Dudley leaves Privet Drive in *Deathly Hallows*. I will explain in chapter eight how Harry serves as Snape's means of transcendence, even salvation, in the *Deathly Hallows* Shrieking Shack death scene.

And Draco Malfoy? The boy Harry hates above all others?

[In Harry's conflict with Draco Malfoy] Rowling is closely following the boarding school story tradition, in which class differences frequently provoke bigotry . . . violence, vengefulness, and snobbery are only parts of Draco's character. He is also the schoolboy

voice of racism and race purity in the Potter *books . . . Draco's*
bigotry, imbibed [from] his parents, is similar to the kinds of
prejudice frequently presented in British school stories as a prob-
lem for the hero or heroine to deal with.[16]

This "unpleasant and incorrigible" character and his prejudice act as Harry's principal foil throughout the seven-book
series. It is no accident that Draco is the first Hogwarts student and wizard his age that Harry meets and that he makes
a cameo appearance in the *Deathly Hallows* epilogue. Draco
chooses to serve the Dark Lord in *Half-Blood Prince*, enthu-
siastically obedient to the "bad faith" of his family name,
just as Harry chooses to be in Gryffindor House rather than
Slytherin during the Sorting his first year.

Their battles throughout the years culminate in the fall of
the House of Malfoy and Draco's agony. Harry feels pity for
him after Dumbledore's death on the tower and rescues him
from the Fiendfyre in the Room of Requirement during the
Battle of Hogwarts. This act of mercy results in Harry's being
able to tell Draco's mother, Narcissa, that her son is still alive,
which news inspires her in turn to deceive the Dark Lord
about Harry's survival at the risk of her life. The Malfoys,
Death Eaters one and all, sit down in peace after the Battle in
the Great Hall, however uncomfortably, with the victors.

Reformed? Redeemed? Sort of. The Malfoys at the end of
Deathly Hallows, like Flashman (Tom Brown's nemesis), who

is expelled from Rugby for drunkenness, seem abashed and broken but have not become champions of the good, true, and beautiful overnight. The *Potter* books and *Tom Brown* both use the hero's antagonist as a foil against which to celebrate the virtues of modest landowners and nongentry or at least the relatively poor and unpretentious.

As much as Draco and his parents are stock players advancing public school story morality, Luna and Neville are more important:

> *Frequently, schoolboy and schoolgirl heroes find themselves defending their weaker comrades from school bullies. Tom Brown's role at Rugby School involves his protection of the saintly and frail George Arthur; Darrell Rivers, in Enid Blyton's* First Term of Malory Towers, *must defend and encourage Sally Hope, who has trouble at home and is the subject of sneers at school. In fact, throughout the* Malory Towers *series, Darrell looks after a succession of troubled and friendless girls who are bullied or mistreated by their heartless and elitist schoolmates . . . Rowling's central character, like those heroes in all conventional school stories, is thus, at least in part, measured by his compassion for underdogs.*[17]

School Story as Morality Tale

Along with these stock players and themes, *Harry Potter* novels, as David Steege puts it, "have one more trait in common with other public school novels, seen especially strongly in *Tom Brown's Schooldays*: a tradition of providing a moral tale as well as a ripping good yarn."

In writing *Tom Brown's Schooldays*, Hughes knowingly preaches to his audience. In his preface, he freely admits: "Why, my whole object in writing at all was to get the chance of preaching!"[18]

Rowling, too, has often been quoted in response to the idea of her books as morality tales. She has said that she "did not conceive it as a moral tale," but that "the morality sprang naturally out of the story." Although she "never set out to preach,"[19] "undeniably, morals are drawn."[20]

What saves Harry in the end are his "free will, courage, and moral certainty."[21] The author values courage "more highly than any other virtue and by that I mean not just physical courage and flashy courage, but moral courage."[22]

Ms. Rowling shudders at the idea that she is a "formula writer"[23] or a moral pedant. Nonetheless, the setting of her stories in a boarding school and the creative but remarkable conformity of these stories in the characters and to the themes of the public school novel genre make the books deliver a predictable moral worldview that C. S. Lewis praised as "training in the stock responses."

As he explained in *A Preface to Paradise Lost*, one of art's "main functions" is to "assist" in the organization of "chosen attitudes," namely, being able to recognize vice and virtue and to praise the latter with truth and beauty and to despise the former with falsehood and ugliness. Such training, fostered by the great poets like Milton and, if Chesterton is to be trusted, even by formulaic schoolboy fiction, yields "all solid virtue and stable pleasure."[24] Sydney, Wordsworth, Horace, and Aristotle all argued that story hits its mark when it is simultaneously "instructing while delighting."

Wouldn't it be odd if a story set at a school wasn't about instruction of some kind and, given its roots in Victorian England, about implicit and explicit moral instruction instead? The students and the readers come to learn—and the schoolboy story instructs and delights.

Harry Potter Not "Just Another Schoolboy Formula Novel"

The *Potter* novels *are* schoolboy fiction, wonderfully reimagined but true to the conventions of the genre all the same. And this setting and Ms. Rowling's conformity to formula *does* tell us a great deal about the literal and the moral meaning of the books.

It is by no means, however, the whole of the literal meaning or of the books' moral layering. We have seen other dimensions on these relatively superficial levels of meaning in the previous chapter discussions of narrative voice and drive and of the formulas and moral weight of "manners and morals" fiction à la Austen, Sayers's character-driven detective stories, and Dickens's orphan novels. The literal level and the devices and set pieces Ms. Rowling borrows from the various traditional genres bleed with moral meaning that informs the reader's experience of the surface story.

The upcoming chapters exploring the explicitly moral, allegorical, and transcendent layers of meaning reveal that dismissing Ms. Rowling's oeuvre as simply schoolboy fiction, as academic critics have, is to miss the source of the novels' power and popularity. What separates Rowling from more formulaic books in the schoolboy genre is her level of planning. She planned her seven books for five years before completing the first novel, *Sorcerer's Stone*. Planning is an integral part of the process for Rowling. In an interview with the *South Australian Advertiser*, she talks about how important it is to her:

> *I do a plan. I plan, I really plan quite meticulously. I know it is sometimes quite boring because when people say to me, "I write stories at school and what advice would you give me to make my stories better?" And I always say and people's faces often fall when I say, "You have to plan," and they say, "Oh, I prefer just writing and seeing where it takes me." Sometimes writing and seeing where it takes you will lead you to some really good ideas but I would say nearly always it won't be as good as if you sat down first and thought: Where do I want to go, what end am I working toward, what would be good, a good start?[25]*

The *Harry Potter* books are anything but thrown together. They're "meticulously planned." There's very little that is accidental or spur of the moment about them.

So what?

Ms. Rowling *is* writing formula schoolboy fiction. But in her years of "meticulous planning" she has layered into the mechanical format, characters, and themes of this tired genre nine other literary conventions from gothic romance to alchemical drama, and the traditional four layers of meaning, to include allegorical satire and symbolist fantasy.

This is not just another *Tom Brown* or even *Tom Brown* "reseen . . . in the magical mirror of Tolkien,"[26] as Harold Bloom would have it. The literal level of meaning we've been exploring in these first three chapters, with their pointers to the moral dimension the surface story inevitably brings with it is just the visible vehicle or stage setting through which and on which Ms. Rowling has worked her multivalent artistry.

Doubt me? Turn the page to discover the Frankenstein monster, vampire, and gothic romance moral meaning tucked into this schoolboy novel. We're about to leave *Tom Brown* and *Malory Towers* for a different dimension in setting and stock response training. On to Transylvania!

PART TWO

The Moral Meaning

CHAPTER FOUR

Gothic Romance: The Spooky Atmosphere Formula from Transylvania

Harry Potter *as an Echo of the Brontë Sisters,* Frankenstein, The Strange Case of Dr. Jekyll and Mr. Hyde, *and* Dracula

Gothic as a literary genre was born in the mid-eighteenth century with the stunning *Castle of Otranto* by Horace Walpole, which almost singlehandedly introduced the devices, themes, and morality of this kind of novel. "Pure gothic" or gothic romance accounts for close to a third of all books written in the late 1700s and early 1800s, believe it or not, and then fades dramatically into near nonexistence. The "machinery" of the pure gothic romance, however, bled into all other genres and became a staple of Dickens, Collins, the Victorian horror writers, the "late gothic" authors, and eventually, we shall see, found a home in the world of *Harry Potter*.

Gothic Literature

"Gothic" can be used meaningfully to describe everything from Samuel Taylor Coleridge's *The Rime of the Ancient Mariner* to bodice-ripping yarns from Victoria Holt, not to mention the macabre horror stories of Poe, Lovecraft, and Stephen King. There are "classic gothic" stories from the nineteenth century that everyone still reads, though; a look at them reveals the common elements of gothic novels that are found everywhere in *Harry Potter*, as well as their admonitory morality. If you could do a word-response test with literature geeks, a test in which for every category named the person has to name a novel, I'm confident that for the word "gothic" most would answer either *Jane Eyre*, *Wuthering Heights*, *Frankenstein*, *The Strange Case of Dr. Jekyll and Mr. Hyde*, or *Dracula*. None of them are "pure gothic"—because they don't contain all the elements that would make them so—but all get their feel or atmosphere from Walpole and his eighteenth-century imitators.[1] Let's look at their individual stories quickly to spot the dominant, recurrent threads before seeing the gothic wool of the *Potter* tapestry and its moral message.

Jane Eyre

Jane Eyre (1847) by Charlotte Brontë is an orphan novel featuring the original "plain Jane" in her rise from abused, adopted child through life's vicissitudes to marriage with her beloved. Taken in by an aunt and uncle at her parents' deaths, she is tormented by her cousins and shrewish aunt when her uncle dies. They send her away to school, but this is hardly an improvement, despite her making a dear friend and finding a sympathetic mentor. The teachers and the school head are sadists and sophists who dislike her, and the boarding students are treated so badly that disease eventually kills many of them, including the dear friend. The school is reformed, and Jane eventually becomes a teacher herself. She leaves the school to become a governess at a Gothic manor to a French child.

The child is the ward of a man twenty years Jane's senior. Edward Rochester is a passionate gentleman who, after a rough start with the manor's new governess, falls in love with her and proposes. Jane is swept off her feet but learns *at her wedding* that Rochester is already married and his mad wife has been kept in the manor attic out of sight. She refuses to become his mistress and flees the manor in the dark of night.

She escapes north to desolate moors and is taken in, near death, by St. John Rivers and his sisters. St. John plans to become a missionary to India and after Jane's physical recovery and miraculous inheritance, he proposes they marry and she join him in India. Jane, though, hears a voice and realizes just in time she still loves Rochester and returns to him.

But he is a humbled man. His confined wife had burned down the manor and died after leaping from the roof; Rochester was crippled and blinded in the fire. In a melodramatic reunion, Jane and Rochester reconcile, and, in their union, he eventually regains sight in one eye.

Wuthering Heights

Wuthering Heights (1847) by Charlotte Brontë 's sister Emily is the story of Heathcliff, a Liverpool gypsy waif adopted by Mr. Earnshaw, the master of the Wuthering Heights estate on the Yorkshire moors. Earnshaw's daughter, Catherine, becomes Heathcliff's companion and friend, but the master's son, Hindley, despises Heathcliff and treats him like a slave when his father dies.

Catherine accepts the proposal of a relatively gentle neighbor, Edgar Linton, despite her belief that Heathcliff is her soul mate ("Whatever our souls are made of, his and mine are the same . . . I *am* Heathcliff—he's always, always in my mind—not as a pleasure, any more than I am always a pleasure to myself—but as my own being" [chapter nine]), and Heathcliff escapes the Heights on hearing only that Catherine believes marriage to him would be "degrading." He returns a few years later a wealthy man, determined to have his revenge on Hindley Earnshaw and Edgar Linton. Hindley has become a drunk at the death of his wife and dies after Heathcliff wins possession of Wuthering Heights. For a more lasting revenge, Heathcliff treats Hindley's orphan son, Hareton, as miserably as the boy's father had treated Heathcliff.

Confused? It gets more complicated and distressing. Heathcliff marries Edgar's sister, Isabella, in order to torture Catherine and Edgar. He treats Isabella cruelly and eventually she escapes, gives birth to Heathcliff's child, and dies some years later. Catherine dies soon after birthing Cathy, Jr. In due time, Heathcliff forces marriage between Cathy, Jr., and Linton, his son by Isabella, and the marriage is, predictably, a disaster. Edgar and Linton die, and widow Cathy is left at Wuthering Heights with Heathcliff and Hareton.

Catherine's ghost haunts Heathcliff literally and figuratively, and, seeing Cathy and Hareton fall in love pushes him to the edge. Heathcliff dies and is buried beside Catherine; their phantoms are seen together on the moors.

From melodrama to horror . . .

Frankenstein

Everyone knows the gist of *Frankenstein or The Modern Prometheus* (1818), or at least thinks they do. The popular version goes something like this: A mad scientist-doctor in a castle on the hill with a hunchbacked assistant and mega-gigawatts of voltage, reanimates a giant sewn together from the parts of corpses. The giant goes on a killing spree before the doctor and villagers hunt him down.

Fortunately, this story isn't the one written by Mary Shelley. Her story is about a young scientist who discovers a way to create life. No castle, no hunchback, no lightning, just an unnamed monstrous giant. The ugliness of his creation causes the doctor to have a breakdown that lasts several months. Sadly, when he recovers, he learns that his younger brother has been murdered. He returns home, and, on a mountaintop, has a heart-to-heart with the monster who wants a bride. So Dr. Frankenstein heads back to the graveyard for monster-fiancée parts. Just before reanimating the stitched-together giantess, though, the scientist has a change of heart and reneges on his promised monster-bride. The monster, not pleased, has his revenge by killing Dr. Frankenstein's bride on their wedding day, as well as the doctor's friend. Dr. Frankenstein chases the monster toward the North Pole and expires on an arctic exploration ship trapped in the ice after telling the tale to the ship's captain. The monster says his pathetic good-bye, incredibly, in the ship's cabin, and escapes after a soliloquy promising his self-destruction.

The Strange Case of Dr. Jekyll and Mr. Hyde

Gothic takes something of a holiday (with the exception of Dickens and Collins, whose latter books are gothic melodramas) until its dramatic reemergence in the late Victorian fin de siècle horror stories made popular by Robert Louis Stevenson's novella, *The Strange Case of Dr. Jekyll and Mr. Hyde* (1886). Here the gentleman scientist Dr. Henry Jekyll, "committed to a profound duplicity of life," discovers a drug that "so potently controlled and shook the very fortress of identity" that it freed him from "certain of the powers that made up my spirit." Dr. Jekyll, with one draught, in other words, could become an ensouled body sans conscience and spirit, by name "Edward Hyde," and with another, revert to the man of body, soul, *and* spirit, Dr. Jekyll.

Mr. Hyde, though, as you'd expect, is more demon than human being. His crimes touch Dr. Jekyll's conscience but do not turn him to a path of abstinence or regret; Hyde's crimes to Jekyll are only Hyde's and he only makes those amends he thinks prudent.

To Jekyll's distress, however, the transformations to Hyde begin to happen spontaneously and are more difficult to reverse. Jekyll the gentleman realizes that Hyde is now the master of his person. Hyde murders a member of Parliament, Jekyll locks himself in his laboratory, the key ingredient in the draughts is lost, and Jekyll-Hyde commits suicide.

Dracula

In Bram Stoker's *Dracula*, Dr. Abraham Van Helsing is called in to combat the Dark Lord. He leads a group of men across London and eventually Europe to destroy Count Dracula. Dracula seduces Mina Harker and gains control of her mind by forcing her to drink his blood. But this mind-link between Mina and Dracula enables Van Helsing to track the count all the way to Transylvania. In a move to protect Mina from Dracula's summoning and influence, Van Helsing places a

Communion wafer on her forehead, but it burns her flesh. Mina cries, "Unclean! Unclean! Even the Almighty shuns my polluted flesh! I must bear this mark of shame upon my forehead until the Judgment Day!" (chapter twenty-two). When Dracula is destroyed, her scar disappears.

And More

Had enough? How about Poe's short story "The Tell-Tale Heart?" In one of the most tightly crafted pieces of horror put to page, Poe's narrator relates his murder of an old man because he couldn't stand the man's "vulture" eye, his "pale blue eye," that made his blood run cold. Madness? No, he insists it's just an "over-acuteness of the senses."

He dismembers the body and conceals the remains under the floorboards of the apartment. The police, having been summoned when the old man's single scream woke the neighbors, see nothing. During their investigation, sitting in the old man's room over the dismembered body asking questions, the narrator hears the dead man's heart, beating louder and louder. Driven to madness, the killer confesses to the nefarious deed.

An Atmosphere of Fear

What do these stories have in common? On the surface, not that much.

Jane Eyre has a hard time both growing up and with

romance, but she marries her true love in the end. Heathcliff and Catherine are star-crossed lovers on the Scottish moors with an unhappy beginning, middle, and ending. Franken-stein creates life, the sewn-together creature turns on its cre-ator, and everybody dies. Dr. Jekyll releases his inner Edward Hyde but cannot put the genie back in the bottle. And *Drac-ula*? The undead are vanquished by sacrament-wielding heroes able simultaneously to embrace science, faith, and the really far-out supernatural weirdness of Eastern European legends. Poe's narrator-murderer seems equally unique and bizarre.

That's quite the spread. Believe it or not, though, all these characters conform to two types and each of the stories is about producing an unsettling atmosphere, "unnerving" all the way to "horrifying."

Ann Tracy, author of *Patterns of Fear in the Gothic Novel*, wrote that gothic literature, ultimately, was about fostering "nameless fears," "familiar anxieties," and an "atmosphere of irrational menace."[2] There are obviously many different ways to produce this atmosphere and its unsettling effects, but "classic gothic" tends to use very similar specific story elements. Few stories have all these elements, however, and many contain only some.

Let's start with the setting.

Gothic stories are usually set—obviously enough—in a Gothic manor or castle. There should be something super-natural or inexplicable at the very least in this manor house and probably a ghost or two will show up eventually. Think of Rochester's mad wife walking the halls of his manor at night.

You can also expect isolated scenes, for example, on alpine glaciers, windswept moors, or arctic expanses. And there is also a sense of confinement. The setting almost certainly will include tight spaces as well to highlight feelings of isolation in a strange place. Dr. Frankenstein tells his whole story in the captain's cabin on a ship trapped in the ice on a voyage to the North Pole. Jekyll/Hyde has the run of misty London but eventually he locks himself in his laboratory to separate himself from all others.

Subterranean passages for escape or adventure, dungeons for holding prisoners unjustly, an attic or especially frightening hole or room are commonplace, too. Jane Eyre is locked by her aunt in the "red room" where her uncle had died, which sends the little girl around the bend. Poe's corpse under the floorboards and the terrifying labyrinth of Dracula's castle are set pieces of fear and dread.

If you venture outside in a gothic novel, you'll find the weather is going to be tempestuous. You'll need a light because most of the action is going to take place at night or in the dark, and the landscape is usually shrouded in mist. Vampires and the undead only walk at night, so *Dracula*'s drama is largely between sundown and sunrise every day. In *Jane Eyre*, the only light you're likely to experience is a fire like the one that destroys Rochester's manor. Hyde's London obscures his double identity in persistent mist and fog. *Wuthering Heights* weather forecasts are something like Seattle's.

Setting and weather are best understood as reflections of the interior life and feelings experienced by the narrator or protagonist. The tight space and violent storm mirror the angst of the confused and disoriented character.

The only joyful item in these madness-inducing landscapes is the possible reunion of principals with their loved ones and families. Inevitably, the gothic heroine is separated from friends and family by choice or circumstances and is reunited with those she loves. *Jane Eyre* models the prototypical gothic romance ending in Jane's reunion with Rochester. Emily Brontë ends *Wuthering Heights* with Catherine and Heathcliff's ghoulish reunion both in their shared grave and the generational echo of Hareton and Cathy, Jr.

And the clichéd gothic trappings . . . an ancestral curse or prophecy; a fascination with tainted or polluted blood; a corpse where it shouldn't be; graveyards; sacrificial bravery and hopeless defiance; memories and dreams galore; a found book with amazing information, even magical properties (a favorite stylistic device is for the story to be told as if it's the diary or record found in an antiquarian's collection); a signature deformity or scar; the stranger, preferably a foreigner from Southern or Eastern Europe—but being Catholic alone will suffice for the exotic; and confusion about the hero or heroine's birth status and origin (you'd think from the number of orphans in these stories that parents in the distant past never lived beyond a child's birth).

Distant past? None of these stories reviewed here were set in medieval times, though that is a gothic favorite. Almost all, though, reflect the gothic social/political tension of an aristocracy or hereditary gentry in decline being displaced by a rising, aggressive merchant class. Here Count Dracula is the archetype, but there are definitely class issues in the Eyre/ Rochester relationship and in Heathcliff's agony in overhearing Catherine say it would be "demeaning" to marry him (and also in Heathcliff's determination to avenge himself by owning the Heights and the Linton ...).

Victims/Heroines and Conscience-Deprived Antiheroes

Here is the formula for your standard "pure" gothic romance from the late eighteenth century onward:

* A young female is stripped of her familial support, her mother usually dead before the novel begins, her father or other guardian dying in the early chapters.

* The lover (if any) who might protect her is sent away or prevented from seeing her.

* Depending upon the period of the novel, she may be kidnapped, fall into the hands of an unscrupulous guardian, go out as a governess, or marry hastily.

* Out in the world her troubles multiply. People want to kill her, rape her, lock her up in a convent for life, and make off with her small fortune.

* Her task is to defend her virtue and liberty and resist evil. She must penetrate disguises by unmasking villains, learning to trust in less-than-obvious heroes, and thereby rebuilding a support system that will restore her to a quiet life.

* With pluck and luck, she manages these near impossibilities and is rewarded with the discovery of lost relatives and/or the promise of reliable domestic love in a household of her own.[3]

Jane Eyre conforms to type here but few of the other tales do. They all have the victimized heroine (sometimes male), though, whose circumstances conspire to put her or him into a trying, seemingly impossible situation from which to escape with virtue and dignity intact. The heroine's job is to resist defiantly and to find the honorable way out, almost always a harrowing flight from a dungeon or a manor, to escape a supernatural evil or just a wicked male in the flesh. Mina Harker—with her histrionic prayers to God about her being "unclean" after drinking Dracula's blood—also conforms to type. Her heroism is in her resistance to the bond of blood and the curse of the vampire within her. She feels God is treating her unfairly despite her trying "to walk in meekness and righteousness all my days. God pity me!" (*Dracula*, chapter twenty-one). These stories, as you can see, are uniformly "theatrical" and "melodramatic."

At the beginning of *Wuthering Heights*, Heathcliff is the suffering orphan all but enslaved by his adoptive father's son. This sets him up to play the "heroine" in the gothic story. However, the son's family then endures Heathcliff's payback for generations. Dr. Jekyll, too, though also a man and despite being *responsible* for being Hyde's victim, takes the "defiant victim" female stock rule.

If the gothic "heroine" (who is sometimes male) is a victim who must resist or escape to protect her virtue or self-respect, the hero is the jerk of the piece, more commonly labeled a "Byronic antihero." Bold, passionate, selfish, demanding to the point of being sadistic, the gothic antihero is notable for overreaching his grasp, especially with respect to his understanding of what it means to be human. *Jane Eyre*? The antihero is Rochester, whose overbearing pride and passion for Jane makes him wish to bring her dishonor. Unable to marry her because of his marriage to the woman in his attic (!), he proposes that she consent to be his mistress. In overstepping traditional morality, he loses Jane, who escapes defiantly and returns triumphantly after Rochester has been humbled and his manor destroyed.

Heathcliff, the adopted and abused son, strives to own all the property and control the lives of those persons and families that kept him from happiness with Catherine. His passion for her and his bottomless hunger for sadistic, manipulative revenge means misery on the moors for three generations.

Dracula, Jekyll, and Frankenstein overreach in a different fashion. They are all scientists who attempt to live as men of reason and passion—mind and body without spirit—and to create the undead man of power without the spiritual faculty of soul.

Dracula, a Transylvanian nobleman and war hero, learned black arts and alchemy centuries ago and cuts a deal "with the Evil One" (chapter eighteen). Living without the interior light of spirit, he has the powers of dark magic but cannot absorb light, hence his inability to cause reflection in a mirror or cast a shadow. He dies at last because of his hubristic attempt at a one-man invasion of Great Britain.

Dr. Jekyll and Victor Frankenstein are more recognizable antiheroes in that their ambitions and overreaching are scientific rather than magical. Unfortunately, their relatively mechanical or formulaic science does not foster or require any kind of wisdom and produces human caricatures that are conscience-deprived monsters.

So, Who Exactly *Are* You?

Another gothic signature is the "doppelgänger" or "character going both ways." This means that one or more characters is a mirror's reflection and inversion of the other. Catherine and Heathcliff, she thinks, are *one person*, remember?

Dr. Jekyll tops this, of course, in being the exact same person biologically as his monstrous doppelgänger. Frankenstein projects his horrifically mistaken and oversized conception of what it means to be human onto his creature, an idea of himself he is obliged to destroy when he recognizes the creature is made in his own fallen image. Count Dracula, the superpowered, supernatural undead man incapable of faith, has his opposite in Dr. Abraham Van Helsing, who is the embodiment of Christian faith and of sacramental vision. In these three pairings, we see the doppelgänger possibilities: internal, projection, and protagonist/antagonist pairing.

With this dual-nature storytelling, however, as you'd guess, we almost always get some confusion or conflation of who the hero and villain are. In *Jane Eyre*, you've got to be pretty cold not to wonder if Rochester isn't as much the victim as Jane when she flees Thornfield. Heathcliff, as mentioned, becomes the monster he does because he is treated as badly as he is by his brother-by-adoption.

Who the heroes and villains are becomes even more confused in *Frankenstein* and *The Strange Case of Dr. Jekyll and Mr. Hyde*. The hero creates the villain, who is the interior, monstrous man hiding inside the hero. In both cases, bizarre science liberates a soulless man-without-conscience to walk the streets unbridled. Which brings us to the morality of gothic fiction. It's all about the life without thought of God. The gothic hero-villain is a story snapshot of fallen man as Calvinists see him. Man is born as an image of God and can grow in God's likeness insofar as he identifies with his spiritual aspect and conscience. Man is depraved, however, and worse than a beast as he forgets God and lives a life consumed by the pursuit of his individual advantage.

"The Gothic world is quintessentially the Fallen world," as one gothic literature authority summarizes it.[4] Let's review our Adam and Eve story. Man once walked with God in the Garden. There was no death; conversation with God was not only a possibility but all that human beings lived for. Adam was expelled from Paradise, though, because of his disobedience. Human beings can only regain Eden by restoring the ability to perceive and speak with God via his darkened and much-diminished spiritual capacity.

The gothic story, in a nutshell, is the Haunted House thrill-show experience written out to highlight for us the facts of our spiritual condition as fallen people living in a world apart from God.

The Gothic Fallen world is characterized by the concentration and magnification of fears and problems inherent in the "normal" world. Hence the two worlds are both effectively dissimilar and latently identical. . . . The Gothic world and the Fallen world are both blighted ones, places of danger, sorrow, and exile, in which the inhabitants' only hope is a rediscovery of and reunion with the Father and the Beloved.[5]

Poe's "The Tell-Tale Heart" is the concentrated version of *Frankenstein, Jekyll,* and *Dracula.* The deranged narrator is rational, clever, and calculating. However superficially sane, he is devoid of conscience or inner light. "Reason, in this world, is a frail and unreliable faculty, perhaps on an average less to be relied upon than the premonitions of excitable heroines."[6] Not only is it "frail and unreliable," it resents the existence and authority of conscience, here symbolized by the old man's "pale blue eye." Reason without the rule of spirit is the servant of passion and works to destroy the single eye and extinguish its light (cf. Matthew 6:22, "The light of the body is the eye: if therefore thine eye be single, thy whole body shall be full of light."). We'll come back to this in chapter ten, of course, when we talk about Dumbledore's "pale blue eye" in Harry's mirror fragment.

Poe's madman succeeds in killing the man, but conscience cannot be extinguished. "The eye of the heart," another name for the faculty of conscience, lives on, and its loud beating drives the murderer to reveal his crimes finally in hysterical obedience.

Likewise Dr. Jekyll and Victor Frankenstein ultimately realize they are primarily that quality or faculty that is absent in their bestial projections and doppelgängers. This revelation (and their inability to regain mastery over their rebellious reason and passions on their own) is a large piece of the didactic moral experience in their books. Gothic stories highlight this retelling of man's fall in the garden by pouring in plot elements that echo the Adam and Eve metanarrative; gardens, snakes, and an expulsion from Paradise after an inability to resist the temptation of power, immortality, or glory, and spiritual falls without hope of recovering self-mastery and redemption are commonplaces.

If you struggle to see the gothic world as the horror comics version of *Genesis* and the Fallen world we live in, the central place of death in these stories, death as an imminent danger or the ever-present backdrop fear, makes the point. All the gothic writers in the Fabulous Five were Christians; it is important to recall, consequently, that a believing Christian imagines him- or herself as living in a place of transition between the Paradise of Eden, where there is no death, and the New Jerusalem of the world to come, in which there can be no corruption, darkness, or death. The life between Eden and Eternity—our world—differs, then, from these worlds most importantly in the presence of death. To drive our human condition home, gothic stories must highlight the fact of our lives we work very hard to ignore, disguise, or otherwise hide from public view: the inevitability of our deaths.[7] The Calvinistic morality of horror and gothic fiction, a genre born at the dawn of modernity, is a wake-up call to the industrial age that has forgotten God and death.

Harry Potter's Cast of Gothic Role-Players

So, are the *Harry Potter* novels gothic? Oh, boy, are they ever. Let's start with the principal players and work our way to the setting and, finally, the gothic narratives permeating every book and the series as a whole.

Severus Snape has his gothic equivalent in the English history classroom of Jane Eyre's school. Miss Scatcherd beats the angelic, long-suffering Helen Burns. Switch out "Scatcherd" and "Burns" in these tormenting scenes of mental and physical cruelty with "Snape" and "Potter" and you have a typical, sadistic Hogwarts Potions class, just shy of the physical violence.

But why is Severus the Potions teacher? Recall his words in Harry's first session in the dungeon: "I can teach you how to bottle fame, brew glory, even stopper death—if you aren't as big a bunch of dunderheads as I usually have to teach" (*Sorcerer's Stone*, chapter eight). He's not kidding or boasting like Lockhart; he can and does "stopper death." This is a wickedly powerful Potions maker, a cross between alchemist and chemist like Frankenstein and Jekyll, and at least as self-important and ambitious. But Severus doesn't create a magical doppelgänger through Potions. His real gothic twin is not Scatcherd,

Jekyll, or Frankenstein but Heathcliff, the lover whose passion is unrequited, who is separated from his beloved by death. Both Heathcliff and Snape act out their unending misery sadistically on those who remind them of past injuries. Heathcliff by force and stealth manipulates for generations every player in *Wuthering Heights* whom he blames for his childhood suffering and his ruined relationship with Catherine. Snape, having vowed to keep Harry alive in memory of Lily Potter, the woman he loved and failed, keeps his word; he never fails, nonetheless, to treat Harry as the stand-in for James Potter, Harry's look-alike, whom Snape despises.

We will discuss the details and meaning of Snape's death in the Shrieking Shack in chapter eight. Here, though, we need only note that with his last request—"Look . . . at . . . me!"—he gazes into Harry's eyes, eyes just like Harry's mother's, and is at last reunited with her in death.

Harry the Gothic "Heroine"

Harry is not like other male gothic figures. He is no Heathcliff, Victor Frankenstein, or Dr. Jekyll. Those madmen each have a plan, however twisted, and the will and drive to bring the plan through to the end. Harry just goes to school and wild stuff happens to him. He resists heroically the terrible things and people that cross his path, but, as a rule, Harry is a victim of circumstances not of his choosing or liking. In this, of course, he is much less the Byronic antihero of gothic romance and more the defiant heroine doing her best to escape the supernatural or masculine shadow tormenting her. If Harry needed a new name, it would be "Jane Eyre."

She is an orphan, beaten up regularly by her male cousin, treated horribly by her aunt, even locked in the "red room" to isolate and punish her. Harry is an orphan, he is Dudley's punching bag as a child, and he lives in a cabinet under his aunt and uncle's stairs. They both are delivered from their families to an extraordinary school where they make their first friends.

But Harry as "defiant victim" resembles Mina Harker from *Dracula* more than Jane Eyre. They both have forehead scars. His unwilling exchange of blood with the Dark Lord at the rebirthing party, which echoes Mina's sharing Dracula's blood, also creates a mind-link conflating their hero-villain identities that is critical in both Mina's and Harry's eventual victory over their nemeses.

Like Mina, too, Harry isn't a supercharged superhero. They are both victims of a bizarre game in which they are, in large part, unwilling players. They depend on their friends for support and in combat. And, like formulaic gothic heroines and overreaching antiheroes, the degree to which they are responsible for their vulnerability and falls to temptation lies in their inability to protect their minds from intrusive tempters and seduction. "When confronted with a tempter, natural or supernatural, of any psychological subtlety, the frail defense of the darkened understanding is exceedingly likely to give way."[8]

Rowling tells this "expelled from Eden" morality tale in *Phoenix*. Harry does not practice Occlumency as instructed by Dumbledore. This disobedience results in, first, Harry's out-of-body experience with a serpent via mind-link in the Ministry of Magic's Department of Mysteries. He refuses even after this to guard his mind from the Dark Lord, who is able finally to deceive him into flying to London on what Harry imagines is a rescue mission. It is instead a trap, and Sirius, whom Harry came to save, dies instead and passes through the veil. Harry's failure to focus on the watchful or *neptic* faculty of soul (traditionally linked to the "eye of the heart" or conscience) results in the death of his godfather.

Harry, though, is just a fallen man coming to understand the world as it is and his need to choose to believe and pursue redemption. Lord Voldemort, like Frankenstein, Dracula, and Jekyll, is a true gothic villain because he acts boldly to pursue an ego immortality divorced from the Spirit.

Of Horcruxes and Hallows

If the *Harry Potter* books were written by Bram Stoker, Harry would be Mina Harker, Dumbledore could easily play Dr. Abraham Van Helsing, and Lord Voldemort would be Dracula. Voldemort is the classic gothic villain. The parallels with

Jekyll and Frankenstein are clear. Tom Riddle, Jr., is an over-reaching Dark Wizard on a quest to live forever. As he tells his Death Eaters at the rebirthing party in *Goblet of Fire:*

> . . . *How could they have believed I would not rise again? They who knew the steps I took, long ago, to guard myself against mortal death? . . . [In Godric's Hollow] I was ripped from my body, I was less than spirit, less than the meanest ghost . . . but still I was alive. What I was, even I do not know . . . I, who have gone further than anybody along the path that leads to immortality. You know my goal—to conquer death. And now, I was tested, and it appeared that one of my experiments had worked . . . for I had not been killed, though the curse should have done it.* (Goblet of Fire, *chapter thirty-three)*

Note his proud scientific language: He is a pioneer in the "experiments" to "conquer death." Like Dr. Frankenstein, though, the creature Voldemort fashions from infamous acts of murder and idolatry is something subhuman.

Frankenstein's creature, an embodiment of the passions and reason of science, lacked conscience, as did Jekyll's Hyde. The spiritual faculty of the human person is uncreated; call it conscience, the active intellect, the eye of the heart, or what you will, it is the divine aspect of the human person. J. K. Rowling calls it love, and Voldemort knows nothing of love.

Love burns the unworthy or polluted in gothic horror.

Remember the scar left on Mina Harker when the Eucharist, representing the God who died in loving sacrifice for his sheep, was placed on her forehead? Voldemort/Quirrell burns in agony when he touches Harry at the end of *Sorcerer's Stone*, Dumbledore explains, because:

> *Your mother died to save you. If there is one thing Voldemort cannot understand, it is love. He didn't realize that love as powerful as your mother's for you leaves its own mark. Not a scar, no visible sign . . . to have been loved so deeply, even though the person who loved us is gone, will give us some protection forever. It is in your very skin. Quirrell, full of hatred, greed, and ambition, sharing his soul with Voldemort, could not touch you for this reason. It was agony to touch a person marked by something so good.*
> (Sorcerer's Stone, *chapter seventeen*)

Voldemort leaps this magical barrier by using Harry's blood to reconstitute himself in *Goblet of Fire*. The admixture creates the "bond of blood" that joins them. When he possesses Harry at the Ministry in *Order of the Phoenix*, however, he is driven away and guards himself against Harry by Occlumency thereafter because of the pain he experiences when Harry remembers Sirius. The love and remorse Harry feels almost destroys the Dark Lord.

Voldemort has become undead and all but immortal, like Stoker's Dracula, through the dark magic of Horcruxes. By committing "the supreme act of evil"—a murder—the soul is torn.

> *Killing rips the soul apart. The wizard intent upon creating a Horcrux would use the damage to his advantage. He would encase the torn portion . . . [into an object with the necessary spell work] . . . then, even if one's body is attacked or destroyed, one cannot die, for part of the soul remains earthbound and undamaged . . .* (Slughorn, Half-Blood Prince, *chapter twenty-three).*

Incredibly, Riddle, Jr., creates one unintentional and six intentional Horcruxes. The Dark Lord's exterior transformation into a person "whiter than a skull, with wide, livid scarlet eyes and a nose flat as a snake's with slits for nostrils" (*Goblet of Fire*, chapter thirty-two) seemed to Dumbledore "only explicable if his soul was mutilated beyond the realms of what we might call 'usual evil . . .'" (*Half-Blood Prince*, chapter twenty-three).

Dracula survives by drinking the life's blood of others and making them undead creatures of darkness like himself. Voldemort, too, must murder to achieve immortality, but, while perhaps not as gruesome as vampirism, Horcrux creation is at least as horrible. The Dark Lord is the satanic cartoon of a materialist who infuses objects with pieces of his own soul, pieces he has acquired via destruction of his neighbor. His "life," such as it is, is entirely *exterior* and material, rather than interior and spiritual. As an allegorical figure, he is the embodiment of our fragmentation, self-estrangement, and alienation—the postmodern, fallen condition gothic literature presents in imaginative form. Voldemort is Rowling's gothic masterpiece.

Steeped in Gothic:
Tales Within Gothic Tales

The *Harry Potter* novels are not only full of gothic touches, but every one of them also has a gothic story inside the story.

First let's look at the gothic touches.

HOGWARTS CASTLE: A gothic novel is set in a castle, manor, or monastery for the most part, preferably far removed from city life. Hogwarts School of Witchcraft and Wizardry exists in its own castle, unplottable to mapmakers. Even if Muggle tourists were to stumble upon it, enchantments prevent them from seeing more than charming ruins. The classrooms and house common rooms are set in towers and dungeons and the castle's grounds and hallways with their huts, suits of armor, torches, and absence of technology are thoroughly medieval.

SUPERNATURAL ATMOSPHERE: With few exceptions, the major players are all magical creatures, which is to say, witches and wizards. Hogwarts has a resident population of ghosts, too, featuring a monk, a poltergeist, and a bathroom spectre. Not enough like Halloween? Harry has a werewolf as a trusted mentor; meets an honest-to-God vampire, Count Sanguini; and even trolls turn up here and there.

HORROR: The supernatural at Hogwarts, it could be argued, isn't any scarier than the old *Addams Family* gothic camp television series. But there's plenty of fright: dementors that suck the souls and joy from a person in a fate worse than death; Voldemort's head under Quirrell's turban; Fenrir Greyback the werewolf eating human beings; not to mention the inconsolable, raw-fleshed baby soul fragment at King's Cross in *Deathly Hallows*.

SUBTERRANEAN PASSAGES: Harry goes underground every year for his annual confrontation with the black hats (except for *Goblet of Fire* when he Portkeys to a graveyard . . .). In *Deathly Hallows*, he goes underground seven times. As a gothic "heroine," Harry is almost defined by his heroic deeds performed in tight spaces underground.

ISOLATION: Every year, sometimes for most of the year, Harry is despised by most of his classmates for something he has done or for things he hasn't done. In *Sorcerer's Stone*, it was losing house points for being out after curfew. In *Chamber of*

Secrets, the rumor is that he is the Heir of Slytherin petrifying Muggle-borns. In *Prisoner of Azkaban*, the need to protect him from Sirius Black is the reason dementors surround the school. In *Goblet of Fire*, he is chosen as the second Gryffindor champion for the Triwizard Tournament even though he is not old enough to have applied. In *Order of the Phoenix*, no one wants to believe Voldemort is back—but Harry tells everyone he has witnessed his return. And, in *Deathly Hallows*, Harry is a hunted man on the run from the Ministry, their Snatchers, and the Death Eaters. For a popular guy, Harry spends a lot of time despised or feared by his peers.

FRAGMENTATION AND REUNION: The most painful chapters of the books are the several times either Harry, Ron, or Hermione decides to exclude a member (for example, Hermione's agony in *Prisoner of Azkaban*) or takes leave voluntarily, spitefully (such as Ron in *Goblet of Fire* and *Deatlhy Hallows*). Their eventual and usually dramatic reconciliations and reunions, in keeping with the gothic formula, are the highs of the whole series. Harry's life as an orphan is highlighted by his always-surprising meeting with shades of his parents: in the mirror in *Sorcerer's Stone*, in the golden web while dueling with Voldemort in *Goblet of Fire*, and on his walk to certain death in *Deathly Hallows*.

PROPHECY, ANCESTRAL CURSE: The Harry/Voldemort relationship and conflict turns on a prophecy about *The One with the Power to Vanquish the Dark Lord*. Hogwarts struggles with its founder's myth and the cross-generational hatred between Slytherin and Gryffindor. The Defense Against the Dark Arts teaching position is clearly cursed. And Professor Trelawney predicts Harry's death at a young age in almost every Divinations class.

TAINTED BLOOD, BOND OF BLOOD: The great divide in the Wizarding world at large is an extension of the Gryffindor/ Slytherin feud. The Pure Bloods of Slytherin maintain that those witches and wizards who are Muggle-born or who have Muggle ancestry in any way are inherently inferior to those who aren't and don't. Issues of "blood purity" and tolerance of Mudbloods define social grouping and standing. It's no accident that Harry ultimately defeats the Dark Lord because of the sacrificial love of his Muggle-born mother.

GRAVEYARD, CORPSES: The pivotal scene for the seven-book series occurs in *Goblet of Fire* in the Little Hangleton graveyard, where Lord Voldemort throws his rebirthing party. Some of the Dark Lord's most horrific weapons are the Inferi, animated corpses that almost pull Harry into the lake and to his death.

DECAY OF ARISTOCRATIC PRIVILEGE, RISE OF BOURGEOI-SIE: Gothic romance celebrates the minor gentry and simple landowner, whose virtues and ambitions for individual rights in inheritance and marriage are in conflict with old money, landed estates, and an aristocracy in decline.[9] Can you say "Malfoys and Weasleys?" The Malfoys have one child because of their caste belief in primogeniture and unwillingness to divide their holdings; they are corrupt, bigoted, and unfailingly patronizing to their social inferiors. The Weasleys are the opposite on all counts. Draco Malfoy, when Hermione points out that he has only been made the Slytherin Seeker because of his father's money, not talent, enrages the Weasleys by calling her "Mudblood." The gothic social argument in a snapshot!

FOREST: The Forbidden Forest that all but surrounds Hogwarts is populated with angry centaurs, a giant, ferocious Acromantulas, and a host of magical creatures running the spectrum from Bowtruckles, Triwizard dragons, and Nifflers to unicorns, Hippogriffs, and Thestrals. It is off-limits because it is a wild place and dangerous to students; Harry, consequently, visits almost every year on detentions, classroom trips, outings with Hagrid, and, finally, to meet his death.

SACRIFICIAL BRAVERY: Hermione says Harry has a "saving people thing" and she has a point; Harry ends every book, it seems, by putting his life on the line to save a friend or keep the Dark Lord from taking over the world. But Harry isn't the only one. Lily dies to save Harry. Ron jumps in the Forest of Dean pool to save Harry's life, and Snape risks his life daily in the last three books as a Death Eater double agent within the Order of the Phoenix. Sacrificial love, loyalty, and bravery are the stock responses *Potter* readers are trained in, beginning to end.

MEMORIES AND DREAMS: Several of the books' mysteries turn on information gained from memories in a Pensieve, and one features a living memory as a principal character (young Riddle in *Chamber of Secrets*). Harry dreams prophetic dreams or has visions through Lord Voldemort's soul fragment when he rests.

FOUND BOOK: In *Chamber of Secrets*, Lucius Malfoy plants Tom Riddle's diary inside one of Ginny Weasley's textbooks. The living memory in it possesses her and frees the basilisk from the Chamber of Secrets. Harry is given a Potions textbook in *Half-Blood Prince* that is brilliantly annotated by the book's mysterious namesake. Harry becomes a Potions whiz kid, learns a spell with which he almost kills Draco, and saves Ron from a death by poisoning.

DOPPELGÄNGERS: The Hogwarts cast of characters is a double-natured bunch. There is a werewolf, a half-giant, a Muggle-born, a double agent, and a "Dumbledore Man" with a Voldemort soul fragment tattooed to his forehead. Besides these Jekyll/Hyde interior doppelgängers, there are also pairs; Dumbledore/Voldemort are a light and darkness set, for example, akin to Van Helsing/Dracula, and Harry's gothic heroine role is complementary both to Snape's Byronic anti-hero part and Voldemort as the gothic overreaching scientist.

SCAR OR TELLTALE MARK: Harry's scar is his connection with the soul of Lord Voldemort. It is also the identifying mark by which every magical person recognizes him.

MYSTERIOUS STRANGER: Consider Black, Lupin, Moody, even Snape as figures who are not what they seem to be at first sight or until known very well.

CONFUSED ORIGIN: Harry is not only an orphan, but also a living mystery. How did he survive the Death Curse as an infant? Harry's life as a survivor leaves everyone scratching their heads.

NIGHT: Rowling has said that Hogwarts had to be a boarding school so the children could have nighttime adventures.[10] Given the number of nights Harry is out in the halls under the Invisibility Cloak, I often wonder how he passed any classes or stayed awake. The naps during Professor Binns's lectures must have helped.

MIST AND FOG: *Half-Blood Prince* opens with the U.K. Prime Minister upset by the chaos erupting all around him inexplicably, not to mention "all this chilly mist in the middle of July . . . It wasn't right, it wasn't normal." He isn't cheered to learn from Cornelius Fudge that the cause of the mist everywhere is breeding dementors, "the creatures that drain hope and happiness out of people" (*Half-Blood Prince*, chapter one).

DISTANT PAST: There isn't time travel into the distant past, but Hogwarts and the Wizarding world have a medieval or Renaissance flavor nonetheless because of the castle and its antiquities and defining characteristics (suits of armor, paintings, the Great Hall, etc.). The robes and absence of technology, too, give everything about the school a nineteenth-century feel, at best.

DEATH: Lupin, Tonks, Sirius, James, Lily, Colin, Fred, Albus, Peter, Alastor, Barty, and Severus, for starters. The books are about death, and characters drop right and left as you'd expect in a series beginning with a double murder . . .

In short, *Harry Potter* is a schoolboy novel steeped, no, make that *saturated* in gothic touches, effects, and clichés. But there's more.

Beyond these gothic touchstones, Ms. Rowling includes gothic romances as stories inside her stories. My favorite is the romance of the Bloody Baron and the Gray Lady, the ghosts of Slytherin House and Ravenclaw Tower respectively (*Deathly Hallows*, chapter thirty-one). In the middle of the Battle of Hogwarts, Harry listens attentively to Helena Ravenclaw's ghost telling the gothic romance that reveals the story of the Baron's agonies and the theft of the Ravenclaw diadem. It has a medieval setting; unrequited love; defiant, victimized maiden escaping and hiding; blood; death in the forest before dishonor—in brief, it has it all.

That is my favorite, but Harry's subterranean adventures in *Sorcerer's Stone* and *Chamber of Secrets* are close seconds. Ginny's being possessed by Tom Riddle, Jr., and taken "miles beneath Hogwarts" despite her heroic resistance only to be rescued by her Prince Charming marks her as Harry's soul mate and fellow gothic romance heroine.

And the story of Severus Snape's life as another Heathcliff, sacrificing himself, not all at once but day by day for years to protect Harry in Lily's memory, and his classroom sadism and his genius as a wizard have made Snape almost more important than Harry in many readers' experience of the book. The Unbreakable Vow he makes with Narcissa Malfoy is a gallant gothic moment and subplot leading to his committing murder-in-obedience on the tower.

Voldemort's mother, Merope Gaunt, lived a life that Ann Radcliffe, the great gothic romance novelist, might have written. Oppressed by father and brother, she is liberated when they are imprisoned for Muggle baiting. Her magic returns, and she wins the attention and affection of the young lord of the local manor with a love potion or charm. Alas, she feels compelled to reveal to him that she has enchanted him literally rather than figuratively—and he leaves her. She is pregnant, destitute, and despairing enough to lose her magic. She dies in childbirth, leaving Tom Riddle, Jr., to grow up in an orphanage.

How about Dumbledore's long-neglected backstory? His sister was tortured by Muggles and becomes mad. The family keeps this a secret, though it means the father dies in Azkaban after revenging himself on her tormentors, because they cannot reveal why he acted as he did. The sister kills the mother accidentally and poor, brilliant Albus, caught at home as a baby-sitter, becomes friends with a Dark wizard intent on world domination! He quarrels, though, with his brother and new friend—and little sister dies in the cross fire. He spends the remainder of his life, like Snape, repenting in service and reflecting mournfully on the loved ones he failed.

Conclusion: The Morality of Gothic Literature

It is a rare gothic novel that pours in so many touchstones of the genre and layers gothic stories within the already-thick atmosphere of the uncanny and sublime. Those that do are either set pieces like *Frankenstein* or a kind of gothic parody, like Jane Austen's *Northanger Abbey*. Austen, Ms. Rowling's favorite writer (see chapter one), puts *Abbey's* heroine, Catherine Morland, in a clichéd gothic scene, a manor house in which she discovers what seems to be a document in secret writing. Because the young woman is a devoted reader of gothic romance, she suspects the worst and sleeps uneasily. She discovers in the morning that the dangerous document is a laundry list. Much of *Abbey* is Austen's gentle mocking of the genre.

Ms. Rowling may be up to the same thing in including so many gothic elements and subplots in the *Potter* novels. Certainly the Grim subplot in *Prisoner*, in which Harry thinks he is being haunted by a Black Dog death omen, which turns out to be his godfather working to protect him from danger rather than supernatural sign, is an echo of gothic parody à la Austen, in which natural explanations always supplant superstitious fears eventually.

But Rowling and Austen, while laughing perhaps at the more comic aspects of the gothic, don't neglect the point of the genre. For both writers, the fears appropriate to our fallen world and atrophied spiritual life—not to mention as women in a man's world (see chapter six)—are real, important, and best expressed with "gothic machinery."

I have demonstrated, I hope, that the heroes of *Harry Potter* are gothic novel stock players and that the author creates the atmosphere of menace in her schoolboy novels both by using every touchstone of the gothic literary tradition and by weaving into her story arc and individual books gothic story subtexts and locations.

What I've neglected to do is discuss how this atmosphere has a specifically moral effect on the reader. The best way to do that is to revisit Ms. Rowling's very gothic first chapters of *Sorcerer's Stone* and the Dursleys' experience of the "Letters from No One."

Aunt Petunia and Uncle Vernon Dursley pride themselves on their normalcy. But they have a private dread that the neighbors will discover that their nephew, Harry, is decidedly abnormal. This fear of public revelation causes them to become sadistic cartoons of respectability and repression to mask their secret. Then the letters begin to arrive.

No postage, no return address, but with alarmingly specific detail on where the letter is to be delivered: "Mr. H. Potter, The Cupboard Under the Stairs." The letters come with the other mail at first, but when Harry does not receive these (which the sender knows, inexplicably), they begin to arrive, en masse, delivered by owls, and, eventually, even through the fireplace chimney in great torrents. Uncle Vernon, already unstable because of his latent fears of his nephew's problem, becomes progressively unhinged—and determined to escape the letters that are besieging his family.

The Dursleys are so unsettled by this magical assault from an unknown quarter that they abandon their home and flee. They wind up, not in a castle or manor house, but in an equally gothic "house on the rock" at sea where they believe they have so isolated themselves in wild nature that they are safe from their faceless, unknown epistolary enemy. Of course, at midnight, in a "ferocious storm," the door to the house is broken down by a bearded giant stranger with a pink umbrella. The story, oddly enough, considering its many gothic elements, is not a scare story per se, even if it does have its gruesome images. It's not just the comic touches like the pink umbrella that keep us from being scared or feeling concern for the Dursleys. They are a despicable lot, we all think, because of the horrible way they treat Harry, who seems a wonderful boy. Harry welcomes the letters. We, consequently, odd as this is in a gothic tale, are rooting for the mysterious, nameless force delivering the mail to win the war with the normal family that feels it is under attack.

What we are cheering for, beyond Harry getting his mail, is that the Muggles will be enlightened by the horror they experience. The Dursleys are allegorical stand-ins for actors in a supernatural drama or, more important, readers of gothic fiction. They are receiving literal and figurative messages from heaven or a supernatural reality they have tried to hide from or deny their whole lives but which is now exploding into their living room in a way that cannot be overlooked, grasped, stopped, or controlled.

Ann Radcliffe wrote that "positive horror" could be "a source of the sublime."[11] Readers scared out of their wits by stories about man-made monsters, men having made themselves monsters, and defiant heroines trapped by cruel men or supernatural forces in subterranean chambers are stunned out of a complacent normalcy that accepts the fallen world of death and sin as "natural." Gothic writers "make a righteous use of the element of horror"[12] to shake their readers awake and to realize the darkened state of their understanding and inattentiveness to conscience and the eye of the heart.

Ultimately, gothic literature is about having the moral courage to see the world as it is and to make the choice to seek a way out. That choice is by definition and tradition a moral one—to flee death and pursue life, to seek light rather than darkness. We see the horror in the world—and in monsters without conscience—and draw away from it. We identify with the defiant heroine resisting the forces working to imprison or diminish her. What is good, true, and beautiful is sharpened in exposure to its absence in the evil of gothic nightmares.

Born centuries ago at the dawn of the age of empiricism and enlightened reason, largely in reaction to the industrial and political revolutions of failed millennialist promise,[13] the gothic in literature, film, architecture, and popular culture is still very much with us. But there are radical differences between the Victorian gothic morality evident in Stoker's *Dracula* and the postmodern vampires of Stephanie Meyer's *Twilight* books or *Buffy the Vampire Slayer*. Having established that *Harry Potter*, if it has to be described in three words, is a "gothic schoolboy novel," let's look at Rowling as a postmodern writer and at the specific moral choices she wants her readers to make for redemption and escape of the fallen world.

CHAPTER FIVE

Harry Potter as Postmodern Epic

*Preaching the Gospel of Tolerance and Inclusiveness—
and Choosing the Metanarrative of Love*

We've just spent two good-sized chapters demonstrating what you probably would have figured out after five minutes of reflection on the question, "What kind of books are the *Harry Potter* novels?" Granted, it hasn't been wasted time if you didn't know about the schoolboy or gothic traditions of English literature in which Ms. Rowling is writing, but, still, to have worked that hard to come up with "*Harry Potter* is schoolboy fiction with a gothic atmosphere?" It seems quite a bit like the scientific studies that demonstrate the surest way to lose weight is to eat less and exercise more. We didn't know that?

But here's the really sad thing. *Harry Potter* isn't a gothic schoolboy series of books. Yes, it's about a schoolboy and his secondary education in a public school, and, sure, it has every gothic fiction gadget from secret closets (can you say "Vanishing Cabinets?") to a castle on the lake.

But the books don't *do* what a schoolboy novel or gothic romance is supposed to do. Not exactly.

The schoolboy or schoolgirl novel, be it *Tom Brown's Schooldays*, penny dreadful, or Enid Blyton serial, is largely a celebration of Victorian morality and ideas of virtue. A gothic romance or horror piece, too, has a supernatural or human enemy that acts as a moral foil; we are confronted with death's grip on the fallen world and our own inadequacy to free ourselves from it. This gothic landslide amounts, in relief, to a call to the life of virtue in hope of redemption, what schoolboy fiction is openly about. Who wants to become the man-made monsters Dracula, Frankenstein, Hyde, or Heathcliff? If we are defiant and resist compromise to the end, à la Jane Eyre, virtue will win out.

Harry Potter certainly has its heroic moments and the evil presented is very real. But as noted in the previous chapter, many of the gothic elements aren't frightening at all; for the most part, they're funny, and often they have the zap or thrill you might get from living room furniture. I mean, if you're horrified by Moaning Myrtle, Peeves, or the Giant Squid,

Hogwarts's "Nessie," you're as oversensitive as Poe's narrator in "The Tell-Tale Heart."

Hogwarts as a school, too, is hard to take seriously. The only things of any value they learn, after all, are lessons they learn outside of formal classes (how to fly on a broom, Apparating, effective Defense Against the Dark Arts spells, etc.). Teachers, as a rule, are sadists, freaks, officious nits, or sufficiently incompetent that they can be all but ignored (see chapter six on satire). Take Professor Trelawney or Dolores Umbridge. *Please.*

That Ms. Rowling isn't writing classic schoolboy or gothic fiction shouldn't be a surprise, though. As these sorts of books were most popular in the nineteenth century, how weird would it be, as a twentieth-century writer aiming to please twenty-first-century readers, if she wrote books just like Bram Stoker, Mary Shelley, or even Enid Blyton?

Very weird. She needs a different hook to catch postmodern readers, a hook at the moral level that will connect with readers the way mystery and Harry's being an orphan did on the surface layer. That hook is Ms. Rowling's delivery of moral lessons we already believe in just by living in this historical period, lessons we learn again in every book we read, advertisement we watch, or news program we listen to.

Let's look at how twenty-first-century schoolboy and gothic books differ from the ones we just reviewed for an idea of how our age differs from Queen Victoria's.

A World Turned Inside Out

Looking around the twenty-first-century bookstores for echoes of gothic horror, schoolboy novels, or anything like a fairy tale with witches or Charlotte Brontë's *Jane Eyre*, I made an amazing discovery. Somewhere around the turn of the last century the world of books was turned inside out. The bad guys of the old books are all new-book good guys, or at least very sympathetic characters to whom we are obliged to give a break for the challenges they're facing. And the good guys seem a little simple.

Vampires are hot right now. But they're not bipedal demons and devils like our friend from Transylvania that the good guys are obliged to decapitate, drive metal stakes into, and defy sacrificially and heroically with the Eucharist. Stephanie Meyer's *Twilight* books hold four of the top five spots on the *New York Times* Bestseller List as I write this; young girls are lining up for repeat viewings of teen heartthrob Robert Pattinson playing boy vamp Edward Cullen in the first *Twilight* film. The vampires in these books are horribly misunderstood superpowered good guys with drinking problems. They're "vegetarian," meaning they drink only animal blood, no human blood allowed. They have to hide who they are lest they suffer persecution by the whacko human beings prejudiced against them.

Dracula is still very bad in *Van Helsing*, the 2004 Universal Pictures blockbuster directed by Stephen Sommers, but Frankenstein's creature? He isn't the horrific figure of gothic romance who conveys what a monster fallen, spiritless man is. The creature is a persecuted victim, attacked by unfeeling villagers, used by Dracula and his brides to animate their "children," and one who does all he can to help the James Bond version of Abraham Van Helsing save the world from a vampire population explosion.

Witches? I grew up believing there were good witches and wizards and bad witches and wizards. Good wizards? Easy: Prospero, the Narnia Star mage, Gandalf, and the Wizard of Oz. I had a harder time with witches, though there were a few good ones like Samantha Stephens (*Bewitched*) and Sabrina (*Sabrina: The Teenage Witch*). What turned me off to witches, probably forever except for *Harry Potter*, was the green-skinned Wicked Witch of the West played by Margaret Hamilton in MGM's 1939 classic Technicolor film, *The Wizard of Oz*.

I remember that film was the only thing I saw on television my senior year at Exeter. We had all grown up with this movie and, though it was exam week, we sat down to watch—teachers, tests, and papers be damned. When Hamilton flew into Munchkinland to get the ruby slippers she felt were hers by right, the boy next to me said, "THAT is a *wicked* wicked-witch." I'm still trying to unwrap all of what he meant by "wicked" in that short sentence, but everyone present agreed with him. I could never drink Maxwell House coffee as a grown-up because Hamilton was their spokesperson. I felt it had to be a nasty brew.

But in the 1995 novel that became the blockbuster 2003 Broadway musical *Wicked: The Untold Story of the Witches of Oz*, the Wicked Witch (named Elphaba) is not the bad guy. She's the horribly misunderstood and misrepresented good witch who has been discriminated against by her religious parents and narrow-minded schoolteachers for her colored skin and free thinking. Who knew?

In *Tom Brown's Schooldays*, the bad guy and Tom's nemesis (much like Draco Malfoy is to Harry) is an older boy named Flashman. After being bullied and burned, Brown and his best friend have their rowdy revenge and Flashman is expelled for drunkenness. Flashy is a vicious, violent, self-important prig, and *Tom Brown* readers can loathe him openly and ardently.

Now, thanks to the twelve volumes of George MacDonald Fraser's *Flashman Papers* (published 1969–2005), we know what happened to Flashman post-Rugby. He's a lifelong cad and a coward, as we'd expect, but, incredibly, in every one of his adventures in wars and scrapes from India and China to Bull Run in the Dakotas, he escapes alive and, get this, *as a hero*. The suggestion seems to be that it is *because* he is such an irresponsible, sex-consumed toady and profligate that he succeeds so spectacularly in the bedroom, boardroom, and battlefield despite himself.

Jane Eyre hasn't survived postmodern revision unscathed, either. In Charlotte Brontë's original novel, Jane's first marriage attempt to Mr. Rochester is prevented, right when the couple is at the altar about to make their vows, by a lawyer and the brother of Bertha, the wife Rochester keeps in the attic. Bertha eventually escapes and succeeds in burning down Thornfield Manor and killing herself, simultaneously blinding and crippling Rochester, but also liberating him to marry Jane Eyre.

In Jean Rhys's *Wide Sargasso Sea* (1966), we learned that the first Mrs. Rochester was the real heroine of her own gothic romance, a white Creole woman whom Rochester married for her money, drove over the mental edge, and imprisoned. The postcolonial version of the tale features Jane and Rochester as racists and colonial suppressors.

Much more fun but in its way as unsettling is Jasper Fforde's *The Eyre Affair* (2001). In an alternate-universe story with more twists than I can possibly summarize here, literary detective Thursday Next (her name) chases literary blackmailer Acheron Hades (ouch) into the pages of *Jane Eyre* via her uncle's invention, the Prose Portal. Hades, to blackmail a literature-obsessed general population, is killing characters in Dickens's *Martin Chuzzlewit* by erasing them from the original manuscript.

In this universe's version of 1985, England and the Russian Empire are still fighting the Crimean War, Wales is a Soviet

Republic, the real author of the Shakespeare plays is contested everywhere, with no little emotion and by almost everyone, and *Jane Eyre* ends with Jane in India with her cousin instead of making up with the blinded Rochester. Thursday's battle at Thornfield Manor with Hades, as you might have guessed, ends up starting the fire that destroys the manor, Acheron tosses Bertha from the roof, and Rochester nearly dies getting Thursday out of the building. Next becomes Rochester's voice that Jane hears, which prevents her from going to India. A new ending to *Jane Eyre* due to reader participation and engagement with the text, literally and figuratively!

In my favorite touch, Thursday realizes she cannot live without her true love and rushes to his wedding—only to find his wedding has been called off because *his bride-to-be* is already married. The Rochesters had sent the lawyer who had broken up their first wedding into the "real world" to stop this one. The boundaries of space, time, text, genre, character, and reader in this book are porous, to say the least.

My point?

All the bad guys in the gothic fiction we discussed in the last chapter are revealed in their twenty-first-century reinventions to be good guys who have been misunderstood. The white hats in these stories, correspondingly, have a dark side we never would have guessed in the originals.

Ms. Rowling is writing stories in the same historical period as these very successful revisionist adaptations of gothic and schoolboy fiction. To get at how her *Harry Potter* stories resemble and differ from Victorian morality tales, we need to think about how we see things differently than Tom Brown and Robert Louis Stevenson did.

We need to look at our own eyeballs, or, at least, at the colored glasses through which we filter reality. With a better idea of how we think, we'll be able to understand Rowling as a writer of our times. As popular as *Harry Potter* is around the world, it's clear her message and meaning resonate profoundly with the fundamental beliefs of our age.

Three qualities of postmodern thinking and literature are at the moral heart of *Harry Potter*. These can also be seen pretty clearly in every popular book, movie, and song of our time. To prove that, let's look at an improbable example: the popular animated television program produced in 1964 from the song "Rudolph the Red-Nosed Reindeer."

Misfits: A Colored Reindeer, an Elf with Lifestyle Issues

According to Rick Goldschmidt, author of *Rudolph the Red-Nosed Reindeer: The Making of the Rankin/Bass Holiday Classic*, "Premiering on NBC December 6, 1964, *Rudolph* has become the longest-running, highest-rated television special in the history of the medium."[1] The story goes something like this: *A young red-nosed reindeer is being ousted from the reindeer games because of his shiny nose. He teams up with Hermey, an elf who wants to be a dentist, and Yukon Cornelius, a prospector. They run into the Abominable Snowman and find a whole island of misfit toys. Rudoph vows to get Santa to help the toys, and he goes back to the North Pole on Christmas Eve. But Santa's sleigh is fogged in. Then Santa looks at Rudolph, and gets a very bright idea . . .* [2]

Let's look at the top three characteristics of postmodern thinking, and how they are reflected in the literature and drama of our time, and how *Rudolph the Red-Nosed Reindeer* exemplifies all three.

The first characteristic is a tendency to question the defining myths of our culture. Defining myths of a culture impose a rational order and hierarchy on those who live within that culture. They are stories around which we organize our ideas of right and wrong, good guys and villains.

This rational order, however, is necessarily oppressive, exclusive, and incomplete because of the way people in power use every social structure (education, right to vote, access to capital, etc.) to hold on to their status. These structures include law and language, art and literature, even movies. No one whose worldview is shaped by belief in this reality can see the world in any way except as confirmation of their core beliefs.

So, what is the grand myth of Rudolph's North Pole? How is it a lie? *Rudolph* is a tale about the evils of unexamined beliefs at the North Pole. Our heroes are Rudolph, a young reindeer, and Hermey, an elf working in Santa's toy workshop. Rudolph can't fit in with the other reindeer because of his "shiny nose." Even his dad, proud Donner, is ashamed of Rudolph's being so different. At the "Reindeer Games"—Quidditch for reindeer—Rudolph is humiliated by his nose even though he is a good flyer.

True reindeer have *black* noses. Nonblack-nosed reindeer are "other," consequently, and "less reindeer" than those whose noses are normal-colored. Remember, this television special first aired in 1964. Rudolph is a minority, oppressed because of his color.

Things aren't much better for Santa's elves. Hermey the elf's nose is the right shade of pink. It's his lifestyle choice that makes him an "other." Hermey hates making toys in Santa's workshop and wants to be a dentist, so he is mocked and marginalized. For Hermey and Rudolph, the happy world of the North Pole is a miserable prison. They reject the defining myth of North Pole culture: that everyone is happy and productive in the places created for them.

The second characteristic of postmodern thinking is: **Nothing is what you think it is, no one is who surface appearances make you think they are.** A tenet of postmodernism is that our perception of reality is untrustworthy. We do not see or sense anything *as it truly is* except through a filter of preconception. Really "knowing," consequently, requires examining the way we think, and how we understand the things we perceive. "Truth" is absolutely relative. In story, our inability to know is best represented by the surprise ending, where we are confronted by our misperceptions and misunderstanding of the people and problems we've read about.

In *Rudolph the Red-Nosed Reindeer*, the "surprise"—which is so characteristic of postmodern fiction that it hardly comes off as surprising—is that the very qualities excluded by the culture of reindeers and elves just happen to be the exact qualities needed to save those communities in their time of desperation. Rudolph, despised by friends and family, saves the day in the storm that would have cancelled Santa's Christmas deliveries.

Hermey saves everyone with his peculiar devotion to dentistry by defanging the Abominable Snowman at story's end. Who could have guessed? Those same qualities that made Rudolph and Hermey misfits were just the characteristics and skills that everyone needed. We missed it because we bought into the prejudices about color-free noses and happy toy-making elves.

The third quality of postmodern thinking is: **Genre blurring: high art and popular entertainment mix.** In architecture it's known as "double-coding" and means mixing in elements of other styles, a Georgian doorway or cornice on a Bauhaus glass-box skyscraper to jar the eye and make the viewer conscious of what is on display. In the literature of our day, the commonplace blurring and mixing of literary genres in one work serves to shake up the reader's preconceived notions of what he or she is reading. It creates a state of slight confusion, a lack of certainty about what can be expected to happen next—and that creates an opening through which writers can drive home larger messages.

When *Rudolph the Red-Nosed Reindeer* first appeared as a Christmas cartoon special in 1964, it was an expansion of a song and a story already very familiar to American viewers. In addition to being a television show derived from a Tin Pan Alley holiday song, *Rudolph* the TV special mixes in two other upside-down elements; it's a stop motion animation play done with dolls rather than a proper Bugs Bunny–type cartoon and, incredibly—to me at least—it *is* a musical. Reindeer, Santa, dentists, misfit toys singing at the North Pole like it is Broadway. I mean how weird is this show? The mixing of genres and media is perfect to deliver the prejudice-blasting morality play because its presentation already has the audience questioning their idea of what they are seeing and thinking.

As you already know from your trip through the first four chapters, Ms. Rowling is a master mixer of genres. She does it, of course, to deliver her postmodern meaning and moral message.

Rowling as a Writer of Her Times

I hope now you can see why we needed those rewrites of *Dracula*, *Frankenstein*, *Tom Brown*, and *Jane Eyre*. You know that Creole woman in the attic was used and abused by the barely suppressed colonial and racist beliefs of Rochester. Vampires and soulless monsters, of course, are misunderstood by the common herd with their ignorant prejudices; turning the story upside-down with the accepted evil as good and vice versa is the means to our re-education in the politically correct prejudice of our time that all prejudice is bad.

Even more than *Rudolph*, *Harry Potter* questions cultural myths, demonstrates to us that we shouldn't think we know what is really going on, and blends all literary genres more than any other work of fiction, perhaps.

Like all cultures, Hogwarts has a Founder's Myth: the story of the Four Founders and the breakup of the once dear friends Salazar Slytherin and Godric Gryffindor. Ms. Rowling asks us to see how this story poisons the minds and hearts of all witches and wizards. This grand narrative causes not only the Gryffindor/Slytherin battle that is the good/evil axis of the storyline, but also turns each magical person into a partisan defending their quarter rather than celebrating the whole. Gryffindor is core, Slytherin is "other" from the Gryffindor side; Pure Bloods are core, all other beings are "other" and "lesser" to the Slytherins. The Death Eaters are Slytherin ideology run amok and truly evil, but Gryffindor pride and machismo are equally divisive. All of them, as partisans, share dismissive attitudes about the "Magical Brethren."

The Sorting Hat, as the vehicle of the Wizarding world's division, says as much about itself in *Phoenix*.

> *Listen closely to my song:*
> *Though condemned I am to split you*
> *Still I worry that it's wrong,*
> *Though I must fulfill my duty*
> *And must quarter every year*
> *Still I wonder whether sorting*
> *May not bring the end I fear.*
> (Order of the Phoenix, *chapter eleven*)

This division-in-keeping-with-legend colors and clouds everyone's thinking or ability to see things as they are (Dumbledore aside). It is the root of Slytherin "wizarding pride" and Muggle-baiting and the inability of the other Hogwarts houses and the Magical Brethren to unite. The Wizarding world's Foundation Myth is divisive and oppressive to the "other." This is the core teaching of the postmodern worldviews we live with today, as expressed in the *Harry Potter* stories.

A case could be made that the Sorting Hat is the real bad guy; Voldemort and the Death Eaters are just understandable consequences of the divisive myth we confirm at the annual sorting.

The *Harry Potter* stories are largely about the many prejudices gripping the magical world of Hogwarts and beyond, consequent to the Four Founders' Myth. Three of the larger prejudices are those against (1) magical people (and creatures) of mixed blood or blood that is otherwise tainted, (2) against the poor, and (3) against those Magical Brethren who are not witches or wizards.

Hogwarts's blood problems, like those outside of the school, can be traced back to the "origin myth" of the Four Founders. One of these four, Salazar Slytherin, wanted only pure-blood wizards in his school house, and, though Slytherin left the school after a disagreement with Gryffindor, his house remains the bastion of wizard prejudice against those witches and wizards of mixed ancestry or those who are Muggle-born. We learned in *Order of the Phoenix* that this prejudice is not limited to Hogwarts but pervades the Wizarding world.

The "N" word among the magical folk is "Mudblood," and Draco Malfoy, the Slytherin boy we love to hate, uses this word to describe Hermione Granger, as Severus Snape did as a student to describe Lily Evans. Other slurs used by "Pure Bloods" are "Half-blood," "Half-breed," and "Muggle-born."

Draco Malfoy doesn't restrict his prejudices to bloodlines, however, in keeping the traditions of his house and beliefs of his family. He is disdainful, too, of those individuals and families who don't have money or worldly goods or a big house. Ron Weasley is the usual target of this prejudice against the poor—and every one of Draco's barbs hits home, it seems, in Ron's heart. Ron, much more than his several siblings and parents, takes his lack of spending money and his hand-me-down wardrobe as if it were a personal failing to be hidden and overcome.

As nasty as these Slytherin prejudices are, they are held by a relatively narrow slice of the population pie. The prejudices identify the evil characters of the book as surely as the Dark Mark tattoo, but they aren't the grand narrative problem that threatens to bring down the Wizarding world.

That "otherness" is the prejudice of good and bad wizards and witches with respect to three-fourths of the world's Magical Brethren, that is, the centaurs, the goblins, and the house-elves. The myth is depicted in the Ministry of Magic as a statue and fount called "The Fountain of Magical Brethren."

Halfway down the hall was a fountain. A group of golden statues, larger than life-size, stood in the middle of a circular pool. Tallest of them all was a noble-looking wizard with his wand pointing straight up in the air. Grouped around him were a beautiful witch, a centaur, a goblin, and a house-elf. The last three were all looking adoringly up at the witch and wizard. Glittering jets of water

were flying from the ends of the two wands, the point of the cen-
taur's arrow, the tip of the goblin's hat, and each of the house-elf's
ears, so that the tinkling hiss of falling water was added to the
pops and cracks of Apparators and the clatter of footsteps as hun-
dreds of witches and wizards, most of whom were wearing glum,
early-morning looks, strode toward a set of golden gates at the far
end of the hall. (Order of the Phoenix, *chapter seven*)

This sculpture represents the overarching belief of witches and wizards about their fellow magical beings or creatures. First, of course, is the fealty of the "adoring" centaur, goblin, and house-elf for the "noble" wizard and "beautiful" witch. As central as this joyful subservience is to the myth, to notice those who are not depicted at all is even more telling about wizard beliefs and exclusivity. There is no giant in the fountain, nor is there a dementor. The nonhuman "brethren" in the fountain have it bad, certainly, but the real "others" in this representation of the magical world are those not even pictured.

After Harry's hearing, he takes a closer look at the statues:

He looked up into the handsome wizard's face, but up close,
Harry thought he looked rather weak and foolish. The witch was
wearing a vapid smile like a beauty contestant, and from what
Harry knew of goblins and centaurs, they were most unlikely to
be caught staring this soppily at humans of any description. Only

the house-elf's attitude of creeping servility looked convincing.
With a grin at the thought of what Hermione would say if she
could see the statue of the elf, Harry turned his money bag upside
*down . . . (*Order of the Phoenix, *chapter nine)*

Ms. Rowling offers us this statue as something that none of the passersby even look up at because it represents the unquestioned and unconscious belief on which the magical world and government rest.

This blind spot in the consciousness of wizards—their exclusive hold of power and misuse of those they think of as "brethren" as well as the totally marginalized others—is the agony of the Wizarding world and the cause of the Voldemort crisis. Lord Voldemort, the Nazilike totalitarian madman of these books, is anything but an incomprehensible and aberrational evil. He is only the logical extension and symptom of the prejudice against nonwizards held by a great many ordinary witches and wizards.

That the statue is destroyed by the combat between Dumbledore and Voldemort at the end of *Order of the Phoenix* is telling. Dumbledore explains to Harry that this myth is a lie—and that the much-uglier truth it fails to represent will have horrible consequences.

"Sirius did not hate Kreacher [his family's house-elf]," said Dum-
bledore. "He regarded him as a servant unworthy of much interest

or notice. Indifference and neglect often do much more damage than outright dislike . . . The fountain we destroyed tonight told a lie. We wizards have mistreated and abused our fellows for too long, and we are now reaping our reward." (Order of the Phoenix, *chapter thirty-seven*)

In case we missed the point, there is a new statue in the Death Eater–dominated Ministry of Magic in *Deathly Hallows:*

The great Atrium seemed darker than Harry remembered it. Previously a golden fountain had filled the center of the hall, casting shimmering spots of light over the polished wooden floor and walls. Now a gigantic statue of black stone dominated the scene. It was rather frightening, this vast sculpture of a witch and a wizard sitting on ornately carved thrones, looking down at the Ministry workers toppling out of fireplaces below them. Engraved in foot-high letters at the base of the statue were the words MAGIC IS MIGHT . . .

Harry looked more closely and realized that what he had thought were decoratively carved thrones were actually mounds of carved humans: hundreds and hundreds of naked bodies, men, women, and children, all with rather stupid, ugly faces, twisted and pressed together to support the weight of the handsomely robed wizards.

*"Muggles," whispered Hermione. "In their rightful place. Come on, let's get going." (*Deathly Hallows, *chapter twelve)*

VoldeWar II is a war between those magical folk who are prejudiced against Muggles, and against witches and wizards with anything but demonstrable Pure Blood status, and the champions of the oppressed. The Nazi-style statuary with suggestions of bodies in Dachau showers isn't meant to be subtle. Prejudice is the core evil, and it is a consequence of believing without question in the Founder's Myth.

Nothing is what you think it is, no one is who surface appearances make you think they are. We're *clueless.* As discussed, Ms. Rowling delivers this message by telling her stories in the third person limited omniscient view, the perspective of a house-elf sitting on Harry's shoulder with a minicam. We see what Harry sees and know what Harry thinks, but because it's not told in the first person, we're lulled into thinking we know what's going on.

Of course, blinded almost totally by our prejudices, we have little idea of what's going on. For clues about the larger picture, we'd be infinitely better off with a house-elf on Dumbledore's or Snape's shoulder—or Voldemort's! We get from Ms. Rowling a never-ending lesson on narrative misdirection. You don't know what's happening. Don't trust what you believe or you'll wind up like Harry, convinced that

Snape killed Dumbledore and that he's not coming back to Hogwarts in *Deathly Hallows*.

Ms. Rowling reinforces our cluelessness by making appearances so deceptive. Between Polyjuice Potion, double agents, and werewolves-in-hiding on the faculty, we can never be sure that people are who they seem to be. And, as with Rudolph and Hermey, it's the freaks who are good guys. The excluded "other" our culture prejudices us against is by definition the postmodern hero. And there isn't a good guy in the *Harry Potter* cast of characters who isn't on the outs with the Pure Blood elites.

Check them out:

The Order of the Phoenix includes a werewolf, an escaped convict, an overtly fecund family of impoverished redheads, a common thief, a Metamorphmagus, a bartender overly fond of goats, a Squib, a half-giant, a magical negro, a Death Eater of unknown allegiance, a paranoid retired Auror with a magical eye and short fuse, all of whom are led by an arguably gay wizard with Machiavellian tendencies.

Dumbledore's Army isn't any closer to being invited to the right parties. You have a brainiac Mudblood, for starters, a crowd of the children from the poor Irish family mentioned above, a nutcase who "believes anything if there is no evidence for it," the boy raised by his grandmother with memory issues and a love for plants, and, of course, they're led by an orphan who grew up with Muggles and has a pronounced history of mental episodes.

Misfits? They make Hermey and Rudolph look conventional. They're all misunderstood and periodically slandered by the *Daily Prophet*, imprisoned or put on trial by the Ministry, and at odds with one another.

They are, as such, the postmodern dream team: Olympic-grade freaks the Nazilike bad guys are obliged to despise and persecute, and we readers are morally bound to understand, even identify with.

Genre Busting

As already noted, Ms. Rowling has said the books spring from a "compost pile" of all the things she has read and, as she said about detective fiction, she's not above bending the rules of any given genre to achieve her story goals. About fantasy fiction she says openly, "I was trying to subvert the genre."[3] She even thinks this is the English tradition:

> *I've taken* horrible *liberties with folklore and mythology, but I'm quite unashamed about that, because British folklore and British mythology is a totally bastard mythology. You know, we've been invaded by people, we've appropriated their gods, we've taken their mythical creatures, and we've soldered them all together to make, what I would say, is one of the richest folklores in the world, because it's so varied. So I feel no compunction about borrowing from that freely, but adding a few things of my own.*[4]

So we get the pile of great books and literature genres behind *Harry Potter* that it is the business of this book to try to sort out. We're not even halfway through and already Harry is the orphan detective hero of a postmodern gothic schoolboy novel written by Jane Austen for children. And it's not just Harry. We've already seen Heathcliff with a touch of Dracula in Severus Snape, but in coming chapters I'll be introducing you to the inner-Dante and Sydney Carton lurking just beneath the surface of the Potions master's scowl.

So what?

The postmodern message of political correctness ("Resist your prejudices! You are a prisoner of your mistaken, unexamined beliefs!") can be a little patronizing and preachy. But, as with *Rudolph*, the combination of our confusion about what kind of book we're reading, our delight in the characters we meet, and our lowered defenses means we don't resent the fire hose of instruction. Rowling's huge message is taken in by her readers, old and young, without the usual skeptical filters in place because, after all, it's a kids' book.

The other reason we don't object, and perhaps the point of this chapter, is that she isn't teaching us anything we don't already believe. Prejudice, courtesy of the air we breathe and the PC messages we receive as intolerance-immunization booster shots daily, everywhere, is the ultimate evil to resist, individually and as a nation and a culture.

Hence the civil rights movement, the Equal Rights

Amendment, pride in having elected a black president (even by those in profound disagreement with him on issues), the Rainbow Coalition, and Barney the Dinosaur. Prejudice is not only the principal evil against which postmoderns battle; our belief that this evil is pervasive, even impossible to avoid or throw off, that prejudice is the "original sin" of the twenty-first century from which we must be delivered by something greater than ourselves—say, government regulation and advanced education—makes us doubt that we can know anything certainly and as it is.

The core postmodern belief is that the cultural assumptions that cloud, distort, and poison our thinking inevitably blind us to people and reality as they are. Only prejudiced and unloving fundamentalists and ideologues think they have a periscope that sees through prejudice to perceive the truth. And these people, who do not embrace relativism and ecumenism as core truths, are the intolerant people postmoderns will not tolerate.

Harry Potter is in this respect the postmodern epic. Ms. Rowling has told us as much in almost every interview she has given since *Deathly Hallows* was published. In the *Time* magazine 2008 "Person of the Year Runner-Up" article, it was put very succinctly:

> *[Y]ou can tell how much this all matters to her, if it weren't already clear from her 4,100-page treatise on tolerance. "I'm*

opposed to fundamentalism in any form," she says. "And that includes in my own religion."[5]

Like most of us, Ms. Rowling's religion, qua postmodern, *is* being "opposed to fundamentalism in any form." She misuses the word "fundamentalism," which refers to a set of beliefs held by a specific, historic sect of Protestant Christians, the way most everyone else does, that is, as a synonym for ignorant, prejudiced people who are intolerant of any beliefs other than their own. She, of course, overlooks the irony that she is talking about these evil fundamentalist folk the way Death Eaters talk about Muggles.

Time magazine still rather overstates the case, as is their wont in highlighting Ms. Rowling's secular agenda, in calling *Harry Potter* a "4,100-page treatise on tolerance." But they do get half the story. The hook that catches readers around the world is the story of Harry—heroic "excluded other"—fighting against the Nazi fundamentalist Pure Blood Death Eaters and their nightmare leader Voldemort.

Why are these bad guys so bad? It isn't just the murders, the nastiness, or the snobbery; it's the poisoned, prejudicial *thinking* that they are better than others because of their blood status that we are obliged to hate. Being "Pure Blood," of course, is just a metaphor for any caste of social class, education, or privilege. They are evil and Dumbledore and Harry are heroic because they are archetypes of our beliefs about good and bad. *Harry* confirms and buttresses in his readers' minds their core beliefs against prejudice and ideological thinking in our time.

The Centrality of Love:
A Step Beyond Postmodernism

One consequence of a narrative that only condemns the inevitable prejudices, intolerance, and violence that come with blinkered thinking is that because nothing can be known for certain, there is no truth per se, and, hence, no good or evil. Only *relative* good and evil based on personal or community advantage are possible in a world without an absolute truth that can be known.

Neglecting the obvious contradiction of "there is no truth" as an absolute statement of truth, relativism bordering on nihilism is one evident consequence of postmodern thinking. One need only talk to a group of teenagers to see their unblinking, unwavering faith in the proposition that everything is relative. Thinking about "good" and "evil" is to be judgmental—and, outside of being a fundamentalist or a Nazi or a Klansman, there isn't much lower one can go than being judgmental.

As much as the *Harry Potter* novels are postmodern, though, there is very little about them you could call "relativist." There is a very real evil in the stories—Lord Voldemort and his Death

Eaters—and resisting them is a necessary and important thing. Those who waffle about fighting are cowards, collaborators, and traitors; virtues of bravery, especially sacrificial courage and love, loyalty, and honesty are celebrated in every book.

Ms. Rowling transcends the contradiction of the postmodern myth by replacing the Pure Blood belief that poisons the Wizarding world with a central narrative of love. In this scheme, love is the central and greatest power, the core reality, and in it there is no constitutive "other." The other, by definition, is embraced by love. The only ones excluded are those who cannot love, and Dumbledore tells Harry flat out, "Do not pity the dead, Harry. Pity the living, and, above all, those who live without love" (*Deathly Hallows*, chapter thirty-five).

But this belief in love is not easily won.

Choose to Believe, Harry!

Here's the problem with love as a core belief: There is no way to get there by argument or demonstration. You have to make a choice to believe in order to get there, and, as skeptical as we are trained to be about our ability to know anything, choosing to believe in something seems ridiculous.

The day after *Deathly Hallows* was published Ms. Rowling told Meredith Vieira of the *Today Show* that the book was largely about her "struggle to believe."

MV: *Harry's also referred to as the Chosen One. So are there religious—*

JKR: *Well, there—there clearly is a religious—undertone. And—it's always been difficult to talk about that because until we reached book seven, views of what happens after death and so on, it would give away a lot of what was coming. So . . . yes, my beliefs and my struggling with religious belief and so on I think is quite apparent in this book.*

MV: *And what is the struggle?*

JKR: *Well my struggle really is to keep believing.*[6]

Her struggle is "quite apparent in this book" because Harry's biggest challenge is to "choose to believe" in Dumbledore. Twice in the beginning of *Deathly Hallows* he is asked to choose to believe and he balks both times.

"Don't believe a word of it!" said Doge at once. "Not a word, Harry! Let nothing tarnish your memories of Albus Dumbledore!"

Harry looked into Doge's earnest, pained face and felt, not reassured, but frustrated. Did Doge really think it was that easy, that Harry could simply choose not to believe? Didn't Doge understand Harry's need to be sure, to know everything? (Deathly Hallows, chapter eight [emphasis on "choose" and "everything" in original])

Ms. Rowling draws our attention to choice and belief again in chapter ten when Harry and Hermione argue about whether to believe like Doge or to join the Skeeter skeptics like Auntie Muriel:

> *"Harry, do you really think you'll get the truth from a malicious old woman like Muriel, or from Rita Skeeter? How can you believe them? You knew Dumbledore!"*
>
> *"I thought I did," he muttered.*
>
> *"But you know how much truth there was in everything Rita wrote about you! Doge is right, how can you let these people tarnish your memories of Dumbledore?"*
>
> *He looked away, trying not to betray the resentment he felt. There it was again: Choose what to believe. He wanted the truth. Why was everybody so determined that he should not get it?* (Deathly Hallows, *chapter ten*)

Harry decides after the debacle in Godric's Hollow, where his faith is broken along with his wand, that he doesn't believe and cannot choose to believe in Dumbledore and his mission:

> *And his fury at Dumbledore broke over him now like lava, scorching him inside, wiping out every other feeling. Out of sheer desperation they had talked themselves into believing . . . that it was all part of some secret path laid out for them by Dumbledore; but there was no map, no plan. Dumbledore had left them to grope in the darkness, to wrestle with unknown and undreamed-of-terrors,*

*alone and unaided: Nothing was explained, nothing was given freely . . ." (*Deathly Hallows, *chapter eighteen)*

After reading "The Greater Good" chapter in Skeeter's *Life and Lies* book, he reaches bottom:

"Look what he asked of me, Hermione! Risk your life, Harry! And again! And again! And don't expect me to explain everything, just trust me blindly, trust that I know what I'm doing, trust me even though I don't trust you! Never the whole truth! Never!
". . . I don't know who he loved, Hermione, but it was never me. This isn't love, the mess he's left me in . . ."
He closed his eyes at her touch, and hated himself for wishing that what she said was true: that Dumbledore had really cared. (*Deathly Hallows, *chapter eighteen)*

And yet in desperation in the Malfoy Manor basement and on reflection in Dobby's grave, Harry does choose to believe. In the golden pink of dawn, Harry makes his decision. He knows but he doesn't seek the Deathly Hallows. He chooses to believe in Dumbledore and in the mission he was assigned:

Harry hesitated. He knew what hung on his decision. There was hardly any time left; now was the moment to decide: Horcruxes or Hallows?

"Griphook," Harry said. "I'll speak to Griphook first."

His heart was racing as if he had been sprinting and had just cleared an enormous obstacle. (Deathly Hallows, *chapter twenty-four)*

Dumbledore may have left him clueless about important things, but he didn't leave him without an important teaching about choice. "It is our choices, Harry, that show what we truly are, far more than our abilities," he says at the end of *Chamber of Secrets.* I think we all understand this in the sense of knowing that choices matter more than birthright. If what we believe about what we cannot know for sure, however, comes down to personal choice, as Harry says, then Dumbledore's teaching about choice is resoundingly relevant. "What we choose to believe" about subjects lacking demonstrations or refutations will "show what we truly are."

For Harry Potter and his readers, the process of overcoming prejudice is actually less vital than the agonizing postmodern dilemma that Harry expresses in a question to Dumbledore in *Hallows*: "Is this real? Or has this been happening inside my head?" (chapter thirty-five). Is this a reality I can count on? Or, in other words, is it just the deluded product or projection of my prejudices and assorted mental filters?

When Harry, while digging Dobby's grave, makes his choice to believe in Dumbledore and pursue Horcruxes rather than Hallows, he follows Dobby's heroic example. Dobby was a self-actualizing house-elf, remember, who, contrary to all programming and house-elf beliefs, chose to believe in Harry Potter. In this choice he won his freedom. Neville, too, in choosing to live his final year at Hogwarts in anticipation of Harry's return and as he imagines Harry would act, chooses to believe in something good, true, and beautiful, something greater than himself. In this choice, Neville achieves heroic stature and the courage to best Voldemort and kill Nagini with the Sword of Gryffindor in the Battle of Hogwarts.

As a postmodern writer, Rowling is obliged to offer prejudice consequent to unexamined belief as the great evil her heroes will resist and her villains will embody. Her series reads, consequently, like the "4,100-page treatise on tolerance" and celebration of misfits that we expect in the politically correct Age of Rudolph, Hermey, and Barney. Ms. Rowling escapes the trap of relativism and there being no ultimate evil, however, by portraying the choices Harry makes to transcend his prejudices and individual imaginings. Becoming his own person in service to truth and virtue is the centerpiece of his final transformation.

The choice that ultimately reveals who we really are is our decision whether or not to believe. Making that choice collapses all metanarratives or prejudice fostering myths other than the resounding metanarrative of love.

From Morality to Metaphor

"Definitely morals are drawn" is the author's fair conclusion[7] about her work. We have the softened didactic message of the schoolboy novel and the never-quite-horrifying but still edifying gothic atmosphere of the stories. *Harry Potter*'s larger moral message, as we'd have to expect, is the primary moral teaching of our historical period, namely, that prejudice is evil and that choosing to believe in reality greater than oneself is the means to transcend it.

We saw as we moved from the "surface" to the "moral" layer of meanings in *Harry Potter* that the two bled together; the setting was a good piece of the morality of the story and couldn't really be separated. Now, as we approach the allegorical layer just underneath the moral, we see a similar blending of morality and allegory. Voldemort and his Death Eaters are de facto Nazi-fundamentalist straw men representing postmodern evils, and Harry, Dumbledore, and friends are the Rainbow Coalition of self-actualizing individuals freeing themselves of their psychological and social bonds. The atmosphere and setting, when understood as postmodern "double coding," become part of the means by which Ms. Rowling draws her simultaneously conventional and, as will see in later chapters, radically traditional moral teaching.

PART THREE

The Allegorical Meaning

CHAPTER SIX

The Satirical *Harry Potter*

*The Allegorical Journey Harry Takes with Gulliver
into Plato's Cave in Order to Make a Point in
Mockery About Government and News Media*

I give plenty of talks about *Harry Potter* at major universities, at fan conventions, and at local libraries and bookstores. There are two or three questions that always come up at these events: I'm always asked if I've met Ms. Rowling, and I'm asked whether she herself told me the things I had just explained. I know why this sort of question comes up. Readers who love the *Harry Potter* novels, but who missed the allegorical, mythic, even religious meanings that I point out, are profoundly skeptical that anyone else was right in having seen it, short of a direct confession from the author.

* * *

Frankly, I understand this skepticism. It isn't every author who deserves such serious digging. Every story has surface hooks, story formulas, and narrative drive—and all of the stories written in the past forty or fifty years have a postmodern moral or two. But allegory and beyond? Believe me: Very few bestsellers reward a look under the hood in search of their hidden political criticism and philosophical meaning.

The original title of Ms. Rowling's first book, *Harry Potter and the Philosopher's Stone,* was changed to *Harry Potter and the Sorcerer's Stone* for the American publication. Her publisher was certain that no American reader would buy a book with the word "philosophy" in the title. But the truth is that it's hard to get a grip on literature in general and *Harry Potter* in particular without a little Plato.

The good news is that Plato was a great storyteller. Plato even insisted in the *Seventh Letter* that he had never written a word of philosophy in his life. His genre of choice was the dialogue, after all, the ancient world equivalent of a screenplay, rather than dry treatises. Plato wrote philosophical dramas featuring Socrates, his teacher, in dynamic question-and-answer sessions with fascinating people, many of whom were well known Athenians. Plato is more like Shakespeare and Steven Spielberg than Spinoza or Spengler. He doesn't dictate doctrine; he tells stories and asks his friends what they think (and then some more questions about what they think . . .).

One of his better stories and probably the most famous is the Cave Allegory (*Republic*, VII, 514a–520a). It goes something like this: Imagine human beings who live deep down in a cave with their heads and necks bound in such a way that they can only look straight ahead and at a wall opposite the entrance. They have no idea they're living in a cave. Their light doesn't come from the entrance but from a fire "burning far above and behind them." In front of this fire there is a wall that acts like a puppet-show box. On the top of the wall, people who are not chained down carry figures of men, animals, and other things so their shadows are projected on the far wall. These shadow projections are the only things the cave prisoners can see and know. The shadows are their reality. "Such men would hold that the truth is nothing other than the shadows of artificial things."

Socrates, who tells the story, then describes a prisoner who is liberated by force, that is, freed from his chains and dragged out from the wall of shadows past the fire and wall over which the figures are held, and up to the cave entrance and out into the light. This is not a happy man. At first, he is unable to see things in the light as they are because he only recognizes image-shadows as reality.

Then, in the light outside the cave, he is all but blinded, ". . . his eyes full of [the sun's] beam and . . . unable to see even one of the things said to be true." Slowly, though, his eyes will adjust to the light and he will be able to see shadows, reflections, objects, people, and finally the stars, moon, sunlight, and the sun itself. Finally, he could understand the sun is "the source of the seasons and the years, and the steward of all things in the visible place, and is in a certain way the cause of all those things he and his companions [in the cave] had been seeing."

In the previous chapter, Socrates has explained a "metaphor of the Sun" in which the sun is a natural cipher for "the Idea of the Good" or God, "what provides the truth to the things known and gives the power to the one who knows."[1] The prisoner able to see and know the sun in the Cave Allegory experiences the illuminating truth that is the "real reality" behind the shadow images in the cave's darkness.

Socrates also makes it clear that this "enlightened" or "illumined" prisoner is in for a very hard time. He's quite happy now that he sees things as they are and feels nothing but pity for his friends back in the hole. But what happens if he goes back into the cave?

First, it's clear that this return would be something he'd try to avoid at all costs. Better a slave in the sunshine than a king in what C. S. Lewis called the "Shadowlands." But if he did go back, he'd be in a fix. While his eyes adjusted, for one thing, he'd seem a moron whose eyes were damaged by his time outside the cave. If he tried to free the other prisoners and help them escape, Socrates is confident that the slaves would kill him rather than question the reality of the shadows.

"Don't be surprised," therefore, that the prisoners who have come back "aren't willing to mind the business of human beings" who think shadows are reality and truth. "Their souls are always eager to spend their time above."[2]

Socrates finally spells out what the Allegory is about. *We* are the people in the cave. Our understanding of reality, the ephemeral quantities of matter and energy we think of as "real things," are just shared beliefs about shadows projected up on the cave wall. The Good, the True, and the Beautiful, the greater reality of things, are only knowable in escaping the cave and knowing the Idea of the Good itself, "what provides the truth to the things known."

What does this have to do with literature?

Good question.

The first part of the answer is in realizing that this isn't just Plato's otherworldly fantasy. This story for shadowlanders like you and me about the nature of reality and how we know (or don't know) is pretty much the Christian consensus. Since much of English literature, from *Beowulf* to Joyce's *Ulysses*, was written by Christian writers for Christian readers, it almost has to be understood in light of Plato's Cave Allegory.

Stories in the Western tradition can be sorted pretty much into two piles: a heap for those that reinforce the delusions of the shadows projected on the cave wall and another for the ones that make us feel our chains, stretch our necks, maybe even give us an imaginative experience of the noetic reality in the sunlight. Reading books is either an enlightening and liberating experience (and, yes, the Cave Allegory is one of the reasons we talk about "enlightenment" the way we do) or just entertainment to distract us from the darkness, smoke, and discomfort of life underground.

Either way, uplifting or dissipating, *everything* written is more or less an allegory. The words on the page, the stories, sentiments, and sentience of them are not the things referred to but signs that make us recall or imagine them. And finding meaning in everything written involves going deeper into the allegory and reflecting on what the story is calling up within us.

If you're reading an average bestseller, the search pretty much ends when the roller coaster action comes to a stop; beyond story and moral (or lack of morals), it's time for another book. The "good stuff," though—what we call "classics" or "great books"—on second, third, and fourth readings reveals political and social commentary or allegory and, in real treasures, an escape from the cave via a truly mythic experience. Mircea Eliade, the great historian of religion, said that all reading in a profane culture like our own serves a mythic or religious function because of our "suspension of disbelief" while reading or watching a movie. This disconnecting from our selfish concerns lifts us to a better place, something like the place religious ritual and sacraments are meant to take us.[3]

He's right, of course. But there are writers who deliberately take us up to the mouth of the cave and force us to look out, who make us return again and again for a refresher course. The books we will be talking about in this second half of *Harry Potter's Bookshelf* to illustrate the allegorical and mythic layers of meaning are the greats. We'll be looking at them because Ms. Rowling has built on them as models, and the *Harry Potter* novels achieve the same resonance in the heart that thrills and engages readers profoundly.

Laughing at Idiots and Self-Important Gits: The Joys of Allegory in Satire

Plato is right, at least in my experience talking to readers, even to *Harry's* biggest fans. Once we move beyond the shadows on the cave wall Ms. Rowling has given us, the surface and moral meanings we've explored so far, most of us don't have the tools, experience, or beliefs to look further. We need an easy and fun stepping-off place to see what's beneath the story. Political criticism or satire is a great place to start. "The main purpose of any satire is to invite the reader to laugh at a particular human vice or folly, in order to invite us to consider an important moral alternative."[4] Satire is about laughing; who doesn't want to laugh, especially at folks who deserve to be laughed at?

To step us into reading *Harry Potter* as allegory, then, I want to start on the straightforward tit-for-tat level of satire. Satire is barely disguised allegory with real-world correspondents—individuals, institutions, and ideas—we're meant to recognize without much effort. Satire is also meant to be ironic.

I start peeling back the allegorical layer of meaning in Ms. Rowling's work this way, then, because the person, organization, or belief being mocked is relatively easy to see and because it's meant to be and *is* very funny. Satire is quite a bit like a political cartoon that shows the faults of a politician, a political party, or a failed policy in the worst possible light. Recognizing her satire makes us more receptive to the less amusing but much more profound and challenging meanings that come with the allegory and symbolism in Ms. Rowling's work.

I also like starting with satire because there is a very long tradition of satire in English letters. From *The Canterbury Tales* to *Harry Potter*, writers have been taking their readers on a journey to a different place to reveal the underside or neglected aspects of the reality we live in. Sometimes this journey means a trip to a "strange new world," as with Gulliver's Lilliput, Butler's Erewhon, and Baum's Oz. As often the journey, like Alice's adventures down a rabbit hole or *Through the Looking Glass* and the Narnia adventures, takes us inside, beneath, and behind the world of appearances and reflection. Or we discover a secret life of animals, say, the esprit de corps of a cadre of the *Watership Down* male rabbits in exodus or the history of the proletarian revolution in *Animal Farm*. Or a combination of all these trips that we get in *The Phantom Tollbooth* and *Harry Potter*: a trip far away as well as "further up and further in" with a menagerie of magical anthropomorphic or just beastly creatures.

The meat of satire is portraying a real-world goon or menace as a laughable caricature in story. The disguise has to be clever enough to be seen through easily enough for those with eyes to see, but not so transparent that there is no pleasure or sense of gleeful accomplishment in the discovery. But the masquerade isn't just for providing puzzle lovers with a challenge. The hidden quality of satire, historically, has been a life insurance policy of sorts for the author, and, as important, it restricts the message to readers for whom the taunt is meant.

Swift is supposed to have said that satire is a mirror in which "everyone can see anyone's face but their own."[5] What better place could there be, then, than in satirical fiction to conceal criticism of those in power?

But *Harry Potter* as political satire? Isn't it just a book for kids?

Harry Potter has quite a thick layer of political allegory in the form of satire, in fact, and that it comes in the guise of a book for children only makes that more credible. As one historian of children's literature has noted, "Many books we shelve as 'children's literature—Grimms' *Fairy Tales* or *Gulliver's Travels* or *Huck Finn*—were born as biting political satire, for adults."[6] And Ms. Rowling has made it clear that she is writing in "political metaphors" for those with the discernment to see it.

First, she insists that she wrote the book for "obsessives" who would turn over every detail for meaning.[7] She also is quite open about the political content of her fantasies—"What did my books preach against throughout? Bigotry, violence, struggles for power, no matter what"[8]—she's quite open about the satire, what she calls "metaphor" instead of allegory.

> **Fan:** *Voldemort's killing of Muggle-borns, it sounds a lot like ethnic cleansing. How much of the series is a political metaphor?*
>
> **JKR:** *Well, it is a political metaphor. But I didn't sit down and think, "I want to re-create Nazi Germany," in the—in the Wizarding world. Because—although there are—quite consciously, overtones of Nazi Germany, there are also associations with other political situations. So I can't really single one out . . .*[9]
>
> **JKR:** *I think that the world of Hogwarts, or my magical world, my community of wizards—it's like the real world in a very distorted mirror.*[10]

Rowling points frequently to the importance of reading the text hidden inside the text. Riddle's diary is smuggled into

Hogwarts between the covers of a textbook. The marginalia
of the Half-Blood Prince's Potions textbook is Harry's life
preserver in that class his sixth year. And Dumbledore leaves
Hermione, the smart character, a copy of *Beedle the Bard* with
confidence that she will be able to figure out its greater meaning in symbols, not to mention the fate-of-the-world relevance
of that meaning, whereas the Ministry would not.

Hermione's cat, Crookshanks, is another pointer to the
"smart reader" being asked to look for political metaphor and
satire especially in the story. Hermione buys the furry ginger
cat, with its bowed legs, grumpy and "oddly squashed" face
that gave it the appearance of a cat who "had run headlong
into a brick wall" (*Prisoner of Azkaban*, chapter four), almost
as an act of charity ("the witch said he's been [in the Magical Menagerie] for ages; no one wanted him"). Given that its
first act in the story is to jump on Ron to get at Scabbers,
it seems cause for buyer's remorse. But it's a good purchase.
Sirius spells it out for Ron in the Shrieking Shack:

> *"This cat isn't mad," said Black hoarsely. He reached out a bony
> hand and stroked Crookshanks's fluffy head. "He's the most intel-
> ligent of his kind I've ever met. He recognized Peter for what he
> was right away. And when he met me, he knew I was no dog. It
> was a while before he trusted me . . . Finally, I managed to com-
> municate to him what I was after, and he's been helping me . . ."*
>
> *"What do you mean?" breathed Hermione.*

"He tried to bring Peter to me, but couldn't . . . so he stole the passwords into Gryffindor Tower for me . . . As I understand it, he took them from a boy's bedside table . . ." (Prisoner of Azkaban, *chapter nineteen*)

So we have a superintelligent cat as the pet of the "cleverest witch of her age" (*Prisoner of Azkaban*, chapter seventeen) that no one appreciates. The most notable aspect of its intelligence is that it is able to discern the reality beneath the deceptive but suggestive surface of people and creatures it meets.

Crookshanks the cat is named for nineteenth-century England's most famous caricaturist and political satirist, George Cruikshanks. Cruikshanks was legendary for his deadly broadside cartoons that pierced the mighty, especially royals and aristocrats, but all the powerful, Whigs and Tories alike. The smart money, consequently, is not betting against the idea that Ms. Rowling, too, is writing political satire, just beneath the skin of her characters, rats and heroes. Let's see if we can make out what Cruikshanks might have seen in the Hogwarts adventures.

Ms. Rowling's Politics

It's a safe bet that Ms. Rowling writes as a political liberal. Her writing pre- and post-*Potter* speaks from the left side of the partisan house. She admires Jessica Mitford (for whom her eldest daughter is named), she worked for Amnesty International as a bilingual secretary and researcher after college,[11] and she has donated as much as a million pounds at a time to the U.K. Labour Party to protect "the poor and vulnerable" from the Conservatives.[12] Keith Olbermann, an American television talking head and *Harry Potter* fan, claims Ms. Rowling "told me the parallels between the Ministry of Magic and its false sense of omniscience and the conduct of the American and British governments were no inferences. She had put them there."[13]

Ms. Rowling has repeatedly said that she is against "fundamentalism of any kind," fundamentalism tending to be a partisan buzzword used to describe the positions of religious people with conservative political beliefs. She said during the presidential primary season that she is "obsessed with the U.S. elections" and "I want a Democrat in the White House."[14] She has agreed that her satirical depiction of the Death Eaters as racists and Nazi-echoes was a pointer to their being "neo-conservative and Thatcherite."[15] One French philosopher and critic has gone so far as to say, "*Harry Potter* is a war-machine against Thatchero-Blairism and the 'American way of life.'"[16]

Where does her satirical slant to the political left show itself? In almost every character-as-caricature we are offered as representatives of government, the justice system, media, and schools. She skewers specific real-world individuals, whole institutions, and human types with big brush strokes and a dark, comic touch.

Did someone mention Margaret Thatcher? Ms. Rowling's experience on the dole as a single mother resulted in a depression that was bad enough that she "contemplated suicide."[17] She felt the "right-wing government" of that time and the media "scapegoated" single mothers as "feckless teenagers who didn't know how to use contraception."[18] The Ministry of Magic and the *Daily Prophet* reflect, as we'll see, her thoughts on government and media, but Lady Thatcher gets special treatment.

Aunt Marge, Uncle Vernon's mustached, self-important, and outrageous sister, a breeder of bulldogs (a mascot or symbol of England because of its determination and fighting tenacity), is easy to see as a Rowling caricature of the former Prime Minister. Her dog, Ripper, isn't lovably tenacious; it is violent and mean-spirited. Just like his mistress. After explaining to the Dursleys after dinner and too many glasses of wine that Harry's runtishness was a function of his poor breeding, she does a little scapegoating on her own:

> *"[Harry's father] didn't work," said Uncle Vernon, with half a glance at Harry. "Unemployed."*
>
> *"As I expected!" said Aunt Marge, taking a huge swig of brandy and wiping her chin on her sleeve. "A no-account,*

good-for-nothing, lazy scrounger who—" (Prisoner of Azkaban, *chapter two)*

Harry loses control at this point and blows her up, literally, like the overinflated bag of wind that she is. What less
could you expect him to do, not only because of the insults
to the memory of his parents, but because of the eugenicist
"breeding" comments only Death Eaters and Voldemort voice
in these books?

Tony Blair gets the more direct treatment. *Half-Blood Prince*
opens at 10 Downing Street, in which the Muggle Prime
Minister meets with Cornelius Fudge and the new Minister
of Magic, Rufus Scrimgeour. (The P.M. is not named and
some say it is meant to be John Major, though U.K. friends
assure me the speech patterns are Blair's.) The Muggle minister is presented as a man concerned only with political praise
and blame, a man wanting to be treated with respect by the
"Other Minister," as he thinks of the Minister of Magic, but
wanting them to fix his problems post-haste. "The President
of a far distant country" is about to call and the P.M. dreads
the conversation to come with "that wretched man."

The institution of government is pilloried more than individuals, of course. On nonsensical things like the thickness
of cauldron bottoms, the importing of magic carpets, and
the organization of "Bread and Quidditch" events like the
Triwizard Tournament, the government lavishes indefinite

resources and manpower. But on the critical issues of the day, namely, the return of Lord Voldemort and the Death Eaters, they rush only to denial and inaction, except to be sure that the *Daily Prophet* is given the correct spin so that the Minister himself doesn't look bad.

The best part of her satirical treatment of U.K. government officials is her depiction of types. There is the ambitious young man on the rise, putting aside thoughts of right, wrong, family obligation, and even common sense to be seen with the right people and to get their attention. I give you Percy Weasley. What sort of man Percy would have turned into if he had continued on this path is visible in the tragic Barty Crouch, Sr., who so neglects his family that his son becomes a Death Eater and a patricide.

Cornelius Fudge, the Minister of Magic for the first five books of the series, is, as Dumbledore says, ". . . blinded by . . . the love of the office you hold, Cornelius!" (*Goblet of Fire*, chapter thirty-six). He becomes a stand-in for Neville Chamberlain, denying Lord Voldemort's ascendancy and evil as Chamberlain did Hitler's. Rufus Scrimgeour, in contrast, is no appeaser and dies heroically after the Ministry is overtaken by Death Eaters. Even he, though, is not interested in winning the war as much as he is in gestures to foster public morale, gestures that include imprisoning the innocent, men like Stan Shunpike; tolerating vicious people like Dolores Umbridge within the Ministry; and holding the items left to

Ron, Harry, and Hermione by Dumbledore in his will. Both Scrimgeour and Fudge are about power, not mercy, justice, or truth.

There *are* good guys in government. Arthur Weasley works in the least important government departments (Misuse of Muggle Artifacts and Head of the Office for the Detection and Confiscation of Counterfeit Defensive Spells and Protective Objects) but manages to write and help pass The Muggle Protection Act. This makes him and his clan "Blood Traitors" to other Pure Blood families. The Aurors, Ministry Dark Wizard hunters, range from the duty-observant street cops like Dawlish to the self-sacrificing heroes like Alastor Moody.

But, taken all together, the Ministry as Rowling presents it is sympathetic to the powerful rather than the needy and vulnerable, to the racist rather than the oppressed, and focused on the trivial and superficial rather than the vital and essential. When the Death Eaters succeed in putting Pius Thicknesse (a name suggesting the religious right, "fundamentalists") under the Imperius curse and take over the Ministry with Thicknesse as Voldemort's puppet, it is no surprise that it quickly becomes a totalitarian, Pure Blood regime.

JOHN GRANGER

Profiteers, Fools, and Blood-Sucking Parasites: Fleet Street in Satirical Story

Ms. Rowling's relationship with the media, by which inclusive term I mean television and print journalists, is a remarkable one. She is a media darling; getting an interview with her is a difficult thing, especially when it is not in association with a charity event or the release of a book or movie—and reporters' gratitude for the privilege is evident. She is rarely asked a hardball question and has not been presented in an unflattering light, to my knowledge, in scores of articles consequent to interviews.

Nevertheless, Ms. Rowling clearly is cautious about the press. She has set up her own website so she can communicate directly to her fans without having to work through the medium or filter of the press. She *does* do interviews and press conferences, online and in person, with nonjournalists— i.e., fans, especially children and young adults, whom she trusts will be kind and attentive to detail rather than having a "selling papers" agenda. She never looks comfortable at designed-for-media events like red carpet charity or theatrical appearances and press conferences.

She has sued newspapers and celebrity photo services to protect her privacy, especially the privacy of her children.[19] The press, as a rule, fawn over her, but they are not her friends. Here is a telling response to a question from a fan about political allegory:

Q: *Many of us older readers have noticed over the years simi-larities between the Death Eaters' tactics and the Nazis from the thirties and forties. Did you use that historical era as a model for Voldemort's reign and what were the lessons that you hope to impart to the next generation?*

A: *It was conscious. I think that if you're, I think most of us if you were asked to name a very evil regime we would think Nazi Germany. There were parallels in the ideology. I wanted Harry to leave our world and find exactly the same problems in the Wizard-ing world. So you have the intent to impose a hierarchy, you have bigotry, and this notion of purity, which is this great fallacy, but it crops up all over the world. People like to think themselves superior and that if they can pride themselves on nothing else, they can pride themselves on perceived purity. So, yeah, that follows a parallel. It wasn't really exclusively that. I think you can see in the Minis-try even before it's taken over, there are parallels to regimes we all know and love. [Laughter and applause.] So you ask what lessons, I suppose. The* Potter *books in general are a prolonged argument for tolerance, a prolonged plea for an end to bigotry, and I think it's one of the reasons that some people don't like the books, but I think that it's a very healthy message to pass on to younger people that you should question authority and you should not assume that the establishment or the press tells you all of the truth.*[20]

She gets her shot in there at the Bush and Blair govern-ments, makes a fist pump for her postmodern celebration of tolerance, but summarizes her message in the axiom "Don't trust the establishment *or the press* to tell you the truth."

When Harry "leaves our world" and finds "exactly the same problems in the Wizarding world," then, it should come as no surprise that one of these problems is an obnoxious, irresponsible, dangerously mean-spirited and unregulated press. And that is exactly what we find there.

But not right away. Though Harry learns about the Wizarding world newspaper, the *Daily Prophet*, the same day he is told by Hagrid he is a wizard (*Sorcerer's Stone,* chapter five) and almost all news of the outside world comes to Hogwarts through this medium, Harry doesn't meet the press, per se, until he becomes an unwilling Hogwarts champion in *Goblet of Fire* (chapter eighteen). Then he meets Ms. Rowling's memorable type and caricature of a Fleet Street reporter, Rita Skeeter.

We actually hear her name mentioned earlier in *Goblet of Fire* (chapter ten) because she writes up a misleading and rumor-laden report in the *Prophet* about the Dark Mark appearing above the Quidditch World Cup campgrounds. We are forewarned, consequently, when she pulls Harry into a Hogwarts broom closet before the weighing of the wands ceremony for Triwizard Tournament champions. Harry gives pedestrian answers to her questions and insists, despite her fishing for a more titillating response, that he hadn't entered the Tournament voluntarily.

Before talking about the story she writes and Rita's further adventures, it's probably best to unwrap the meaning of her name. The photographer accompanying her to Hogwarts on this visit is called "Bozo," and the reporter with the acid-tipped Quick-Quotes-Quill has a tag that is just as disparaging and revealing. In brief, "Rita Skeeter" should be said aloud: "Read-a-Squiter," i.e., "Read a Mosquito." The cameraman is a buffoonish clown and the journalist is a bloodsucking parasite that, at best, is a nuisance, and, as often as not, spreads diseases that could be fatal. If the insect analogy seems far-fetched to you, Rita is revealed in later chapters to be an Animagus who turns herself into a bug.

Not a name you'd give someone you liked, right? And Rita is not someone we're meant to like.

The article she writes, as you'd expect, has little to nothing to do with what Harry said and everything to do with a story Ms. Skeeter knew would be a "wow." She makes up "facts" and quotations whole cloth (e.g., that Harry was the only Gryffindor champion, cried about his parents at night, etc.), which proves to be the source of teasing and embarrassment for Harry. Because everyone seems to believe everything they read in the *Prophet,* though they know it is a rag.

Rita writes stories in *Goblet of Fire* about Hagrid being a half-giant, about Harry's being "disturbed and dangerous," and about Hermione as something of a tart who toys with the affections of both Viktor Krum and Harry Potter. This last bit was a mistake on Skeeter's part because Hermione figures out how Rita listens in on their conversations unseen via a "bug." She captures Skeeter, an unregistered Animagus, in her beetle form and exacts pledges of journalist abstinence from her to "see if she can't break the habit of writing horrible lies about people" (*Goblet of Fire*, chapter thirty-seven).

Ms. Rowling, however, is only warming up in her story-portrait of the press as evil. In *Order of the Phoenix*, by innuendo, asides, and suggestion as well as in written reports, the *Prophet* becomes the voice of the Ministry in doing everything possible, even without their star reporter, to diminish the respect witches and wizards feel for Harry Potter and Albus Dumbledore. The Ministry doesn't want to acknowledge that Voldemort has returned, so those who have seen that he has come back have to be discounted as witnesses. The *Prophet* obliges both in disparaging the boy and his headmaster and in not covering any news of Voldemort's rebirthing or Cedric's death at the Tournament.

Incredibly, the strategy works. When Harry returns to school, he finds that he has very few friends, even in Gryffindor. All have been seduced and hypnotized by newspaper reports questioning his honesty and portraying him as a braggart and attention seeker. Hermione decides to go on a media-manipulation campaign through Rita Skeeter and *The Quibbler*. Rita's comments about journalism in their conversation about an interview with Harry are telling:

"There's no market for a story [about the truth]," said Rita coldly.

"You mean the Prophet *won't print it because Fudge won't let them," said Hermione irritably.*

Rita gave Hermione a long, hard look. Then, leaning forward across the table toward her, she said in a businesslike tone, "All right, Fudge is leaning on the Prophet, *but it comes to the same thing. They won't print a story that shows Harry in a good light. Nobody wants to read it. It's against the public mood. This last Azkaban breakout has got people quite worried enough. People just don't want to believe You-Know-Who's back."*

"So the Daily Prophet *exists to tell people what they want to hear, does it?" said Hermione scathingly.*

Rita sat up straight again, her eyebrows raised, and drained her glass of firewhisky.

"The Prophet *exists to sell itself, you silly girl," she said coldly.*
(Order of the Phoenix, *chapter twenty-five)*

The media, in a nutshell, tells people what they want to hear, and reporters and editors will sell the truth down the river *any time* to make money. Ouch. When the Ministry goes under the Dark Lord's control in Harry's seventh year, the *Prophet* falls into line as well. "Don't trust the establishment *or the press* to tell you the truth." The media, in Rowling's satirical treatment, is joined at the hip to the powerful, to bozos, and to parasites on the body politic that are to be used, if necessary, but kept at arm's length if not farther. "The *Prophet* is bound to report the truth occasionally," said Dumbledore, "if only accidentally" (*Half-Blood Prince*, chapter seventeen).

The Book Most Like *Harry Potter*

Ms. Rowling offers Hermione's aggressive approach to media as the best way to deal with this beast. Rather than suffer its poisons patiently, it is better, she suggests, to use new or alternative media to better control your story and to foster relationships with journalists you can trust (or blackmail!).

Ms. Rowling's political and social allegory within and beneath her story line are not as dark as Orwell's picture of 1948 reality projected into his nightmare *1984* or even his relatively comic portrayal of political revolution in *Animal Farm*. These are bleak satires compared to *Harry Potter* because the arrows travel much deeper into their subjects and the wounds are mortal.

A book that is a mean between dark Orwell and light Lewis Carroll, whose *Alice* adventures are delightful but whose satirical bite has almost completely evaporated with time, is Jonathan Swift's *Gulliver's Travels,* published in 1726. When I am asked what other books most remind me of *Harry Potter,* the top three are *Emma, A Tale of Two Cities,* and *Gulliver's Travels*—and, of those three, the satirical journeys of Lemuel Gulliver are probably the closest match to Harry's.

Why? First of all, it's funny in ways *Emma* and *A Tale of*

Two Cities, as set pieces, cannot be. If you're not amused by Swift's various stories, it's time for a sense of humor transplant. Gulliver, in his seriousness and the variety of voices in which he speaks fluently and convincingly (scientist, lawyer, world traveler, doctor, philosophical disputant, courtier, etc.), is a cartoon character for the ages.

Travels, too, is a book written like *Harry Potter,* as a mélange of several genres. On the surface, it is a parody of the travel books that were so popular in its day. Because it is obviously fantasy, it invites shelving with children's books as a harmless fairy tale, but it has been read as a novel, as science fiction, as philosophical treatise, and, of course, as political and social satire.

But it is the satire for which Swift is famous, even if few people outside the Ivory Tower read it except as entertainment. Funny as it is, Swift meant the book to be a poke in the eye both to his targets in their specific foolishness and to his readers just as human beings. Gulliver's comment in text that "... my principal Design was to Inform, and not to amuse thee" (*Travels,* XII) echoes Swift's aside in a letter to Alexander Pope (September 29, 1725), that "the chief end I propose to myself in all my labors is to vex the world rather than divert it."

And vexatious he certainly is! Like Rowling, Swift caricatures historical individuals and events, institutions of power and prejudice, as well as types of people and specific attitudes or beliefs. I don't intend to write a "Hidden Key" text to *Gulliver's Travels* (not very surprisingly, given its popularity on publication, explanations to the satire were in print within months) but just to give you an idea of the variety of Swift's targets:

* In "The Voyage to Lilliput," part one of the book's four parts, he tells in allegorical form the history of the War of Spanish Succession. Lilliput and Blefuscu are England and France, the Big-endians and Little-endians are Catholic and Protestant partisans, and the high heels and low heels courtiers are Tories and Whigs, respectively.

* In "The Voyage to Laputa," part three, Swift mocks both the Royal Society of Science and the court of King George I in his description of the floating island of Laputa. The ridiculous experiments and scientific investigations Gulliver describes as Laputan Academy concerns are not Swift inventions; incredibly, almost all have been confirmed by historians of science as activities of the Royal Society in Swift's day.[21]

* In almost every country, Swift takes aim at aristocrats, lawyers, courtiers, scientists, medical doctors, and soldiers. In Lilliput and Laputa, these types are despicable and shown in the worst satiric light. In Brobdignab and the Land of the Houyhnhnm, parts two and four

of *Travels,* in contrast, we see their ideal equivalents. Brobdignabians are giants, and the Houyhnhnm are noble, almost otherworldly horses exclusively guided by their reason.

And it is with these enlightened horses that Swift delivers his version of the Cave Allegory.

Houyhnhnm and Yahoos: Enlightenment Reason and Romantic Fancy

Gulliver sets sail on his fourth adventure as captain of his own vessel but suffers the terrible fate of a mutiny among his scurvy crew and is put ashore on an unknown shore with nothing but clean clothes and a short sword. Gulliver is set upon by savage, hairy creatures on all fours who back him up against a tree—then climb the tree to avoid his sword and to defecate on him. He is rescued by a horse.

The horses in this world are rational animals, much more rational and noble than anything human of any size Lemuel has met so far, and the savage animals are Yahoos, wild human beings the horses use as work animals (though they are difficult to train and control). The Houyhnhnm Master who adopts Gulliver despite his Yahoo appearance teaches him the language and the truly civilized ways of the Houyhnhnms.

The horses, in fact, are citizens of Plato's ideal country in his *Republic*. They have no money, they have strict castes, and they raise and educate their children in common. Gulliver's dialogue with the horse he calls his Master with the greatest possible deference is an echo of the dialogue in the *Republic* during which Plato describes the best form of government.

Gulliver, the cave dweller who has seen the Sun in the land of the Houyhnhnms, cannot forget what he has seen truly and experienced with his Master when he returns to the "cave" of his home in Britain. He decides to live in the stable in seeming cruel disregard for his family—a rational, almost laudable choice, when we understand that *Gulliver's Travels* is only an extended and more involved retelling of Plato's Cave Allegory. Swift is savaging the "rationalists" and "humanists" of the seventeenth and eighteenth centuries who are proud of their "scientific discoveries" in the cave and imagine themselves more enlightened than their "superstitious" contemporaries of traditional faith and classical virtues. Even for a world traveler, life in a confined stable with honest horses is far preferable than the company of the proud Yahoos.

Harry and the Houyhnhnms: Satire as Stunning Blow, Warning Shot, and Dark Zebra

Swift takes no prisoners in *Gulliver's Travels*. In what one writer has called "second person satire," he is trying to bring the reader to Gulliver's epiphany that he is a Yahoo who, while capable of reason, has very little to be proud of with respect to the attainment of reason. "Pride" for a Yahoo is death, or, worse, acceptance of a life sentence chained in the cave.

"[*Gulliver's Travels*] prevailing tone is quarrelsome and disorienting, programmed to vex rather than to divert, and it is the antithesis of more conventional satirical styles which purport to engage the reader's solidarity."[22] Ms. Rowling, as we learned in our chapter on Austen and narrative misdirection, has chosen to tell her stories from a specific perspective that will draw the reader in, rather than poke him or her in the eye. Rowling and Swift as allegorists have very similar goals in mind for their heroes; how they tell their stories reflects the different relationship we are meant to have with their heroes. If every satirist is painting a picture of man as a zebra, Swift is with those satirists who think man is a black horse with attitude on which you can paint white stripes. This is usually called a Menippean satire and is a specific category of allegory in which the "story" is essentially a vehicle for scenes in which the ridiculous are shown to be stupid or, better, they sound off à la Gilderoy Lockhart and reveal themselves in outrageous speech. It's more like *Saturday Night Live* than a coherent drama; but the knives are all buried, quite humorously, in their targets.

We could call the satire Ms. Rowling uses, in contrast, "Cruikshankian." It isn't the focus of the books; it's largely incidental to the central story arc. The Cruikshankian satire's man-zebra is a white horse on which the artist paints black stripes. Ms. Rowling satirizes, even ridicules teachers, politicians, judges and jailors, and Fleet Street reporters in stories told in her "distorted mirror" but only, perhaps, because they were features in her story already. Unlike Gulliver's adventures, which clearly were designed to deliver blows on specific targets, the *Harry Potter* books don't have satire as the main focus. Her hero's story, unlike Swift's, isn't about human *inability* to transcend ourselves; Harry's apotheosis is about man reaching his destination rather than falling short of it.[23]

That is the larger story of *Harry Potter*, which, though it shares the traditional or at least antimodern view of Swift's *Gulliver* in its satirical depiction of individuals and types as proud Yahoos from the shadowlands, is an allegory without visible or one-to-one correspondences. And it is this parable or fairy-tale quality of Ms. Rowling's Hogwarts adventures that we turn to next.

CHAPTER SEVEN

Harry Potter as an Everyman Allegory

Harry, Hogwarts, and Company as Medieval Types for Reader Reflection and Edification

Latin, that most magical of languages, has a single word that defines and explains what allegory means: *alieniloquium*, literally, "saying one thing to mean another." C. S. Lewis defined "allegory" as:

> By an allegory I mean a composition (whether pictorial or literary) in which immaterial realities are represented by feigned physical objects, e.g., a pictured Cupid allegorically represents erotic love (which in reality is an experience, not an object occupying a given area of space) or, in Bunyan a giant represents Despair.[1]

We started down the road to allegory with satire because both are devices that employ literary language to refer to something else, be they specific individuals, ideas and ideologies, or types of people holding certain beliefs. Both provide the reader with something to interpret, a puzzle even, and allow the reader a certain sense of triumph once they have decoded the author's potential message. But while satire is often used to be critical of someone or something specific, allegory has its greater power in nonspecific referents that draw the reader into the message and meaning of the book.

Allegory can extend and deepen the moral meaning of the story and point to something greater. For an example of this larger view, let's look through the allegorical lens at the gothic setting and devices of *Harry Potter*. Without straining our eyes, we should be able to make out a world of antimodern, even traditional religious meaning in that castle with ghosts and suits of armor.

Subversive Texts Dressed Up in Fairy-Tale Garments

Like the *Harry Potter* series, many, I dare say "most," great children's fiction, and books often labeled as such, are, as Jill Lepore wrote in *The New Yorker*, "utterly bound up in the medieval."[2] From Tolkien to Lewis, from Norton Juster's *The Phantom Tollbooth* to Brian Jacques's *Redwall* series, the fantasy setting of these books resembles the Middle Ages more closely than it does our modern day.

It doesn't take more than a moment's reflection on favorite books to recognize this trend. Alice's trip through the looking glass and her adventures with the chessboard characters there are essentially a side trip into feudalism—kings, queens, knights, and knaves. And each escape and sojourn into Narnia with the Pevensie children and Eustace Scrubb, like *The Lord of the Rings* epic, is another journey into an imaginary Middle Ages that is set as a critical foil to our own age.

There is a pattern here that I hope you are catching: the Battle of the Books between life, love, and laughter against the forces of antiseptic reason and scientism.

The medieval backdrop as a critical foil set up against our technological times is an echo of Jane Austen's subtle critique of Hume's empiricism (see chapter two), of the "fallen man" morality of gothic romance and horror opposed to humanism and materialism (chapter four), and Swift's broadsides and satirical swipes against the Enlightenment thinkers (chapter six). The poets and Romantic visionaries since Swift have retreated behind the high barricades of popular fictions and poesy to carry on the traditional critique of the mores and advances of their time, a subversive war against the dominion of scientific, analytical reason shorn of love, conscience, virtue, and imagination.

What is it about a medieval setting—the castles, monks,

and feudal trappings—that makes it the vehicle it is for critiques of modernity? Two things.

First, to scientists and nonbelievers (to simplify and generalize), medieval Europe, focused as it was culturally (at least relatively speaking) on matters of faith, was an age of superstition and subjective nonsense. The Romantics chose the medieval setting, in other words, as the stage for antimodern dramas because the scientists whose inhuman rationalism they were fighting had chosen the "Dark Ages" they decided were "dark" as their enemy and counterpoint. Second, the medieval period serves as an excellent literary foil because of that time period's art and literature. Unlike modern naturalist paintings and realist novels that are largely devoid of poetry, the art of the Middle Ages is suffused with the sacred and spiritual and song. The people's worldview and the art corresponding to it were relatively otherworldly, which is the reason, of course, that the rationalists consider it a "dark" time and the Romantic reactionaries thought it a fitting place of resistance.

Biblical Allegory in *Harry Potter*: Medieval Mystery Play, *Everyman*, and *Pilgrim's Progress*

The castle and technology-free setting of Hogwarts have an obvious medieval message contra modernity. It's nothing, though, compared to the stories themselves, which several

times seem to be allegorical entertainments written in imitation of the plays, poems, and prose of the Middle Ages.

With the spiritual and intangible taking such precedence
in a society centered around the Church and scripture, medieval people saw this world as a "shadowland" existence. There
was a greater life to come that sometimes revealed itself in the
saints, in nature, and in art, and it was this life toward which,
culturally and nominally at least, minds and hearts were ori-
ented. Medieval folk, consequently, looked to the theatre, the
plastic arts, story, and song for clarification about how they
were to achieve salvation and eternal life.

D. W. Robertson, Jr., explains that characters in medieval
dramas, then, are not to be understood as realistic portraits,
individual personalities, or even types per se. They are instead
exempla, "stories with an implication,"[3] or exemplars of vice or
virtue. They are allegories, or the *alieniloquium*, in which we
are meant to see pictures for our reflection and edification.[4]

This is easier to see in the morality plays and novels of the
English tradition than it is in the wider-read works of Chaucer or Shakespeare. *Everyman* (c.1480) is typical of this purely
allegorical genre. In it, God sends Death to call the character named Everyman to judgment. Everyman begs Death
for time to put his life in order but only gets permission to
seek companions who will testify to his merits before God.
He seeks out Fellowship, Kindred, Good Deeds, and Knowledge, among others, and after confessing, receives the jewel

of Penance. This animates Good Deeds sufficiently that she is able to accompany Everyman to Heaven. In case anyone in the audience missed the point, a Doctor ("learned man" in Latin) explains the importance of good deeds in spiritual life at performance's end.

Perhaps the most important written work in English letters (having never gone out of print) is also pure allegory. John Bunyan's *The Pilgrim's Progress from This World to That Which Is to Come* (1678) follows Christian on his pilgrimage from the City of Destruction to the Celestial City. Christian is a figure like Everyman; he lacks individual quirks or personality but represents humanity in toto on his spiritual quest. Like Everyman, he encounters figurative characters as both guides (Hopeful, the Evangelist) and as characters representing the challenges, opportunities, and points of passage along the way from the fallen world to heaven's paradise.

Rowling uses similar allegorical devices that at once reference the preceding works and help build the depth of her own series. Remember in *Sorcerer's Stone* when Harry and Draco are in the Forbidden Forest at night serving a detention with Hagrid? They stumble onto a unicorn that has been killed and a man in serpent form who is drinking its blood. Firenze, the centaur, rescues Harry from what we learn later was Quirreldemort and explains to him why anyone would drink unicorn's blood.

The brilliance of this is in its allegorical meaning, which, sadly, a medieval audience might understand better than Rowling's own. It's a fairly straightforward dramatization of St. Paul's teaching in his First Letter to the Corinthians on receiving the blood of Christ properly. The snake man is a stand-in for fallen man or even the devil in the Garden of Eden. The unicorn in the Western tradition is a symbol of Christ. The life-giving blood of the unicorn is the Blood of Christ in the Eucharist. Paul writes about those who receive the Blood of Christ unworthily that they are damned: "For he that eateth and drinketh unworthily, eateth and drinketh damnation to himself, not discerning the Lord's body" (1 Corinthians 11:29, KJV). Rowling here drops a biblical mystery play into her postmodern drama to make vivid the godless horror and desperation of Harry's enemy.

A "mystery play" is the term given for a depiction of a story acted out straight or very close to the scriptural account; think "Passion dramas" or just a staging of Adam and Eve's expulsion from Eden or the Nativity in Bethlehem. A "morality play," in contrast, is a depiction like *Pilgrim's Progress* and *Everyman* in which a person representing all humanity or "man" meets characters representing challenges and opportunities on what evangelicals call the "Christian Walk." Ms. Rowling gives us two of these, one at the end of *Chamber of Secrets*, the other in Harry's walk into the Forbidden Forest in *Deathly Hallows*.

The *Chamber of Secrets* drama is a *morality* play because the hero, Harry descending into Slytherin's long-closed basilisk berth to save the fair maiden, is in large part an Everyman drama. All men and women, like Harry, are called to make a choice to confront the demons in their basements and to act sacrificially and lovingly for what is true, good, beautiful, and sacred. The *mystery* play component is that Harry's defeat of the basilisk and Tom Riddle, Jr., like the adventure with the centaur and unicorn, is a staging of biblical teaching in dramatic, allegorical form. Harry's victory because of his faith and his ascent from the depths of the Chamber cavern, the satanic serpent's lair, to the heavenly Hogwarts via the Resurrection phoenix is a transparency of how a Christian finds salvation in Christ.[5]

Deathly Hallows, as we'll discuss in chapter nine, is built on a scaffolding of alchemical events laid over the Christian calendar. Key events happen in Harry's transformation on Christmas Eve, Theophany, and Easter. The climax of the story takes place, not on the calendar date for the Crucifixion but in a depiction of it in story form. Ms. Rowling has said several times that Harry's walk into the forest in *Deathly Hallows* (chapter thirty-four) was the most difficult and rewarding chapter of the books for her. It is largely a retelling of the Crucifixion of Christ.[6]

In essence, chapter thirty-four, titled "The Forest Again," is simultaneously a retelling of the Crucifixion and a story of the death of a Christian Everyman. Harry's choices, and successful struggle to believe, have transformed him into a transparency of the God-man in whom he believes. "The Forest Again" tells us how:

* Harry has Garden of Gethsemane desires and chooses to act in obedience as savior.

* Harry walks the Via Dolorosa, stumbles, and is helped by Lily, his mother.

* Harry dies sacrificially and without resistance to defeat the Dark Lord, as Christ died on the Cross.

Ms. Rowling inevitably tells Harry's story in language resonant with the Passion gospels. The chapter following it is titled "King's Cross," in case we missed the Calvary message, and, when Harry returns to the forest from his conversation with Dumbledore, we get even more. Narcissa Malfoy's "nails pierced him," so we are left with a fallen savior pierced by nails, a Cross, and despairing disciples. Other than a plaited crown of thorns, I'm not sure how she could have made her allegorical point more obvious.

Perhaps it is having Harry, her Everyman figure, in imitation of Bunyan's Christian throwing off his pack of sins at the "Place of Deliverance," losing the scar/Horcrux by having died to himself and offered his life as a sacrifice to save his friends. This death to self, an interior victory resulting in resurrection and eternal life, is a story echo of Matthew 16:25, "For whoever wishes to save his life will lose it; but whoever loses his life for My sake will find it" and of John 15:13: "Greater love hath no man than this, that a man lay down his life for his friends."

The Allegorist's Tale: Harry Potter as a Canterbury Pilgrim

Bunyan's characters, as he tells us plainly in his *Apology* or preface to *Progress*, are allegories and metaphors but no less "solid" in meaning or value for being story transparencies.[7] Chaucer, whose *Canterbury Tales* (c.1400) predates Bunyan by two hundred years and *Everyman* by the better part of a century, is, if anything, more allegorical in intention though with more developed and literal characters. Chaucer was famous even in his day for his poetic achievement in *Tales* and for his use of "sentence," which, as Robertson explains, is the "solidity" of allegorical meaning beneath the surface story and morals. A book's "sentence" is what we arrive at "as the result of allegorical interpretation"[8] and is Chaucer's claim to fame.

If Ms. Rowling hadn't pointed to Chaucer herself and to "The Pardoner's Tale" specifically as an influence on her last novel,[9] we might have guessed as much from the frequent departures she makes within her narrative for characters to tell stories themselves. We have Hagrid explaining his extended vacation among the giants, Kreacher detailing how Master Regulus had died, and Helena Ravenclaw's gothic romance about the Bloody Baron. If we still miss the Chaucer connection, Ms. Rowling gives us four chapter titles that end with "Tale" as a specific hat-tip toward the *Canterbury Tales*.[10]

That Ms. Rowling suggests "The Pardoner's Tale" was an important influence invites greater attention. Not too surprisingly, there are surface, moral, and allegorical correspondences between "The Pardoner's Tale," Ms. Rowling's "Tale of the Three Brothers," and *Harry Potter*'s story arc viewed as a whole.

The surface story told by Chaucer's "Pardoner" is about three men, disgusted by the death of a mutual friend, who head out to find Death and destroy him. They meet an Old Man who says he just saw Death in the graveyard under a tree. At the tree in the graveyard, the three friends find bags of gold rather than the enemy they expect. Long story short, two of the men kill the third to split his share of the gold. The third man has his posthumous revenge because he had poisoned the two men's wine. All three set out to destroy Death but were brought to their own deaths, spiritual and physical, by greed.

"The Tale of the Three Brothers" from *The Tales of Beedle the Bard*, and featured in *Deathly Hallows*, is also about meeting Death. Rowling's tale involves three brothers who bridge a previously uncrossable river with their magic. Death meets them on the bridge, feigns awe at their accomplishment, and grants them three wishes. The oldest chooses an unbeatable wand, which coupled with the brother's arrogance, results in his being murdered. The middle brother "asked for the power to recall others from Death," which eventually causes his suicide after he is "driven mad with hopeless longing" for the shadow of a woman he had called back from beyond the veil. The youngest brother, "the humblest and also the wisest," asked only for a gift that would keep Death from following him. The Invisibility Cloak he receives conceals him from Death until he is an old man and chooses to take it off; he greeted Death then "as an old friend, and went with him gladly, and equals, they departed this life" (*Deathly Hallows*, chapter twenty-one).

Taken as a whole, the *Harry Potter* novels are the story, too, of three men and their battle with death. Tom Riddle, Jr., pursues a personal immortality through power, murder, and dark magic. As a young man, Albus Dumbledore had pursued the Deathly Hallows to become "Master of Death." Harry Potter, the descendant and heir of the brother who had received the Invisibility Cloak, succeeds in winning the three Hallows and vanquishing Voldemort, if not Death per se. Riddle's megalomaniacal search to cheat death results in his death, Dumbledore's sister is killed consequent to his fascination with power, and Harry becomes "the true master of death, because the true master does not seek to run away from Death" (*Deathly Hallows*, chapter thirty-five).[11] "The Tale of the Three Brothers" is, in a way, a synopsis of all seven books.

Chaucer's story has a different ending and a different stated moral (the Pardoner is preaching that cupidity [greed] is the root of all evil), but the implicit instruction or *sentence* of the story is a match with Rowling's: Seeking to defeat or master death willfully is the short cut to an early demise. Chaucer further highlights "the denial of the Spirit" in the pursuit of immortality and fortune by having the Pardoner himself be an allegory of its anti-greed moral.[12]

The Pardoner's example, the allegory alongside the allegorical sermon, is also a testimony to the need for allegory. The Pardoner understands the surface and moral meanings of his tale, not to mention Christian doctrine and scripture, but as D. W. Robertson writes in *A Preface to Chaucer*, he misses "the spirit of Christ beneath the letter of the text" and pursues "the corporal rather than the intelligible."[13] "The Pardoner's Tale," because the narrator has clearly missed the point of his allegorical story, is an ironic argument within an allegory. Ms. Rowling, in her allegorical children's story, "The Tale of the Three Brothers," within her allegorical children's series of books, *Harry Potter*, makes the same argument.

Soul Allegory: The Brothers Karamazov; *Star Trek*; and Harry, Ron, and Hermione

Everyman, Canterbury Tales, and *The Pilgrim's Progress* may be familiar to every great books geek and literature major, but I understand if you're suspicious that their overtly Christian messages signal that their allegorical artistry may be a bit dated. Allegory and the medieval setting as a delivery for same, though, are as relevant as the greatest novel ever written and as current as the most successful science fiction television shows and movies ever made.

The novel is Fyodor Dostoevsky's *The Brothers Karamazov*. In brief, *Brothers* is a murder mystery involving the death of Fyodor Karamazov, the father of Dmitri, Ivan, and Alyosha Karamazov, three brothers who have grown up separately and seem to be from different planets with respect to their temperaments. In a writer as realistic and plainspoken as Dostoevsky, where's the allegory in that?

Your best bet, I hope you see by now, would be to find the medieval fable told by one of the characters and work your way out from there. In the chapter titled "The Grand Inquisitor" (book five, chapter five), Ivan, the philosopher and journalist, sits down with his younger brother Alyosha, a monastery novice, and tells him a parable from fifteenth-century Seville. The story is that Christ Himself returns to Spain and reveals Himself by raising the dead. A cardinal of the Catho-

lic Church, the Grand Inquisitor, has him arrested and inter-
rogates him.

Ivan sympathizes with the cardinal, who explains to his
unwelcome God that the Church is obliged to execute Him
the next day lest He derail the mission of the Church. The
cardinal, like Ivan, is a well-meaning atheist and guardian of the greater good. The Catholic Church, to him, has
vanquished freedom that men could never achieve through
Christ's promises and miracles and has ensured happiness on
earth via obedience.

Christ's response? He says nothing but kisses the cardinal.
The Inquisitor, stunned and shamed, releases Him and tells
him to "Go and come no more . . . Come not at all, never,
never!" Ivan explains that Jesus' kiss "glows in [the cardinal's
heart], but the old man adheres to his ideas."

Like Rowling's use of allegory in the *Harry Potter* series,
Dostoevsky's allegory works on several levels. On the surface,
Ivan's parable about the Catholic cardinal and a church that
would murder Christ lest He urge the peasants to true freedom is about the Roman Catholic Church versus Orthodox
Christianity. By extension, the story is a parable decrying
European ideas of socialism and the greater good that were
already growing in Russia and would lead to the communist
revolution. Dostoevsky is no ecumenist; he equates Catholicism with atheism and an antifaith, an opinion that was more
consensus than controversy to his Russian readers.[14]

At a deeper level, Ivan's cardinal is his self-portrait, a skeptic educated in Europe; the story's Christ is Alyosha. Ivan's opinions are put in the mouth of the cardinal and Alyosha sits quietly in the place of Christ. Alyosha confirms that this is his understanding of Ivan's story by kissing Ivan at chapter's end.

More importantly and profoundly, the story of Ivan and Alyosha and the parable Ivan tells within the story are allegorical transparencies about the soul.[15] Ivan and Alyosha are stand-ins for the soul's capacity for reason and spiritual experience, what we call "mind" and "spirit." Add in passionate, unbridled Dmitri, and the Karamazov brothers are a triptych of the soul's carnal, rational, and spiritual faculties and the book is the story of their relationship to each other, as well as the relationship of Russia's military, educated class, and church.

This body-mind-spirit triptych, soul faculties of one person in three-character allegory, is not Dostoevsky's invention. Plato, you'll recall, is the fountain of all literature as well as philosophy, right? See the Chariot Allegory in Plato's *Phaedrus* (246a–254e) for the originals of Dmitri (the black horse), Ivan (the white horse), and Alyosha (the charioteer). This triptych is a model for a host of twentieth-century imitators, Rowling included.

This three-part soul allegory is as evident in futuristic and fantasy storytelling as it is in ancient philosophy. Science fiction? Think *Star Trek:* Kirk is spirit, Spock is mind, and "Bones" is the carnal part of man. How about *Star Wars*? Luke Skywalker, Mr. Trust the Force, is spirit; Princess Leia is will and smarts; and Hans Solo, the he-man, is looking out for number one. The characters on Mount Doom—the hobbits Frodo and Sam, and Gollum—are Tolkien's images of spirit, will, and fallen passions. Rowling falls into this tradition with her own spiritual triptych: Harry as spirit, Ron as body, and brainy Hermione, of course, as mind.

The Struggle to Believe in Tennyson's *Idylls*, Dostoevsky's *Brothers*, and *Deathly Hallows*

There aren't many medieval Christians or people of childlike faith in Ms. Rowling's twenty-first-century reading audience. Even her younger readers, I suspect, are more skeptical, perhaps even jaded, than they were a mere twenty years ago. Their struggle as thinking people with spiritual aspirations is not a cut-and-dried "do you believe or don't you?" question and answer; but, as profoundly skeptical people qua postmoderns, how do you acquire and sustain anything like traditional faith? Allegorical writing, to be relevant for these readers, needs to portray this struggle more than as a plastic morality play. The best writers have been doing just this since the dawn of the modern age.

We've already met Ivan Karamazov and seen him both tell a parable about the conflict of reason and spirit and act as reason in the allegory of *The Brothers Karamazov*. Ivan, as reason, struggles to believe, and, as Dostoevsky depicts him, his European and modern ideas drive him mad. Ivan is confronted by a nightmare of the devil who is "the incarnation of myself, but only of one side of me . . . of my thoughts and feelings, but only the nastiest and stupidest of them" (*Brothers*, book eleven, chapter nine, "The Devil: Ivan Fyodorovich's Nightmare"). The nightmare is that Ivan at once believes the devil is only a hallucination from his delirium and believes he is the devil and can answer questions like, "Is there a God or not?" Alyosha, the spirit figure in the triptych of the brothers' collective soul, wakes him from this intellectual atheist's nightmare.

Returning to the English tradition, Alfred, Lord Tennyson, employs allegory to describe the struggle with belief in both the Arthurian *Idylls of the King*'s conclusion "The Passing of Arthur" and "In Memoriam." *Idylls* is a poem that is the photographic negative of "In Memoriam." "In Memoriam" is Tennyson's record of his successful struggle with keeping faith and living in faith after the death of his friend, Arthur Hallam. *Idylls* is the elegy of a kingdom destroyed by those not keeping faith: in marriage, as knights, or as subjects. "Both poems not only emphasize man's essential need to believe but also those forces which make it so difficult for him to do so."[16]

In *Idylls* King Arthur and Sir Bedivere's struggles, in brief, are to believe and to trust, albeit on different scales. Arthur, in the idyll before "Passing," forgives Guinevere and is, in an otherworldly manner, reconciled with her despite her betrayal. He leaves her to lead the remnants of his Table against the forces of Mordred, a foe incapable of fealty.[17] The battle is one of mist and confusion, before which Arthur comes close to despair. Sir Bedivere proclaims his fealty, however, and, moved by Sir Bedivere's faith in him, the king attacks and slays Mordred. He receives a mortal blow himself, not unlike Harry's battle with the basilisk in *Chamber of Secrets*.

The king is taken to a chapel. There Arthur orders Bedivere to throw his sword, Excalibur, into the lake. Twice Bedivere balks and attempts to deceive the king. He hides the sword, unable to rationalize its loss because of its beauty, value, history, and because Arthur is not in his right mind. Instead, Bedivere rationalizes his disobedience and disloyalty. Arthur, however, sees through Bedivere's lie and demands he throw the sword in the water. Bedivere at last complies, and the Lady of the Lake catches it and comes for Arthur.

Bedivere is rewarded with the sight of Arthur boarding a vessel that sails to Avalon, the Isle of the Blessed, where the sword was forged. In the allegory of a struggle to believe, Bedivere, the surviving knight of Arthur's Round Table, is the Christian of the end times and Arthur is the Christ. Arthur destroys Mordred in response to Bedivere's faith but is almost allowed to die because of Bedivere's inability to trust in his instruction to the end. Arthur survives on the thread of such halting faith.

Similarly, Harry is an allegory of the modern struggle to believe rather than a cardboard depiction of faith. Rowling gives Harry's first appearance in *Deathly Hallows* the chapter title "In Memoriam" to clarify that "my struggling with religious belief and so on I think is quite apparent in this book."[18] Harry's trouble in *Deathly Hallows*, his interior agony, has less to do with Horcrux hunting or the long camping trip with Ron and Hermione than it does with his crisis of faith.

In brief, Dumbledore serves as a stand-in for God; Harry, as he learns more about the late great headmaster, changes from the "Dumbledore man" he said he was in *Half-Blood Prince* to feeling certain at his nadir that Dumbledore never loved him.

And his fury at Dumbledore broke over him now like lava, scorching him inside, wiping out every other feeling. Out of sheer desperation they had talked themselves into believing . . . that it was all part of some secret path laid out for them by Dumbledore; but there was no map, no plan. Dumbledore had left them to grope in the darkness, to wrestle with unknown and undreamed-of terrors, alone and unaided: Nothing was explained, nothing was given freely . . .

"Look what he asked from me, Hermione! Risk your life,

Harry! And again! And again! And don't expect me to explain everything, just trust me blindly, trust that I know what I'm doing, trust me even though I don't trust you! Never the whole truth! Never!

"... *I don't know who he loved, Hermione, but it was never me. This isn't love, the mess he's left me in ...*"

... *He closed his eyes at her touch, and hated himself for wishing that what she said was true: that Dumbledore had really cared.* (Deathly Hallows, *chapter eighteen*)

In the denouement of *Chamber of Secrets*, Dumbledore had told Harry that "it is our choices, Harry, that show what we truly are, far more than our abilities." Choice is clearly a major theme throughout the series but it is only in *Deathly Hallows* that we learn that the essential choice is not about being kind to Muggles or choosing not to kick your house-elf; it is the choice to believe that makes all the difference.

Harry is counseled by both Elphias Doge and Hermione to "choose to believe" in Dumbledore. He finds the idea of choosing what you believe so nonsensical that he "could simply *choose* not to believe" (*Deathly Hallows*, chapter eight, emphasis on "choose" in original). Ms. Rowling draws our attention to choice and belief again in chapter ten, "Kreacher's Tale," when Harry and Hermione argue about whether to believe like Doge or join the Skeeter skeptics like Auntie Muriel: "There it was again: Choose what to believe. He wanted the truth. Why was everybody so determined that he should not get it?" To Harry at this stage, "choosing" a belief means turning a blind eye to reality. He wants to know facts, not choose beliefs.

Harry decides, however, after the events in the basement at Malfoy Manor, that he must choose to believe or not to believe because he doesn't have and can't get the facts he needs to know for sure. On Easter morning, in a grave that he had chosen to dig by hand to honor Dobby's sacrifice, he chooses to believe in Dumbledore and put aside his doubts. He recalls later:

> *Harry kept quiet. He did not want to express the doubts and uncertainties about Dumbledore that had riddled him for months now. He had made his choice as he dug Dobby's grave, he had decided to continue along the winding, dangerous path indicated for him by Albus Dumbledore, to accept that he had not been told everything that he wanted to know, but simply to trust. He had no desire to doubt again; he did not want to hear anything that would deflect him from his purpose.* (Deathly Hallows, *chapter twenty-eight)*

And it is this choice to put aside doubts, to trust and believe, that makes all the difference. His Easter decision to trust in something greater than himself is the cause of his consequent transformation, ability to walk into the woods as a Christian Everyman, to rise from the dead and defeat Lord Voldemort. That allegorical mystery play, though, at story's end is just part of the modern struggle to believe allegory that is the heart of the book.

What If I Missed All That?

What if you don't get the meaning or see the correspondents of this sort of allegory? Well, don't feel bad. Most people don't pick it up on their first or second pass. If we don't see Harry as an Everyman or as a Christ figure, we can still experience the sacrificial love he shows and the purification he experiences during his willing death in the forest. If we don't "see" Christ, we can still understand that he acts out of love for his friends.

Believe it or not, though, allegory is just the stepping-off place for the real depths of reading experience, the anagogical layer and mythic meaning. Grab your branch of Gubraithian Fire and your indestructible goblin helmet, gifts you picked up from Ms. Rowling's Giants after discovering the allegorical elements of "Hagrid's Tale" (*Order of the Phoenix*, chapter twenty), to explore what legendary art and literary critic John Ruskin called the jewels available only to those doing the "deep mining" of meditative and close reading,[19] our experience of the Hero's Journey, literary alchemy, and magical, spiritual core reality beneath the surface of everything existent in Harry's adventures.

PART FOUR

The Mythic or Anagogical Meaning

CHAPTER EIGHT

The Magical Center of the Circle

*The Mythic Meaning of Harry's Hero's Journeys
from Privet Drive to King's Cross*

I'll admit that the first time I opened each Harry Potter novel I wasn't reading for substance or to find any deep, hidden meaning. I turned the pages as fast as I could because I was on the edge of my seat with excitement about how Harry and friends would solve the mystery and survive the inevitable confrontation with the Wizarding world's forces of evil.

But even on the initial speed-reads there are what seem to be fascinating and inexplicable comments or events in the story line. I always fold a page corner to mark these passages so I can find them easily after putting the children to bed. (My first readings of the last four books were to my children

after "Midnight Madness" parties at local bookstores.) Here
are three examples:

* In *Deathly Hallows,* the Ravenclaw common room door
  asks two questions, "Which came first, the phoenix or
  the flame?" and "Where do Vanished objects go?" Luna
  answers the first successfully ("A circle has no beginning"), and Professor McGonagall handles the second
  ("Into nonbeing, which is to say, everything"). The door
  compliments Luna on her "reasoning" and McGonagall
  on her "phrasing."

* After Harry's sacrifice in the Forbidden Forest, he
  wakes up in a palace he thinks "looks like" King's Cross
  station. He asks Dumbledore at the end of their conversation there if his experience has been "real" "or has this
  been happening inside my head?" Dumbledore responds
  as he fades into the mist, "Of course it is happening
  inside your head, Harry, but why on earth should that
  mean that it is not real?" Huh?

* And what about all the eyeballs in *Deathly Hallows*?
  The blue eye of Dumbledore in the mirror fragment,
  the disembodied eye of Mad-Eye Moody, the "triangular eye" of the Hallows symbol, Snape's love for Lily's
  green eyes, and the red eyes of Tom Riddle, Jr., in the
  locket Horcrux. What's up with that?

These mysteries do not have surface, moral, or allegorical explanations. They require the meditative "slow mining" that John Ruskin says is rewarded by the best art and literature with jewels of meaning.

[The maxim that story teaches better than sermon is true] not of the Iliad *only, but of all other great art whatsoever. For all pieces of such art are didactic in the purest way, indirectly and occultly; so that, first, you shall only be bettered by them if you are already hard at work at bettering yourself; and when you are bettered by them, it shall be partly with a general acceptance of their influence, so constant and subtle that you shall be no more conscious of it than of the healthy digestion of food; and partly by a gift of unexpected truth, which you shall only find by slow mining for it—which is withheld on purpose, and close-locked, that you may not get it till you have forged the key of it in a furnace of your own heating.[1]*

Ruskin is the giant of iconographical criticism, and this remark of his about the deepest meanings of art is worth unpacking. He says first that the teaching or "didactic" quality of art in its "purest" sense isn't overt teaching at all but something hidden, even occultic. Mark Twain, in advice to writers, urges them to this kind of covert meaning: "If you would have your fiction live forever, you must neither overtly preach nor overtly teach; but you must *covertly* preach and *covertly* teach."[2]

Further, discovering this meaning, Ruskin suggests, is not so much a function of cleverness or prior learning as it is a measure of the reader's intention and acceptance. You will be able to "forge the key" to unlock the covert meaning of a writer's work "if you are already hard at work bettering yourself." Grasping this meaning will be less an "aha!" or "got it!" epiphany than something analogous to our assimilation of food: a "constant and subtle" and largely unconscious transformation.

The artistry here will not be surface fireworks; just the contrary. As Lewis wrote in *The Literary Impact of the Authorised Version,* "An influence which cannot evade our consciousness will not go very deep."[3] Expanding on Ruskin's gustatory analogy, Martin Lings, the Shakespeare scholar, says great art is not teaching at all; instead, it is offering a sample of nourishing food that is wisdom each receives to the degree their intentions and capacities allow:

> *In considering how Shakespeare conveys his message to us we must remember that the true function of art is not didactic. A great drama or epic may contain little or much teaching of a didactic kind, but it does not rely on that teaching in order to gain its ultimate effect. Its function is not so much to define spiritual wisdom as to give us a taste of that wisdom, each according to his capacity.*[4]

But Ruskin adds that there is some effort involved in this process beyond a willingness to receive it. We readers need to become sensitive to the clues in the text that the author leaves as pointers for those with eyes to see—little mysteries like the Ravenclaw door's questions and the marble bag of eyeballs rolling around in *Deathly Hallows*.

As we begin the three-chapter anagogical section of *Bookshelf*, in which we will be looking for the hidden spiritual wisdom of these stories ("anagogical" literally meaning "uplifting" or "edifying"), let's start with the door questions and Luna's answer: "A circle has no beginning." Circles, it turns out, are in all literature the preferred esoteric shape for "hero's journey" stories—including Harry's, and are the setting of his most dramatic confrontations with Lord Voldemort. Ms. Rowling didn't make this up herself but lifts it from her favorite writers, ancient and modern.

The Secret Garden at Hogwarts School of Witchcraft and Wizardry

When asked at the dawn of Potter-mania about the possibility of *Harry Potter* movies, Ms. Rowling revealed her familiarity with the best-known books of Frances Hodgson Burnett:

> *Among the things that swayed me to Warner Bros. were the movies* A Little Princess *and* The Secret Garden . . . *They treated the books with respect and made changes where it absolutely made sense.*[5]

Though to my knowledge she has never mentioned Ms. Burnett or her children's classics as sources or inspiration for *Harry Potter*, this remark reflects her intimacy with each book. She knows them well enough to have been impressed with the changes a movie production made as departures from the original. Even without this comment, though, there are sufficiently substantial echoes of *Secret Garden* in *Harry Potter* that the connection can be made without the author's drawing our attention to it.

Secret Garden's cast of characters is a model for Harry, Ron, and Hermione. Both adventures are the stories of two young boys and a girl—in *Garden* the boys are Colin and Dickon, and the girl is Mary. *Garden* takes place in a single year, early spring to late summer, and involves three children ten to twelve years old. The *Potter* adventures, though seven years long, begin when Harry, Ron, and Hermione are eleven years old and are largely the tale of this "terrible trio," as Snape calls them.

Colin and Harry both own mansions, and both houses feature the painting of a mother behind a curtain that is disturbing to the son. Colin and Mary repeatedly describe the manor as a "queer place" and Colin has covered the picture of his mother's smiling face because "sometimes I don't like to see her looking at me. She smiles too much when I am ill and miserable. Besides, she is mine and I don't want everyone to see her" (chapter thirteen, "I am Colin").

Later, Colin pulls back the curtain in the moonlight and leaves the painting for all to see; "I want to see her laughing like that all the time. I think she must have been a sort of Magic person perhaps." In correspondence, the House of Black that Harry inherits at Sirius's death is certainly an odd place, and the painting of Sirius's mother in the entry hall is kept behind moth-eaten velvet curtains. She is definitely "a sort of Magic person," albeit the worst sort.

The most obvious and persuasive echo-pointing-to-influence in Burnett's stories, however, are in the eyes of her lead characters. Sara Crewe in *Princess* has "big, wonderful" and "solemn" green eyes that everyone admires and notes on first meeting her in that book. Colin Craven's eyes, though gray rather than green, repeatedly and by almost every character in *Garden*, are said to resemble the eyes of his late mother, Lilias, the woman in the portrait. Lilias's death precipitated Colin's birth and it is suggested several times that she is watching over him still. Harry's mum was named Lily, of course, his green eyes are always said to be "just like his mother's," her death saved Harry's young life from the Dark Lord, and she walks Harry to his destiny in the Forbidden Forest.

Which brings us finally to the magic of circles. Everyone who enters the walled Secret Garden of Burnett's story—including animals and invalids—looks around and around and around in wonder. Colin's "prayer-meetings" and scientific experiments to explore and invoke the Magic (always capitalized) of the place, too, are held in what Burnett calls "a mystic circle."

It all seemed most majestic and mysterious when they sat down in their circle. Ben Weatherstaff felt as if he had somehow been led into appearing at a prayer-meeting. Ordinarily he was very fixed in being what he called "agen' prayer-meetin's" but this being the Rajah's affair he did not resent it and was indeed inclined to be gratified at being called upon to assist. Mistress Mary felt solemnly enraptured. Dickon held his rabbit in his arm, and perhaps he made some charmer's signal no one heard, for when he sat down, cross-legged like the rest, the crow, the fox, the squirrels and the lamb slowly drew near and made part of the circle, settling each into a place of rest as if of their own desire.

"The 'creatures' have come," said Colin gravely. "They want to help us."

Colin really looked quite beautiful, Mary thought. He held his head high as if he felt like a sort of priest and his strange eyes had a wonderful look in them. The light shone on him through the tree canopy.

In Theosophy, the spirituality that largely shaped Ms. Burnett's personal philosophy, study groups are called "circles." The chanting, processions, incantations, and lectures on Magic in the "mystic circle under the plum tree canopy" in *Garden* are romantic pictures of Theosophical Society meetings. Colin has an especially intense epiphany one day after his lecture in the circle in which he realizes "I'm well! I'm well" and "I shall live forever and ever!" The older gardener then recommends he sing the Anglican doxology, "Praise God from Whom all blessings flow," as celebration. Colin is wonderfully taken with this Christian anthem he has never heard, saying ". . . it means just what I mean . . ." about the Magic and that "it's my song!"

Ms. Rowling's magic is not New Thought or Theosophical, as we'll see in a minute. But Rowling's magic, like Burnett's "Magic," has a circle-laden esoteric edge to it that may be as Christian as the doxology. To get there we need only read a little E. Nesbit, a Rowling favorite, for the passage we need to gain an understanding of Luna's answer to the Ravenclaw door.

"I Think I Identify with E. Nesbit More Than Any Other Writer"

The author with whom Ms. Rowling says, "I identify most," is not her favorite writer, Jane Austen, or the "self-taught socialist" Jessica Mitford, after whom Rowling's first child is named.[6] The distinction of being the storyteller Rowling models herself on as a novelist belongs to a writer of very "funny fairy tales," E. Nesbit.[7] "I identify with the way that she writes. Her children are very real children and she was quite a groundbreaker in her day."[8]

Nesbit's influences are everywhere in Rowling's work. When Harry is facing a year at St. Brutus' Secure Center for Incurably Criminal Boys, Nesbit readers think of Maurice being sent away to Dr. Strongitharm's School for Backward and Difficult Boys in "The Cathood of Maurice" (*The Magic World*, 1912). Fawkes the Phoenix has the name he does almost certainly because the phoenix in Nesbit's *The Phoenix and the Carpet* (1904) is discovered in that story on Guy Fawkes Day. But it is Edith Nesbit's "groundbreaking" work of writing fantasy stories featuring real children rather than cardboard Dick and Jane figures in her magical adventures that has been the greatest influence on Rowling. Nesbit's most famous magical series is a trilogy, sometimes called the *Psammead* after a magical creature in these stories, in which books five very lifelike (and very funny) children argue with and help one another escape death or worse in the ancient past, the far-flung future, and at the British Museum.

Edith Nesbit does not fit our stereotype of a Victorian children's book author. For starters, she had an open marriage and her life turned on political issues. She was a founding member of the Fabian Society, the egg from which the U.K. Labor Party eventually hatched. Travis Prinzi argues cogently in his brilliant *Harry Potter and Imagination* (Zossima, 2009) that Ms. Rowling's political argument in her *Harry Potter* stories is for the gradual-change socialism endorsed by Nesbit's Fabian group. As Rowling names most of Dumbledore's

Order of the Phoenix for historical leaders of the Fabian Society, she isn't being especially subtle on the point.[9]

Beyond being a leader of what was then relatively radical politics, Ms. Nesbit was also a member of the Order of the Golden Dawn. You can think of this group as something like the literary wing of the Theosophical Society, because its members included Bram Stoker, Charles Williams, Arnold Bennett, and William Yeats. The purpose of the Order, in a nutshell, was working magic, by liturgy, ritual, and invocation to affect a relationship or communion with the divine. Dumbledore's secret Order of the Phoenix, because the phoenix as "resurrection bird" is a hermetic symbol of Christ, is a story echo of the Golden Dawn.

Which brings us to Nesbit's magic circle.

In *The Story of the Amulet*, one of Nesbit's best-loved books, five children discover an Egyptian amulet. They are instructed to sit in a circle, and one of them speaks an ancient word. The room is plunged into darkness.

But before the children had got over the sudden shock of it enough to be frightened, a faint, beautiful light began to show in the middle of the circle, and at the same moment a faint, beautiful voice began to speak.

Like Frances Hodgson Burnett, Nesbit believes in the magical properties of "mystic circles." To understand this, we have to talk about sacred geometry to unwrap the metaphysical symbolism of the circle and the center.

So we're all on the same page, here is a little Euclid to define what it is we mean by "circle" and "center": *A circle is the uniform radiation of a spaceless point, the center, into space.* All points of a circle are equidistant from a center point, right? This center, then, really *defines* the circle, of which point the circle is only a radiation or extension. Think of a ripple moving away from a rock dropped in the pond. The rock at the center both causes and defines the circle rippling away from it. A circle, which is visible, is only intelligible and understandable because of the defining and spaceless center that is usually invisible and unknowable in itself.

So far, so good, I hope. Now for the harder part. The reason magicians (or children wanting to speak to a magical object) would sit in a circle looking to the center is to invoke the power of the center. As its radiation or visible aspect, the circle is *essentially* the same thing as its defining center or origin. If magic has a shape, it is a circle and it is the circle's unplottable and defining center that is the heart and power of the magic. Sitting in a circle and saying the magic word, believe it or not, is the symbolic equivalent of saying God's Name.

The circle is a traditional and profound representation of God as Trinity in Christian art and literature. God the Father is the Center, the Word or *Logos* is the visible circle or sphere, and the Holy Spirit is the radiation proceeding from the center. The Father is only knowable through His Word and because of the Holy Spirit. St. Bonaventure describes God as a sphere whose center is everywhere and whose periphery is nowhere.[10]

Nesbit's circle center in *Amulet* is especially heavy on the hermetic Christian symbolism. The center of her circle reveals itself as otherworldly light and speech. Similarly, Christians believe that the Creative Principle, the second person or hypostasis of the Trinity, is the *Logos* or "Word" and that this principle is the "light of the world," "which lighteth every man that cometh into the world" (John 1:9, KJV). Jesus of Nazareth is the incarnation of this divine light and speech that was "in the beginning" with God. Nesbit here is telling this fundamental Christian doctrine in story form; the magic "voice" and "light" here is an aspect of the cosmic *Logos* that creates all things and is the substance of human thought.

Do most readers see this? Probably not. Burnett's and Nesbit's associations with occult groups and doctrines make it a fair reading, though. And internal evidence, which is to say, what we know from Harry's adventures rather than from a Rowling interview, points to her treading a similar path. The high points of the *Potter* epic involve story circles: the circular structure of each year's hero's journey, and even Harry's name.

The Rowling Story Circle: Harry's
Battles with Lord Voldemort

The high points of the novels that are circular are Harry's two face-to-face wand wars with the Dark Lord, first in the *Goblet of Fire* graveyard and last in their Battle of Hogwarts fight to the finish. Harry, as you'll recall, has been Portkeyed unwillingly to the graveyard where his blood is used as the critical ingredient in Voldemort's rebirthing potion. Born again, if you will, the Dark Lord summons his Death Eaters to him and they form a circle around him while he speaks:

> Each of [the Death Eaters approached] Voldemort on his knees and [kissed] his robes, before backing away and standing up, forming a silent circle, which enclosed Tom Riddle's grave, Harry, Voldemort, and the sobbing and twitching heap that was Wormtail. (Goblet of Fire, *chapter thirty-three*)

Voldemort tells this unholy gathering the story of his resurrection and begins to torture Harry before challenging him to a duel. Harry decides to die "upright like his father, and he was going to die trying to defend himself, even if no defense was possible . . ." (*Goblet of Fire*, chapter thirty-four). To Harry's surprise and Voldemort's, his desperate "Expelliarmus!" meets the Dark Lord's death curse and "a narrow beam of light connected the two wands, neither red nor green, but bright, deep gold." Wands joined by golden light, the combatants are raised out of the circle to rest on a "patch of ground that was clear and free of graves."

The Death Eaters quickly reform their dark magic circle, but the "golden thread connecting Harry and Voldemort splintered." It encloses them in a sphere of golden light, "a golden, dome-shaped web, a cage of light." The web, a creation of the phoenix feather wand-cores, begins to emit phoenix song, an inspiring song of hope Harry feels is "inside him instead of just around him." Through the magic of *Priori Incantatem*, the shades of people Voldemort has murdered—including Harry's parents—rise from the Dark Lord's wand after Harry has willed light from the connecting thread to enter it.

Harry escapes miraculously but we see the same battle three years later in Hogwarts's Great Hall. In the melee and maelstrom of duels, flying bodies, and curses, Voldemort is described as being in the "center of the battle." When Harry reveals himself, the "crowd was afraid, and silence fell abruptly and completely as Voldemort and Harry looked at each other, and began, at the same moment, to circle each other" (*Deathly Hallows*, chapter thirty-six). Throughout the rematch, they continue "moving sideways, both of them, in that perfect circle, maintaining the same distance from each other . . ."

The battle, truth be told, is less a duel than a debate—with Harry doing almost all the talking. He tutors the Dark Lord in all the things he does not know about Dumbledore, Snape, wand-lore, and, incredibly, repentance. Harry invites him, almost begs him to " 'Think, and try for some remorse, Riddle . . .' Of all the things that Harry had said to him, beyond any revelation or taunt, nothing had shocked Voldemort like this."

At the moment of resolution, dawn breaks and light floods the circle:

> *A red-gold glow burst suddenly across the enchanted sky above them as an edge of dazzling sun appeared over the sill of the nearest window. The light hit both of them in the faces at the same time, so that Voldemort's was suddenly a flaming blur. Harry heard the high voice shriek as he too yelled his best hope to the heavens, pointing Draco's wand:*
>
> "Avadra Kedavra!"
>
> "Expelliarmus!"
>
> *The bang was like a cannon blast, and the golden flames that erupted between them, at the dead center of the circle they had been treading, marked the point where the spells collided. Harry saw Voldemort's green jet meet his own spell, saw the Elder Wand fly high, dark against the sunrise, spinning across the enchanted ceiling like the head of Nagini, spinning through the air toward the master it would not kill who had come to take full possession of it at last.* (Deathly Hallows, *chapter thirty-six)*

The first thing to note is how many similarities there are between this illuminated circle and the golden dome battle scene of *Goblet of Fire*'s graveyard. They use the exact same spells, for instance, and their spells meet at a point between them, from which center "golden flames" and "golden light" break forth. We have a symbolic circle, not to mention a "Golden Dawn."

In both *Goblet of Fire* and *Deathly Hallows*, Harry has chosen to die, to give up his individual life, in order to defeat the Dark Lord. Harry tutors his foe and calls him to repentance, "to feel some remorse," because he has become the power of the circle's center, the creative *Logos*, of light, knowledge, and conscience. He knows the wand-cores, which in Goblet share feathers of a phoenix, and therefore are representations of Christ, will do his will, because he has identified himself with the Word-Center of the same essential substance.

Privet Drive to King's Cross:
The Rowling Ten-Step Hero's Journey

This wouldn't be much of an argument if it were just the big battle scenes between Harry and Voldemort that were circular. Every *Harry Potter* adventure is a circle, and like Odysseus's, Aeneas's, and Dante's adventures before him, each conforms to the three steps of separation from the mundane world to the mystical, initiation there, and divine return, usually with a trip to the underworld thrown in.

In each book Harry *separates* from his Muggle home

on Privet Drive, is *initiated* and transformed in a series of magical trials and adventures, and *returns* to Muggledom at the end of the school year. Ms. Rowling's annual journey formula for Harry, though, is more detailed than a mechanical hop from Privet Drive to Hogwarts and back to King's Cross. Harry's journey has *ten* distinct steps we see every year:

1. **Privet Drive:** Home Sweet Home!

2. **Magical Escape:** the intrusion of the magical world into profane existence—and the adventure begins!

3. **Mystery:** Harry, Ron, and Hermione's extracurricular assignment each year.

4. **Crisis:** the mystery comes to a head—and Harry chooses to do the right, difficult thing!

5. **Underground:** Harry and one or both of his two friends go underground to confront the evil to be overcome!

6. **Battle:** and we have a fight!

7. **Loss and Death:** a fight Harry loses every single year . . . and seems to die.

8. **Resurrection:** but he rises from the dead, in the presence of a symbol of Christ.

9. **Dumbledore Denouement:** the headmaster explains what happened that Harry missed.

10. **King's Cross:** Harry rides the Hogwarts Express back to the conjunction of his magical and Muggle lives.

Here I just want to point out three curious things about how *Deathly Hallows* satisfies this formula before getting to the power of the circle and Luna's answer to the Ravenclaw common room door.

First, the ten steps above can be divided pretty neatly into the divisions of separation (steps one and two), initiation (three to eight), and return (nine and ten). The fifth step, though, "going underground," is a bit of a head-scratcher. Sure, Odysseus journeys to the land of the dead, Aeneas follows suit, and Dante, boy, does he go underground! There is even the pointer to Christ's Harrowing of Hades.

But in the Rowling formula, "going underground" can seem bizarre. We go through the trap door that Fluffy protects in *Sorcerer's Stone*. In *Chamber of Secrets*, it's down the long slide under the sink in Myrtle's bathroom to the Chamber of Secrets, again, "miles beneath Hogwarts." *Prisoner of Azkaban* has the most token underground travel—through the roots beneath the Whomping Willow to the tunnel leading to the Shrieking Shack. Harry doesn't go underground in *Goblet of Fire* but to a graveyard, which, because most of the people "present" *are* underground, has the same symbolic weight. In *Order of the Phoenix*, Harry and friends battle the Death Eaters in the Department of Mysteries in the lowest level of the Ministry of Magic. Dumbledore takes Harry into a subterranean cave and lake in *Half-Blood Prince* before making his notable descent from the Astronomy Tower.

What is Ms. Rowling after here? I think it's safe to assume if we see an event or action recur without fail in each book, we know it has been put there intentionally. The answer is the series finale, *Deathly Hallows*, in which Harry spends a lot of time underground.

In *Deathly Hallows* Harry and friends go underground again and again. And again. I counted seven times. They flush themselves into the Ministry and descend to the Wizengamot chambers to rescue the Cattermoles. Harry and Ron dive into the pool in the Forest of Dean to get the Sword of Gryffindor. There's a regular reunion in the dungeon beneath Malfoy Manor. Harry digs himself a hole to get underground and bury Dobby. The Terrific Trio and Griphook descend to the depths below Gringotts to liberate and hitch a ride on a pale dragon. We get back into the Shrieking Shack via the tunnel beneath the Whomping Willow. And Harry enters the London "underground" in King's Cross, his imagined "underworld" and very real *and* "in his head" meeting place with the late headmaster (King's Cross is the busiest platform on the London underground subway system).

In every one of these trips, a spelunker ascends in a lifesaving rescue (the Cattermoles, Harry from the pool, Dobby's group rescue from the Malfoys, and the Gringotts dragon), with an invaluable magical object (the Sword of Gryffindor—twice—the cup Horcrux, and Snape's memories), or forever changed (Ron post-baptism, Harry after burying Dobby, Harry rising from King's Cross). Could the previous six novels' underground passages have just been foreshadowing all these descents in *Deathly Hallows*? Hold on to this question. We'll have to come back to it.

Second, another signature of Ms. Rowling's hero's journey is Harry's annual figurative death and resurrection from the dead in the presence of a symbol of Christ. There are two lines we read in every book, I think. (Maybe three, if you include Hermione's pleas for Ron and Harry to read *Hogwarts: A History*.) One is ". . . and Harry's scar hurt worse than it had ever hurt before." The other and more important repeatable line is Harry's dying thought, ". . . so this is what it's like to die." Battling Quirrell, fanged by a basilisk, kissed by a dementor, tortured by the reborn Dark Lord, possessed by Voldemort in the Ministry, carried by the Inferi into the lake, and just flat-out killed by Voldemort in the finale, Harry dies a figurative death in every single book.

And in every book except the last, he comes back from this faux death either because of or just in the vicinity of a symbol of Christ. I'll talk more about that symbolism in a moment, but here you just have to note that for six books, Harry's resurrection is cued or caused by a potent Christian reference. Fawkes the Phoenix plays this part in *Chamber of Secrets, Goblet of Fire*, and *Order of the Phoenix*. It's a Philosopher Stone in his pocket in the first book, a stag Patronus in *Prisoner of Azkaban*, and both a Hippogriff and the Half-Blood Prince in *Half-Blood Prince*. [For explanations of these symbols, see *How Harry Cast His Spell*, chapter nine (Tyndale, 2008).]

And *Deathly Hallows*?

In *Deathly Hallows*, Harry doesn't rise from the dead *in the presence of* a symbol of Christ. As we saw in the last chapter, he rises *as* a symbol of Christ. I think it's safe to say here that all the previous deaths and resurrections were just pointers and prefigurings of Harry's ultimate victory, his "mastery of death." Ms. Rowling has said that the last third of *Deathly Hallows* was the fixed part of the storyline that drove every other element of the previous books. All the stories do point to Harry's trip into "The Forest Again."

Third, two violations of journey formula happen at the end of *Half-Blood Prince*: we don't get our meeting with Dumbledore (he's attending his own funeral) and we don't go to King's Cross station. That omission is understandable; as Ms. Rowling said before the finale, books six and seven slide together at the end into one story. We make up for it, though, in *Deathly Hallows*, where we get *two* Dumbledore denouement scenes and *two* trips to King's Cross. Harry's encounter with his mentor at his King's Cross vision is the most curious of these scenes and trips.

On her Open Book Tour press conference in Los Angeles, Rowling said she thought the Christian content of the books was "obvious."[11] I think we can all agree that Harry's arriving at "King's Cross" after his sacrificial death in love for his friends points to Calvary and not an especially obscure reference. But why meet with Dumbledore there, and underground?

To answer those questions, I think we have to discuss why poets and novelists return again and again to the hero's journey. If you grasp the spiritual meaning of the circle, you'll understand Luna's answer to the Ravenclaw door as well as why Harry's final return from the dead *guaranteed* his eventual victory over the Dark Lord.

Mythic Return: The Power of the Circle Center

The hero's journey isn't a story formula, ultimately, or just a mechanical structure on which to hang a plot. It's really about the symbolism of the circle and the center we discussed above.

Harry's adventure completes a circle every year: from his life with the Dursleys at Privet Drive, through his adventures in the magical world, back to being picked up by the Dursleys at King's Cross Station at year's end. If you have a piece of paper handy, draw a circle with the beginning point at the bottom being the Dursleys, Hogwarts being diametrically across from it (up in Scotland?), and the circle coming to a close again at the Dursleys, who meet Harry at King's Cross.

Now every hero's journey is a figurative, completed circle, if not a geometric one, and from what we've discussed before and seen in *Secret Garden,* in *Amulet,* and in Harry's circular showdowns with the Dark Lord, the circle is a symbol of God and creation, specifically of the unknown center defining and creating the visible circle.

And this has *what* to do with Harry's annual journey?

A hero completing a circular journey has ritually arrived by his circumnavigation at the defining center because the circle he or she has completed is one with the center. To repeat myself: As its radiation or visible aspect, the circle is *essentially* the same thing as its defining center or origin. If magic has a shape, it is a circle and it is the circle's unplottable and defining center that is the heart and power of the magic.

Harry ends every year and the story has its most important turn at King's *Cross* because the cross, like the circle, is defined by the center point at which a horizontal and vertical line meet. Draw a cross in your hero's journey circle to divide that circle into four pie pieces. This point that defines the cross, the circle, and the end of the journey brings the hero into the "sacred space" or point creating the world.

Harry makes this trip to the crossing point defining the circle of his journey *seven* times. I explain the symbolism and importance of the number seven in *Unlocking Harry Potter*; but, as you've read the stories, you know how central the number seven is: the number of Quidditch players, Horcruxes, Years of Magical Education, Harry-clones escaping Privet Drive in *Deathly Hallows*, etc. If you've studied Arithmancy with Professor Vector or Pythagoras or even Lord Voldemort, you know this is the most "magically powerful" number.

Having completed the circle and achieved the center the seventh time, this last time by sacrificing himself without hope of gain, Harry, in effect, has executed his ego or died to himself, thereby returning to the center or transpersonal self before Voldemort kills him. Harry survives the Killing Curse *again*. How? In the story, it's a function of his connection with the sacrificial death of his first savior, Lily Potter, and the magic of this sacrifice that exists in her blood, blood that flows in both Voldemort and Harry. No doubt this is a tip of the hat to the goddesses of Homer and Virgil and Dante's green-eyed Beatrice, who save their respective heroes.

I think it is as credible—and maybe even easier to understand—to look at Harry's survival within the context of his repeated circular journeys. From this view, Harry survives as the center because no point on the circle can destroy the center defining that circle. By transcending himself, Harry steps out of time and space, if you will, and into eternity and the infinite of the Origin, which Ms. Rowling portrays quite appropriately as a place called King's Cross.

When Harry tells Dumbledore he thinks they are at King's Cross, do you remember the headmaster's reaction?

"King's Cross Station!" Dumbledore was chuckling immoderately.
*"Good gracious, really?" (*Deathly Hallows, *chapter thirty-five)*

Dumbledore, unlike Harry, undoubtedly has studied Arithmancy, sacred geometry, and Christian scripture (hence the tombstone verses in Godric's Hollow). Of course, he finds Harry's intuitive choice of "locations" (after his sacrifice makes him "master of death") quite humorous. Dumbledore laughs because the hero's journey is a circle for much the same reason that the events of Calvary (the King's Cross) have their meaning and why Christ died on a geometric cross. In achieving the symbolic Center, Harry has become, if not one, then "not two" with the transcendent Absolute.

By choosing to return to time and space after this apotheosis, Harry broke the power of the Dark Lord. Harry went underground repeatedly in *Deathly Hallows*, most importantly in choosing to dig Dobby's grave on Easter morning, because each descent into the underworld was a dying to himself from which, remember, he either saved lives, recovered lost treasure, or was enlightened. Imagine the world as a circle; every descent was Harry's movement toward the center and source of life and away from the periphery of ego and the fear of death.

It's important to note that the end of *Deathly Hallows* is not just the completion of Harry's journey in his seventh year, but the joining of the circle with the beginning of his journey in *Sorcerer's Stone*. There are too many connecting points and echoes to go into here, but you probably noticed in the first book that Hagrid carries Harry's body from the ruins of his childhood home to safety on Sirius's motorcycle and he escorted Harry from his about-to-be-destroyed house on Privet Drive on the same motorcycle and, in the last, carries Harry's body from the Forbidden Forest to Hogwarts as an echo of that event.

Harry returns to Godric's Hollow in *Deathly Hallows* for the first time since Hagrid took him to the Dursleys and learns on Christmas morning what happened to him and his parents on that Halloween long ago. Ted Lupin becomes the philosophical orphan whose parents were murdered by the Dark Lord's Death Eaters, completing and repeating another circle.

There is Neville Longbottom, too. In *Sorcerer's Stone*, Dumbledore awards Gryffindor House the five points it needs to overcome Slytherin, because of Neville's courage. In *Deathly Hallows*, of course, it is Neville's courage and faith in the face of almost certain death that brings him the Sword of Gryffindor to destroy the Nagini, the last Horcrux.

And remember Harry's "resurrection" in *Sorcerer's Stone*? He doesn't quite get to King's Cross in his first year, but it does take him *three days* to return to life. No doubt, Dumbledore "chuckled immoderately" then on the Chosen One's rising on the third day.

The hero's journey in *Harry Potter*, especially the journey he starts and finishes in *Deathly Hallows*, which also completes the circle and finds the center and crossing point of the whole series, explains in large part why we love the books and why Voldemort couldn't defeat Harry in the end. Having achieved the Absolute and Transcendent unity and whole, the origin of life, Harry could not be defeated by the peripheral fraction of a man fearing death that Voldemort had become.

And we, having experienced Harry's journey alongside him, had some imaginative experience of our own hope of defeating death. No wonder we read and reread these books! Privet Drive to King's Cross is the journey from a "private" or ego-driven conception of self to the illuminating experience of the point defining the circle, the Cross, and everything in existence. Sacrificing ourselves in love for our friends alongside Harry, we perceive and experience the eternal verities as much as our spiritual capacity allows.

Conclusion: The Mystical Questions of the Ravenclaw Common Room Door

I certainly understand if you're skeptical about the anagogical meaning of the circle and Harry's hero's journey. Harry's becoming the mythic defining point and Creative Principle has to seem a bit of a stretch for what almost all of us think of as a series of entertaining stories for children. I'm satisfied if at this point you're just willing to suspend your disbelief in a larger meaning to the stories, a spiritual meaning to which readers respond.

Think back to the Ravenclaw door's questions and the answers of Luna and Professor McGonagall, though, if you just cannot believe that Ms. Rowling put these metaphysical meanings of the circle in her story as did Homer, Virgil, and Dante, and, more recently, Frances Hodgson Burnett and E. Nesbit.

The eagle in the door asks Luna, "Which came first, the phoenix or the flame?" Right away, we have to acknowledge the wizarding equivalent of the chicken-and-egg joke—and that Ms. Rowling's version involves a phoenix, a symbol of Christ the Center, and flame, the word she uses to describe the light coming from the center of Voldemort's and Harry's last stand. Think Gubraithian Fire, the nonconsuming flame in *Order of the Phoenix*'s allegory-within-the-story, "Hagrid's Tale," and the lights of Mounts Sinai and Tabor.

Luna's answer—"A circle has no beginning"—is as illuminating. A circle has no start or finish in itself but is defined by an origin that cannot be seen—the "no beginning," which is the sacred center. The door congratulates her on her "reasoning" because she has put her finger on the *Logos* that is the fount of all knowledge and reason. There is nothing rational per se in her symbolic answer.

The door later asks McGonagall "Where do Vanished objects go?" Her answer—"Into nonbeing, which is to say, everything"—is, again, to point to the Divine Center that cannot be known in itself that St. Bonaventure says is every-where and the origin of everything existent. The door compli-ments the professor on her "phrasing" because the Word that is beyond being and the unity of existence is divine speech.

Wildly metaphysical, I know. But Burnett and Nesbit are not freaks or even especially peculiar in pointing to a divine reality greater than matter and energy that is the light in every person (John 1:9). They choose to deliver this message, though, in story, like the Divine Center who taught in para-bles, so that those with ears to hear might hear it and the rest might enjoy a good story.

Burnett wrote once that literature "offered a far greater significance to the happiness of men and women than any sci-entific discovery can give them."[12] I don't doubt that she was referring to the reader's experience of identifying with char-acters transformed by magic and illuminated by the center.

Harry Potter's name means "Heir of the Potter," which, because "potter" is a biblical metaphor for God, "shaper of the human vessel," used from the Book of Genesis to Revelations, points to his being a Christian everyman and spiritual seeker. In the next two chapters, we'll go "further up and further in" on our slow-mining adventure to unveil the anagogical mean-ing of his adventures as his transformation from God's image to his likeness. The first stop on that tour is to visit Shake-speare and Dickens to reveal how Rowling's stories are liter-ary alchemy about Harry's change from spiritual lead to gold.

CHAPTER NINE

Harry Potter as Alchemical Reading Magic

*Shakespeare, Dickens, and the Artistry Changing
Readers' Hearts from Lead to Gold*

The *Potter* magic formula Ms. Rowling uses is hard to deny. Every year we journey from Privet Drive, to a magical escape, to a mystery ending in confrontation, to a loss—no, to a victory and resurrection. Other than the end of *Half-Blood Prince*—the book Ms. Rowling says really slides right into *Deathly Hallows*—we always wind up at King's Cross and, figuratively, at the point defining the cross and the circular journey.

The alchemy Ms. Rowling uses as each story's scaffolding and structure is more obscure. Because of a misspent childhood, I knew enough about the history of alchemy and the stream of literary alchemy in English letters that I recognized it in Ms. Rowling's work even before I knew the first book was originally titled *Philosopher's Stone* rather than *Sorcerer's Stone*.

I learned quickly, though, that however obvious this was to me, readers found the idea that Ms. Rowling was writing in the alchemical tradition of Shakespeare, Donne, Blake, Yeats, and Joyce more than just hard to believe. Fandom critics and at least one notable academic thought—and said loudly and publicly—that the idea of a hermetic "hidden key" to these children's books was absurd. Then, in February 2007, Lisa Bunker, a librarian in Arizona who headed a worldwide staff of Internet mavens collecting Ms. Rowling's every statement for Accio-Quote.org, found an interview from 1998 in which Ms. Rowling talked about alchemy:

> *I've never wanted to be a witch, but an alchemist, now that's a different matter. To invent this Wizarding world, I've learned a ridiculous amount about alchemy. Perhaps much of it I'll never use in the books, but I have to know what magic can and cannot do in order to set the parameters and establish the stories' internal logic.*[1]

That's as close as we're going to get, I'm afraid, to an affirmation from the author that the books are alchemical in structure. Let's talk about what literary alchemy is in light of historical "lead-to-gold" alchemy, how Ms. Rowling actually uses it in her novels, and to explore the uplifting meaning and mythic effect it has on readers.

Alchemy: What It Was and Wasn't

I grew up in twentieth-century America and was indoctrinated by inoculation like everyone else with the popular ideas that define our age. Every age has them. Perhaps the most important spell or charm that entrances us as modern people is the belief that nature, specifically matter and energy, is all that exists.

Alchemy is everything that scientific naturalism and materialism are not. It is the modern empirical worldview turned inside out.[2] Alchemy, in a nutshell, was the science of working toward the perfection of the alchemist's soul. This heroic venture is all but impossible today, because the way we look at reality makes the concept itself almost an absurdity. Unlike the medieval alchemists, we moderns and postmoderns see things with a clear subject/object distinction; that is, we believe you and I and that table are entirely different things and there is no connection or relation between them. The knowing subject is one thing and the observed object is completely "other."

To the alchemist that was not the case. His efforts in changing lead to gold were based on the premise that he, as the subject, would go through the same types of changes and purifications as the materials he was working with. In sympathy with these metallurgical transitions and resolutions of contraries, his soul would be purified in correspondence as long as he was working in a prayerful state within the mysteries (sacraments) of his revealed tradition.

Historically there was an Arabic alchemy, a Chinese alchemy, a Kabbalistic, as well as a Christian alchemy; each differed superficially with respect to their spiritual traditions. In every one, however, the alchemist was working with a sacred natural science or physics to advance his spiritual purification.

This was only possible because he looked at the metal he was working with as something with which he was not "other" but with which he was in relationship. The alchemist and the lead becoming gold were imitating and accelerating the work of the Creator. The alchemist's aim was to create a bridge so that as lead changes to gold, or material perfection, his soul in sympathy would go through similar transformations and purifications.

To the alchemist, lead is hard darkness and gold is light made solid; sanctification beyond salvation or virtue is the illumination of the soul, its identification and communion with the light of the world in all men (John 1:9), that light shining into our spiritual darkness. Just as the Circle is the extension of and essentially identical with the Center, and the hero by completing his initiatory journey takes on the divine qualities of the Creative Principle, so the alchemist, in directing the resolution of contraries that are the visible activity of the Word in creation, becomes the eternal light and knowledge of the defining point.

Alchemy and English Literature: The Drama Connection

Metallurgical alchemy as a sacred science was never an American adventure. It was history long before the pilgrims set sail. This spiritual science went into precipitous decline from the Renaissance through the Enlightenment when it was eclipsed by the materialist view and priorities of modern chemistry. American readers, consequently, are almost unaware of alchemy. This is perhaps no great loss, but it does have one consequence that touches on *Harry Potter* fans: Alchemy is near the heart of great English fiction.

English literature is rich in alchemical language, references, themes, and symbols from Chaucer to Rowling; to be ignorant of this language and imagery is to miss out on the depths and heights of Shakespeare, Blake, Donne, Milton, even C. S. Lewis and James Joyce. Ms. Rowling, as I will demonstrate in a moment, is not ignorant of literary alchemy. The *Harry Potter* books individually and as a series are built on alchemical structures, written in alchemical language, and have alchemical themes at their core.[3]

I think the connection is probably most clear in drama. Eliade even suggests that the alchemical work grew out of initiatory dramas of the Greek mystery religions.[4] Shakespeare doesn't just make asides to alchemy in his plays; many if not most of them are written on alchemical skeletons and themes. *The Tempest, Romeo and Juliet, Antony and Cleopatra, Two Gentlemen of Verona, The Comedy of Errors, Love's Labour's Lost*, and *The Merchant of Venice* come to mind.[5]

Shakespeare and Ben Jonson, among others, used alchemical imagery and themes because they understood that the work of theatre in human transformation was similar to alchemical work. Alchemical work, of course, claimed to be more than just an imaginative experience, but the idea of purification by identification or correspondence with an object and its transformations is "spot on" with the purpose of theatre. We identify with the characters, and we are transformed.

Dominant Contraries to Be Resolved

Alchemists, like all traditional people, thought of the visible world as a reflection of the Creator's nature. God is transcendent or "other," totally apart and distinct from us as creatures, and, at the same time, He is even closer to us than our breath, the cause of our existence. In His unity, God is the resolution of these absolute contraries and every aspect of creation has the fingerprint of contraries on their way to resolution. The revealed religious traditions, in this view, are means of humanity's return to the still point of love and peace out of which the contraries of time and space, male and female, heaven and earth, as well as all the complements of sense perception (hot/cold, near/far, loud/quiet, hard/soft, sweet/salty) proceed.

Literary alchemy is a snapshot of this apotheosis by alchemical transformation. It presents in story form the contrary aspects to be resolved as external contraries in the community, as internal conflicts to be resolved, or as both. In *Harry Potter*, the Wizarding world is divided largely along the Gryffindor/Slytherin divide, which extends ultimately to the militant factions of these tribes—Dumbledore's Order of the Phoenix (with Harry's Dumbledore's Army the junior varsity squad) and Voldemort's Death Eaters. Internally, this is represented in Harry's mind, as he is both Gryffindor icon and the bearer of a Lord Voldemort soul fragment with its attendant powers and abilities. The drama of the seven books is how both of these conflicts, in the world at large and within Harry, will be resolved—and this resolution of all contraries is a signature of alchemical drama.

Three Stages of Transformation and Their Alchemical Colors

Harry's annual hero's journey, consequently, is also the cycle of his alchemical transformation—and each stage of the work has a character or more than one character named for that stage's indicative color. The first stage of the alchemical work is dissolution, usually called the "*nigredo*" or the black stage. In the black, initial stage, "the body of the impure metal, the matter for the Stone, or the old, outmoded state of being is killed, putrefied, and dissolved into the original substance of creation, the *prima materia*, in order that it may be renovated and reborn in a new form."[6] Sirius Black is named for this stage of the work; the book in which he died, *Order of the Phoenix*, as we'll see in a second, was the *nigredo* novel of the series.

The second stage of alchemical transformation of lead into gold is the "*albedo*" or white work. It follows the ablution or washing of the calcified matter at the bottom of the alembic, the washing of which causes it to show the "peacock's tail" (cauda pavonis) or the colors of the rainbow before turning a brilliant white. "When the matter reaches the *albedo* it has become pure and spotless."[7] Albus Dumbledore is the character with the "white" name; "Albus" is Latin for "white, resplendent."

Frequently used symbols of the *albedo* stage of the work in pictorial representations and descriptions of it are luna (Latin for "moon") and a lily. I'll explain how *Half-Blood Prince* was Albus's book in many ways because it featured his tutorials with Harry—and because of his fall from the Astronomy Tower, planned or unplanned, at book's end. The real work of alchemy is accomplished in the wedding or resolution of contraries in the white stage, a victory that is revealed in the crisis of the red.

The third and last stage of the chemical work is the "*rubedo*" or the red stage.

> *When the matter of the stone has been purified and made spotless at the* albedo *it is then ready to be reunited with the spirit (or the already united spirit and soul). With the fixation, crystalliza-tion, or embodiment of the eternal spirit, form is bestowed upon the pure, but as yet formless matter of the Stone. At this union, the supreme chemical wedding, the body is resurrected into eter-nal life. As the heat of the fire is increased, the divine red tincture flushes the white stone with its rich, red colour . . . The reddening of the white matter is also frequently likened to staining with blood.*[8]

Rubeus Hagrid has the red name; "*rubeus*" is Latin for "red" (the Latin for "black," of course, is "*niger*" so Sirius's name is translated to the English "black" for obvious reasons). Rufus Scrimgeour also has red meaning and we should note that Fred Weasley's name is "Red" if we drop one letter. A com-mon symbol of the red work and the Philosopher's Stone is the red lion, which is, of course, the house mascot for Gryffindor.

The formula for each book in the series is a trip through these three alchemical stages.

In the individual books, the black stage, or *nigredo*, is almost always launched on Privet Drive, where Harry is treated horribly. The work of breaking Harry down continues each year when he gets to Hogwarts and Severus Snape takes over, a black figure if there ever was one. But Hogwarts is also the home of Albus "the White" Dumbledore, and Hogwarts is where Harry is purified of the failing identified at the Dursleys as he, Ron, and Hermione solve that year's mystery. The understanding he gains through these trials is revealed in the book's crisis—the confrontation with the bad guys—in which he always dies a figurative death and is reborn. From Privet Drive to his chat with Dumbledore at book's end, Harry is purified and transformed. The series taken altogether has a black, white, and red stage, too: *Order of the Phoenix* is the black book of the series, *Half-Blood Prince* is the white, and *Deathly Hallows* is the *rubedo* or red stage. Let's review them quickly.

The *nigredo*, again, is the stage in which the subject is broken down, stripped of all but the essential qualities for purification in the *albedo* or white work. *Order of the Phoenix*, darkest and most disturbing of all the *Harry Potter* novels, is this stage in the series; Ms. Rowling cues us to this not only in the plot points, all of which are about Harry's loss of his identity, but in the blackness of the book. No small part of it takes place in the House of Black and it ends, of course, with the death of Sirius Black.

More important, though, is that *Order of the Phoenix* details Harry's near complete dissolution. Every idea he has of himself is taken from him. Dolores Umbridge teaches him that Hogwarts can be hell. He learns his father was a jerk. No Quidditch! Ron and Hermione outrank him on the Hogwarts totem pole. The entire "girl thing" eludes him except for agonizing confusion and heartbreak. Everything, in brief, is a nightmare for him in his fifth year. His self-understanding and identity are shattered—except, at the very end, after Sirius's death and with it any hope of a family life with his godfather, Harry learns about the prophecy. That understanding replaces everything else. And that's the end of the black work.

When *Half-Blood Prince* begins, we feel we are in a different universe. Albus Dumbledore is not only back in Harry's life, he comes to pick him up at Privet Drive! The headmaster, largely absent in *Order of the Phoenix*, is everywhere in *Half-Blood Prince*. This is his book, which, given the meaning of his name and the work that is accomplished, might be called the "white book." And, like Sirius at the end of the "black book," Albus dies at the end of the "white."

Through the tutorials with Dumbledore and the tasks he is given, Harry comes to a whole new understanding of himself in terms of the prophecy and his relationship to Lord Voldemort. Harry doesn't get the whole truth from the headmaster, but at the end of *Half-Blood Prince*, he has been transformed from a boy who doesn't believe Dumbledore will show up to one who defiantly tells the Minister of Magic, "I'm a Dumbledore man through and through."

A Quarreling Couple and
an Alchemical Wedding

The American publisher's decision to change the title from *Philosopher's Stone* to *Sorcerer's Stone* obscures the alchemical title. Which is a shame because if the man in the street knows anything about alchemy, it is that alchemists pursued the Philosopher's Stone to turn lead into gold. The characters, too, point right at alchemy. Albus Dumbledore, we learn on the first train ride to Hogwarts when Harry reads his Chocolate Frog Card, is an alchemist of some renown. This relationship, it turns out, is the key to unraveling the mystery of what is hidden at Hogwarts in Harry's first year.

Those alchemical pointers are right on the surface. But there are important alchemical red flags just beneath the surface of the story, most notably—characters representing alchemical mercury and sulfur, and the alchemical wedding.

The alchemical transformation of metals is a series of purifications of a base metal from lead into gold that is accomplished by dissolving and recongealing the metal via the action of two principal reagents. These reagents reflect the masculine and feminine polarity of existence; "alchemical sulfur" represents the masculine, impulsive, red pole, and "quicksilver" or "alchemical mercury," the feminine and cool complementary antagonist. Together and separately these reagents and catalysts advance the work of purifying a base metal into "corporeal light" or gold.

Alchemical literature often features one or more pairs of characters with these qualities who bicker (in alchemical texts, the reagents are actually called the "quarreling couple"). The bickering alchemical pair in *Harry Potter* is Ron and Hermione. "Hermione" is the feminine form of "Hermes," who besides being the Greek messenger god (Mercury), was also the name of the great alchemist Hermes Trismegistos in whose name countless alchemical works were written through the centuries. Her initials (Hg) and her parents being dentists (who use mercury in their work) point to mercury, feminine intelligence, the part Hermione plays in Harry's alchemical transformation.

Ron, the redheaded, passionate boy, is a cipher for alchemical sulfur. Together with Hermione, and in their disagreements and separation, he acts to transform Harry from lead to gold in each book, as discussed above. For readers who wondered whether Hermione was meant for Ron or Harry in the end, this point suggests the eventual love match of Ron and Hermione.

"Medieval alchemists adopted from the Arabs the theory that all metals were a synthesis of mercury and sulfur, whose union might achieve various degrees of harmony. A perfectly harmonious marriage of the mother and father of metals might produce gold."[9] When Ron and Hermione stop quarreling and hook up, as we saw first in *Half-Blood Prince* and finally in the Battle of Hogwarts, Harry's "perfection" is near.

The alchemical wedding doesn't have to be of this pair, certainly, but we need to see a marriage of contraries that is somehow sacramental. It should also end in death and the appearance of a child—the philosophical orphan.

The *rubedo* as the final stage of the Great Work features the wedding of the Red King and White Woman, their copulation and death, and the birth of the orphan. The "chemical wedding" is an image central to alchemy, from Shakespeare's *Romeo and Juliet* (1595) to Lindsay Clarke's *The Chymical Wedding* (1997). Bill and Fleur's wedding is this marriage of choleric Weasley and phlegmatic Gaul, the Red King and White Woman of the formula we see onstage in *Deathly Hallows*. The marriage and death of Tonks and Lupin are what give us Teddy Lupin, philosophical orphan.

The chemical marriage of the imbalanced "quarreling couple" of masculine sulfur and feminine quicksilver results in opposing qualities being reconciled and resolved; they must "die" and be "reborn" before recombining in a perfected golden unity. The end of alchemy is the creation of the Philosopher's Stone, which is the transcendence of this imbalance, impurity, and polarity. It is also, you recall, about the creation of the transcendent alchemist, the saintly God/man often represented by a hermaphrodite or "s/he," a person who is *both* male and female. Here polarity is not resolved as much as it is transcended and embodied in a harmonious unity, an incarnation of love and peace.

We'll talk again at chapter's end about whether Harry has transcended his internal Gryffindor/Slytherin divide and become the Hogwarts hermaphrodite and Philosopher's Stone. Don't bet against it.

Doppelgängers

In chapter four we discussed this staple of nineteenth-century gothic and romantic fiction, about a creature or pair of creatures that have complementary figures or shadows, and whose shadows reveal aspects of their character otherwise invisible. Think of Stevenson's *Jekyll & Hyde*, Stoker's Count Dracula, Shelley's Dr. Frankenstein and his monster. Rowling points to these shadows in her principal characters in a variety of ways: as Animagi, half-breeds, Mudbloods, threshold characters living in two worlds (Squibs and rebels and double agents), twins, multicross magical creatures, and, most important, Harry and Voldemort, sharing blood and soul pieces.

Many characters in Potterworld—itself divided between magical and Muggle domains—have twins or antagonistic complements, and many others live a double existence between worlds. This pairing is a marker of literary alchemy and points to the anagogical meaning of such work.

Transformation by Sacrifice:
Death to Ego and Persona

The alchemical work is about changing the soul from lead to gold—from spiritual atrophy and failing to dynamic virtue—in order to create a person whose character is the conjunction of all contraries. Becoming an embodiment of opposites, the alchemist gains the image and likeness of God. In literary alchemy, therefore, we should look for a hero (or lovers) who dies to ego concerns, sacrificially and out of love for others, a hero who becomes semi-divine in this sacrifice. In *Harry Potter*, we see just that in the title character's transformations and near deaths in each and every book—Harry's "people saving thing."

This pattern of loving sacrifice and Harry's acceptance of even the *pursuit* of death holds from *Philosopher's Stone* to *Deathly Hallows*. Before we look at *Deathly Hallows* as the alchemical *rubedo* of the series and at Harry's walk into the forest in this hermetic light, here are two notable alchemical texts you've probably read to illustrate the five qualities I've highlighted with Harry.

Romeo and Juliet and *A Tale of Two Cities*:
The Peace of Verona, Paris, and London

As you'd expect in an alchemical writer, Ms. Rowling knows her Shakespeare, and it was Shakespeare who unleashed a flood of alchemical references into English literature. A quick look at *Romeo and Juliet*, the Shakespeare play most familiar to American readers and moviegoers, illustrates this point.

The play has five acts but the three colored stages of alchemy are hard to miss. You remember Romeo's melancholic beginnings, his black bile, and the strife and division in the streets of Verona. *Nigredo!* The white stage begins when the young lovers meet. The agonizing, violent division between Capulets and Montagues is joined when this couple is bound by the sacrament of marriage in Friar Lawrence's chapel. The story is essentially over when they're married in the church service and the marriage is consummated. But the accomplishments of the white stage that are hidden have to be revealed on a larger stage in the crucible of the red stage. Through the deaths of Romeo and Juliet in the Capulet tomb, greater life comes to Verona. Juliet's parents and Romeo's father promise to erect golden statues of the star-crossed lovers and the city is at peace at last: black depression and division, wedding white, blood red, and gold statues.

The quarreling couple is Mercutio (Mercury, right?) and Tybalt, the two reagents whose combat and death act as catalysts to the resolution of the drama. And it is love, the resolution of male and female contrary identities and individualities, that becomes the star-crossed sacrifice of the drama. Neither Romeo nor Juliet is either Capulet or Montague as they profess in the balcony scene but the union of these contraries. Check off "Resolution and Transformation in Sacrificial Death."

Is this sort of thing obvious to audiences at the plays? Hardly. But it is a large part of the uplifting spiritual punch that the play delivers. Identifying with this couple (as their parents do in the end), with their love and sacred union, we are made less partisan in spirit. We aren't turned into gold statues, figures of solid light, as Romeo and Juliet are, but we have experienced vicariously and alchemically their love and light.

I don't recall ever reading or hearing of a remark by Ms. Rowling about *Romeo and Juliet*. Dickens's *A Tale of Two Cities*, on the other hand, is a book that she mentions frequently.[10]

She told the Radio 4 literary programme "With Great Pleasure" that one Sunday [in Paris] she stayed in her room all day reading A Tale of Two Cities *by Charles Dickens. "When I emerged in the evening I walked straight into Fernando, who looked absolutely horrified. I had mascara down my face and he assumed I had just received news of a death, which I had—Sydney Carton's." The unhappy Carton had taken the place of Charles Darnay at the*

*guillotine because of his love for Darnay's wife, Lucie, and by his
ultimate sacrifice finds salvation. He says, "It is a far, far better
thing that I do, than I have ever done; it is a far, far better rest
that I go to, than I have ever known." Joanne considers this "the
most perfect last line of a book ever written" and one that invari-
ably makes her cry.[11]*

There is a connection here between Rowling, Shakespeare,
and Dickens, especially his *Tale*. Dickens was a Shakespeare
lover, and there was a London Shakespearean revival in the
early nineteenth century at a time when Dickens was in love
with the stage. He even produced, directed, and played a
major part in an amateur production of *The Merry Wives of
Windsor*.

In *A Tale of Two Cities*, one of his shortest, most theatrical works, Dickens attempts alchemical drama in the manner
of Shakespeare. *Tale* has all the hallmarks of *a Shakespearean presentation* of the "resolution of contraries." It has the five
qualities of literary alchemy I noted above, in spades.

Three Stages of Transformation: Dickens presents his *Tale*
in three books and each corresponds to a stage in the work.
The first book, "Recalled to Life," is about the recovery of
a man, Dr. Alexandre Manette, who was "buried alive" in
the Bastille and about the darkness in both England and
France of the time. The second is about the doppelgänger
of Darnay and Carton and how each loves Lucie Manette,

the doctor's doting daughter, who is almost always dressed in white and whose hair gives the second book its title: "The Golden Thread." *Tale's* third book is the crucible of revolutionary Paris, and contains Carton's spectacular and sublime sacrifice to save the wedded Charles and Lucie. It's a play in three acts about the resolution of contraries, a play featuring a wedding in the second act and a sacrificial death that "saves" a city in some fashion in the third. Dickens is writing according to strict alchemical formula.

Dominant Contraries: There are three lines from Dickens that most everyone knows, and two of them are the first and last lines of *A Tale of Two Cities* (*Christmas Carol*'s "God bless us, every one!" is the other). The famous opening announces that the book is about contraries and contrasts, in case the title slipped by you: "It was the best of times, it was the worst of times . . ." As the title tells us, the novel is about London and Paris in conflict, both on the grand political scale and on the domestic scale of the principal characters.

Doppelgängers and an Alchemical Wedding

In addition to creating double-natured individuals, Dickens pairs up characters to highlight qualities of each as foils to one another. Sydney Carton and Charles Darnay are good likenesses of one another but inversions in spirit: Darnay the French aristocrat who has abandoned his caste rather than accept injustice, and Carton the brilliant English lawyer whose drinking and sloth prevent his rise in station. Miss Lucie Manette and Madame Defarge are contrasted as French women of light and darkness to illustrate the possible responses to barbarous times.

The marriage of Lucie and Charles is the alchemical wedding, but the more important and substantial pledging of troth and sacrifice is made by Carton to Lucie:

> *"It is useless to say it, I know, but it rises out of my soul. For you, and for any dear to you, I would do anything."* (A Tale of Two Cities, *book two, chapter thirteen*)

Carton may not be Lucie's husband, but his confessing his love to her and his willingness to die, not only for her, but to save a life she loves, is his transcendence of self and ego. He is a new man because of love.

Resurrection Figures

Throw a rock at a lineup of the characters in *A Tale of Two Cities* and odds are pretty good you're going to hit a character who could be said to have died and risen from the dead. The first book is titled "Recalled to Life" because Dr. Alexandre Manette is rescued from his living death in the Bastille. Charles Darnay is rescued from almost certain death, too, by a bizarre legal stratagem of Carton's that discredits a lying witness.

Jarvis Lorry describes the effect of his association with the Manettes as being like a Lazarus raised from his tomb. Jerry Cruncher is a grave robber, the meaning of which Dickens is sure to drill home by calling him a "Resurrection Man." Miss Pross, believe it or not, achieves something like an apotheosis in her sacrificial hand-to-hand combat with Madame Defarge.

But it is Carton that both rises from the death of his dissipation and drunkenness in anticipation of a greater reward and life that we remember. Having purchased the vapours he needs to sedate Darnay to change places with him, Carton walks the streets of Paris and recalls his hope of resurrection in Christ, his illumination at dawn.

The Alchemy of *Deathly Hallows*: The *Rubedo* and Climax of Harry's Perfection

Dickens closes *A Tale of Two Cities* with the prophetic vision Carton experiences at the guillotine. It includes perhaps the most famous single exit line in all literature: "It is a far, far better thing that I do, than I have ever done; it is a far, far better rest that I go to than I have ever known." The end of the *Potter* epic reflects this—the ending Ms. Rowling says is the best in all literature.

Like the Darnays, Ginny and Harry name one of their

sons for the two men who sacrificed themselves literally and figuratively to save and serve Harry, as Sidney Carton did Charles Darnay. Albus Severus Potter's bipolar name, serpentine initials, and concerned questions to his father at King's Cross station in the *Deathly Hallows* epilogue suggest that he, too, is a Gryffindor/Slytherin union. Albus Severus reflects the greater interior victory of Harry, Severus, and Albus in the last book of the series.

How does the alchemy in *Deathly Hallows* bring us to Harry's final "All was well?" *Deathly Hallows*, as the last, is the red book or *rubedo* of the series. As in *Romeo and Juliet* and *A Tale of Two Cities*, a wedding has to be revealed, contraries have to be resolved, and a death to self must lead to greater life. We should expect to see a Philosopher's Stone and a philosophical orphan, as well. The *rubedo* of *Deathly Hallows* is the crisis of the whole series— and it is everything alchemical we could have hoped for.

We start with Bill and Fleur's alchemical wedding, in which France and England again are married, here in the *sitzkrieg* before the shooting war with Voldemort's Nazis begins. The first seven chapters of *Deathly Hallows* lead up to this union of opposites, of choler and phlegm. As you'd expect, the wedding itself is a meeting of contraries, of solar and lunar. That's why, in addition to the Gallic/Briton jokes, we have the lunar Lovegoods show up in sunlight-bright yellow. Luna, the moon dressed as the sun, explains that it's good luck to wear gold at a wedding. This isn't just loony Luna; everything at the wedding is golden: the floor, the poles, the band jackets, the bridesmaids' dresses, even Tonks's hair.

We have a long way to go, though, before the Slytherin and Gryffindor opposites are united in Harry's son. The wedding breaks up when Kingsley's lynx Patronus arrives with the message that Rufus Scrimgeour is dead and the Death Eater blitzkrieg has begun. With this wedding and the death of the first character whose name means red, the real action of the alchemical work in *Deathly Hallows* begins.

The rest of the book can be interpreted in black, white, and red stages. The *nigredo* stage stretches painfully from chapter nine, "A Place to Hide," to chapter eighteen, "The Life and Lies of Albus Dumbledore." Harry's purification and illumination begin in chapter nineteen, "The Silver Doe," and end with the trio's return to Hogsmead in chapter twenty-eight, "The Missing Mirror." The crisis of the book, and of the series, is in Harry's return to Hogwarts, the destruction of the remaining Horcruxes, and victory over Lord Voldemort, as told in the last eight chapters of *Deathly Hallows*.

The ten *nigredo* chapters are as dark and gothic as any reader could want. We get a trip to the House of Black, we visit the Orwellian "Magic Is Might" black statue in the new Ministry (accessible only by flush toilet . . .), and we go camping, where, for some reason, it's always night, or overcast, or the three friends can't get along. Ron finally leaves, in a painful dissolution. Ask anyone what the longest part of *Deathly Hallows* is. The answer is always "the camping trip." It lasts eight chapters (fourteen through twenty-one) but three are agony, the three after Ron departs.

The chapters about Harry's trip with Hermione to Godric's Hollow are the climax of the *nigredo* and end with Harry's crisis of faith. We left Harry at the end of *Half-Blood Prince* proclaiming that he was "a Dumbledore man." In *Deathly Hallows*, he has his private agonizing doubts. He reads one article by Rita Skeeter and his faith is shaken. He talks to Aunt Muriel and Dogbreath at the wedding, and his faith takes another blow. And now he is struggling to believe in Dumbledore at all.

At the end of the *nigredo*, when Harry reads *The Life and Lies of Albus Dumbledore*, he denies Dumbledore, denies that he loves Albus, denies that Dumbledore loved him, etc. Harry's holly-and-phoenix wand has been broken in battle with Nagini and he is left with a broken wand, a broken piece of mirror, and shattered faith. He keeps these fragments, though, in a bag around his neck and close to his heart. He denies Dumbledore, denies his mission, and, in something like despair, he keeps these remnants or relics of the person who once was close to his heart.

And just when despair is closing in, the *nigredo* ends with the brilliance reflecting off the Silver Doe in the snow-covered Forest of Dean. This chapter, a meeting of Christian, alchemical, and Arthurian images in one spot, is probably the height of Ms. Rowling's achievement as a writer. Ron the Baptist saving Harry, Ron's exorcism in destroying the Horcrux, Harry's death to self and discovery of remorse, repentance, faith, and love in Dobby's grave on Easter morning, and the pale dragon in Gringott's are all images of purification, with water on hand or nearby.

The white stone on the red earth of Dobby's grave and the dragon's "milkily" pink eyes are chromatic signs of the story's movement from white to red. The *rubedo* of *Deathly Hallows* begins, I think, when Harry refuses to listen to Aberforth's complaints and criticism of his brother, Albus. When Harry shows his faith and his choice to believe, Neville appears to take him into the castle, and the battle for Hogwarts begins. You could say the red stage really begins when Rubeus, the half-giant whose name means "red," flies through the window of Hogwarts Castle.

In this battle, which includes Harry's sacrifice in the Forbidden Forest and his ultimate victory over Voldemort, the contraries are resolved and all the houses sit down at one table. The battle also causes the creation of the "philosophical orphan" when Nymphadora and Remus Lupin are killed. And we get a Philosopher's Stone, too; Hermione and Ron's daughter, we learn in the epilogue, is named "Rose," which is another name for the Stone.

Three quick alchemical points: The complete transformation in the last novel of the series shows how the world has been changed by Harry's internal victory and destruction of the scar Horcrux. Lord Voldemort tortures and murders the Hogwarts Muggle Studies teacher in the first chapter of the book. Her name is Charity Burbage and her corpse is dinner for Nagini. Charity or "love" is destroyed by "death." Harry's death to self in Dobby's burial, revealed in his willing self-sacrifice before Voldemort, breaks death's power. Lily and Harry's sacrificial and selfless love sustains life and has its victory over death.

We see a complete transformation in Harry, too. He is a Dumbledore man by confession as the story begins, but his disbelief and lack of trust come to the fore after his fight with Nagini in Godric's Hollow. After choosing to believe, however, when digging Dobby's grave he becomes almost Christlike in dying and rising from the dead to vanquish death. Even the near-omnipotent Dumbledore begs Harry's forgiveness and tells him he has known for a long time that Harry was "the better man." Harry was made the better man by achieving the Gryffindor/Slytherin union within himself, as demonstrated by his naming his son Albus Severus Potter. He becomes the conjunction of contraries.

When he fights Lord Voldemort in the Great Hall, Harry has achieved an understanding and perspective that is essentially all-knowing. Voldemort, in contrast, has the limited ego view that we had at the end of every previous book. Remember, to a classicist and postmodern like Rowling, "knowing" is in large part a measure of "being." In resolving the core polarity of the Wizarding world, Harry both goes to and becomes the circle and cross's point of origin and metaphysical principle. Becoming relatively omniscient, Harry is the de facto Philosopher's Stone and, as such, virtually omnipotent.

Conclusion: Why the Alchemy Matters

Literary alchemy isn't something that we were all born knowing. Seeing how it works requires a certain receptivity as well as some serious "slow mining." It rewards the effort, however, with answers to important questions beyond the meaning of Hermione's name and why her parents are dentists.

The popularity of these books cannot be explained, I think, with "what great stories" and how much we love the characters, at least not without an in-depth look at what we mean by "great stories." It's not the eloquence of the prose or even the moral viewpoint of the stories, beyond reproach though that may be—how brave and bold is it to be against prejudice and to advocate freedom versus slavery? We read and reread Harry's adventures because of our profound engagement with these stories and the resonance we feel at our core with their meaning. That level of engagement is a function of artistry, and the alchemy setting the "parameters of magic" and "internal logic" of the series is a key part of Rowling's artistry.

More than circles and journeys, literary alchemy imbedded in the fabric of the story gives us both a more profound way of seeing reality and, more important, an experience of that view and reality via our identification with Harry. We join Harry, the hero, as he is transformed by the quarreling couple and the distillation, purification, and crucible experiences he has, and we are transformed by the alchemy of story just as the alchemist was by his purifying metallurgy and Shakespeare's audiences were by cathartic drama.

There is one more bit of anagogical artistry that touches on Harry as a symbol of transformational, even sacramental vision. We'll need to look at the marble bag full of disembodied eyeballs in *Deathly Hallows* to understand this vision and to explain Dumbledore's cryptic comments at King's Cross about reality.

CHAPTER TEN

The Secret of the Mirror
and the Seeing Eye

Ms. Rowling's Debt to the Subversive
Fantasy Writers of the English Tradition

Outside of Jane Austen, the most frequently mentioned author in Ms. Rowling's many interviews is Elizabeth Goudge, and the most frequently mentioned book is that author's *The Little White Horse. Horse* was the Carnegie Medal winner for children's fiction in 1946, but odds are good that you have never heard of this book and, if you have, that you never would have except for Ms. Rowling's enthusiastic and repeated endorsements of it. Because of her push, the book has seen a great revival and will be coming soon to a theater near you as a major motion picture.

In interview after interview, Ms. Rowling praises *The*

Little White Horse. She has repeatedly said that it was her favorite book as a child.[1] She has said that the book overall is "very well-constructed and clever" and, most important for our purposes, that "perhaps more than any other book, it has a direct influence on the *Harry Potter* books."[2] Thus, we are obliged to look at *The Little White Horse* very closely to discover the cleverness of its construction and the ways in which it corresponds with the *Potter* story.

The story, in brief, is this: Maria Merryweather, a child orphan accompanied by her tutor, Miss Heliotrope, and little dog, Wiggins, travels from familiar London in 1842 to magical Silverydew valley by passing through a secret hillside tunnel separating the outer and inner worlds. She is welcomed to the palatial Moonacre Manor by her much older cousin, Sir Benjamin. He is a Sun Merryweather. You see, some Merryweathers were born at midday and were thus known as Sun Merryweathers. Those born at midnight were the Moon Merryweathers.

Though Sir Benjamin is the incarnation of charity and generosity, Moonacre Manor and the valley, as you might expect in the gothic landscape of the story, are burdened by unresolved antagonisms born in medieval times. There is discord between the Sun and Moon Merryweathers and their conflict with Monsieur Cocq de Noir of the Pine Woods and his band of thieves. The Old Parson tells Maria the legend of Sir Wrolf, Black William, and the Moon Princess that explains the conflict.

According to the tale, Sir Wrolf was given the village of Silverydew and the estate on which Moonacre Manor was built, but was not satisfied with anything less than the whole valley. In an attempt to win more land, Sir Wrolf offered to buy the Pine Woods Forest and castle from Black William, whose family had owned the forest since William the Conqueror had awarded the land to their Norman clan. When his offer was rebuffed, Sir Wrolf turned the "lovely valley" into something like a "battlefield, with the turf of the green meadows stained red with blood, the harvest fields neglected, and gardens choked with weeds" as the servants of Wrolf and William fought whenever they met.

Sir Wrolf finally decided to win the Pine Woods by marrying Sir William's daughter, who, as fair as her father was dark, had been dubbed the "Moon Princess." At their wedding, she gave him a large tawny dog and brought a necklace of "moony pearls" as her dowry. He gave her a fairy horse, a unicorn that had been caught in the thorn tree on Paradise Hill.

There was only love and joy in Silverydew until Black William took another wife and she bore him a male heir. The Moon Princess would not inherit the Pine Woods or castle! Sir Wrolf was enraged. In his anger, he revealed that his motivation in courting his bride had been greed and pride, not love. Sir William and his wife and heir disappeared. Equally proud and upset at her husband's greed and suspecting him of murdering her father, the princess, after giving birth to Sir Wrolf's heir, left Moonacre Manor on her little white horse. Black William's descendants eventually returned to living in the forest.

In each generation a Moon Princess returns to Moonacre to unite the two sides of the family; her Moon Merryweathers with the Sun Merryweathers. And in each generation she succeeds, but only temporarily. She then goes away like the original Moon Princess.

Maria is this generation's Moon Princess, and the Old Parson believes she can unite the opposites and resolve the contraries of centuries. Maria takes up her part as Moon Princess with gusto. On her first day at the manor she had discovered a painting over the fireplace mantel that "showed a little pure-white horse and a brave-looking tawny animal rather like Wrolf [Sir Benjamin's lion in residence] cantering along a forest glade together." She asks Sir Benjamin the meaning of the words carved in the mantel, "The brave soul and the pure spirit shall with a merry and a loving heart inherit the kingdom together." He tells her it is the family motto and "perhaps, a device for linking together those four qualities that go to making up perfection—courage, purity, love, and joy."

Maria, consequently, sets about uniting the divided lion and unicorn by linking these four qualities and undoing the sins of Sir Wrolf. She agrees to marry Robin, the poor boy who is the son of Loveday Minette, the Moon Princess of the previous generation who had quarreled with Sir Benjamin before her marriage to him.

The biggest challenge of the book, of course, is reconciling the descendants of Black William, the evil poachers and thieves in the Pine Woods led by the evil Monsieur Cocq de Noir, to the Merryweathers. Maria makes two trips into the forest to confront Monsieur Cocq de Noir and convince him to give up his evil ways. The first ends disastrously with the castle lord trying to capture Maria and Robin and throw them in his dungeon. Only the return of the first Moon Princess's pearls, which he believes are his by right and proof that Sir Wrolf did not kill Black William ages ago, will make him change his evil ways. Maria finds the string of pearls hidden in the Moonacre Manor well and discovers Black William's secret cave and ship that prove that Wrolf did not murder William. Eventually everyone agrees to reconcile.

All of the separated and quarreling couples are then united. Loveday Minette and Sir Benjamin, Miss Heliotrope and the Old Parson, Maria and Robin, all pictures of the lion and the unicorn, all marry and live happily ever after. Now that we have a basic understanding of *The Little White Horse*, we can see the many ways in which it corresponds with the *Harry Potter* tales.

Echoed Story Points in *The Little White Horse* and *Harry Potter*

The shades of *The Little White Horse* in *Harry Potter* range from the trivial hat-tip in items like living chess pieces to the scaffolding of the stories and the symbolism of the principal character in each. Ms. Rowling wasn't kidding or even being especially generous when she said *The Little White Horse* has a "direct influence on the *Harry Potter* books."

Obvious echoes include the evil lurking in the Pine Woods behind Moonacre Manor that Sir Benjamin tells Maria she is not allowed to enter and the Forbidden Forest bordering Hogwarts. The evil men in *Horse*'s forest are referred to as "they" by the good guys for most of the story just as He-Who-Must-Not-Be-Named remained a nameless taboo through the *Potter* epic. More important, the great chasm and conflict in the world is between the descendants of Black William and Sir Wrolf Merryweather in *Horse,* which sees its equivalent in the Wizarding world divide between the Houses of Godric Gryffindor and Salazar Slytherin, two of Hogwarts's founders.

To bridge this divide, both worlds require alchemical magic. Moonacre Manor has its quarreling couple of Sun and Moon Merryweathers (Sir Benjamin and later Robin as the sun, Loveday Minette and then Maria as the moon), the brave soul and pure spirit unable to join themselves into a union that will help them "inherit the kingdom together." Every page of *Horse*, it seems, includes at least one and oftentimes more than one mention of this essential polarity of gold and silver, sun and moon, flushed and pale, or hot and dry versus cold and moist.

Harry's world is similarly represented with Ron and Hermione as a sulfuric and mercurial quarreling couple in a world with a central division and antagonism. Both the Wizarding world and Silverydew valley require a savior from the "outer world," and Maria Merryweather and Harry Potter could be fraternal twins in this respect. Both are orphans who become aware at a young age that they belong in a world hidden within the mundane existence in which they have grown up. Maria travels by carriage through the tunnel to Silverydew valley and Moonacre Manor; Harry passes through the barrier at King's Cross Station for the Hogwarts Express train to Hogwarts castle and Hogsmeade. Both are secret passages to a more wonderful, magical place where the orphan-saviors have a great destiny.

Maria soon learns that the people of the village think she is the prophesied deliverer, the Moon Princess of her generation: "Be you the one, my dear?" they whisper to her after her first trip to the Silverydew church (*Horse*, chapter three, part two). Harry, "The Boy Who Lived," of course, is known almost universally as the "Chosen One." And this is only the beginning of their list of likenesses:

* Maria is a natural horseback rider, her birthright it seems as a Merryweather. Harry is a born Seeker, broom flyer, and Quidditch player, supposedly gifts he has inherited from his father, James.

* Both Maria at Moonacre and the students at Hogwarts are served by invisible servants who are attentive to their every need. Maria's helpers are eventually revealed to be Loveday Minette and Marmaduke Scarlet and the Hogwarts's keepers and cooks turn out to be the house-elves.

* Both worlds have lions that take care of the hero or heroine. At Hogwarts Harry lives in Gryffindor House, whose symbol is a red lion. Maria, by looking into the eyes of Wrolf, the tawny manor lion, becomes his "possession" and the subject of his special protection. The red lion in alchemical symbolism is a token of the "elixir of life" and is used in heraldic devices as a symbol of Christ, whose blood means eternal life to believers. Wrolf the lion appears at Moonacre Manor on Christmas morning once each generation before the Moon Princess arrives at the manor.

* Each book has its unicorn that takes on the allegorical role of Christ. Harry discovers a slain unicorn in the Forbidden Forest and a serpentine creature drinking its

blood for physical salvation. Maria's unicorn saves her life from the evil men of the forest (much as the Stag Patronus saves Harry in *Prisoner of Azkaban*) and again by illuminating the dark heart of Cocq de Noir on her walk with him into the forest.

* Maria meets Loveday Minette, the previous generation's Moon Princess, at the Old Parson's house and becomes her close friend. Harry's friend Luna Lovegood resembles Loveday in appearance and in both the sound and meaning of her name ("Luna" means "moon" in Latin).

* Both books have nonspeaking magical animals besides a red lion, most especially a cat of notable intelligence. Sirius calls Crookshanks "the most intelligent of his kind I ever met" (*Prisoner of Azkaban*, chapter nineteen), and Maria admires the brilliant cat Zachariah as "no ordinary cat," an estimation qualifying as risible understatement (*Horse*, chapter ten, part two).

* Both Maria and Harry live in worlds where the generations echo previous generations in characters and in their relationships. Harry's father had two close friends and a hanger-on with a Slytherin rival; Harry does, too. Maria and Robin are generational reflections of Sir Benjamin and Loveday and all the Sun and Moon

Merryweathers back to Sir Wrolf and the Moon Princess, all in conflict with Black William's descendants in the Dark Forest.

* Harry is tutored by Albus Dumbledore, the greatest wizard of his age, who recognizes and fosters Harry's ability to defeat Lord Voldemort. Maria is given private instruction about her destiny by the Old Parson, the "true king of this small kingdom" as Sir Benjamin puts it. The Old Parson is the spiritual director of all of Silverydew and he reveals to Maria the prophesied role she is to play in uniting the Merryweathers and ending the curse of Sir Wrolf.

* On her first trip into the forest, Maria finds the answer to the mystery of what happened to Black William by following a rabbit, in Alice fashion, "down a rabbit hole" at the base of a pine tree into a cavern wonderland (*Horse*, chapter ten, part four). Harry's first adventure in *Sorcerer's Stone* ends with him traveling "through the trapdoor" "miles under the school" and discovering the answers to that year's mysteries (*Sorcerer's Stone*, chapter sixteen).

* Harry's penultimate, solo, and sacrificial confrontation with Voldemort comes in the Forbidden Forest in a chapter titled, "The Forest Again." Maria makes her second trip into the forest by herself and bets her life and freedom to master Cocq de Noir.

If I had to choose the main similarity between Harry and Maria, though, it would be that they are both the spirit aspect in the story triptych of mind, body, and spirit. I've already discussed Harry as the Alyosha/Kirk/Frodo of his adventures and the spiritual leader of Hermione, who is the mind, and of Ron, who is the body or the passions (see chapters seven and eight). Maria plays a similar role in *Horse*.

Maria, as described in the Merryweather family motto and emblem, is "pure spirit," the elusive unicorn; Sir Benjamin Merryweather is the lion, a "brave soul," subject to Maria's direction in almost everything; and Monsieur Cocq de Noir is the darkness of the unconscious passions. She masters her Merryweather anger, pride, and curiosity, putting off her Voldemort Horcrux, if you will, transcending her persona and ego to be the savior of her small Silverydew world.

Goudge reflects Maria's unique spiritual capacity in her eyes and the ability she has to see things others cannot. Most notably, of course, her ability to see the little white horse, the unicorn of the Moon Maiden. But she also connects with every principal character and sees their fundamental or potential goodness by looking in their eyes; and they, in turn, recognize who she is by looking into her eyes. Ms. Rowling echoes this linking of eyes and spiritual vision throughout her books.

Severus Snape and Lily's Green Eyes

The overwhelming symbolism of *Deathly Hallows* is not solar and lunar, silver and gold allusions as it is in *Little White Horse* but one of sight and, weirdly, eyeballs. There is Mad-Eye Moody's disembodied eye that Harry rescues and buries, the "triangular eye" of the Hallows symbol, and the demonic eyes of Tom Riddle, Jr., in the locket Horcrux. There are two other images in *Deathly Hallows* that I want to focus on here because of their literary relevance and their transcendental significance.

The first of these *Deathly Hallows* eye symbols is the green eyes of Harry's mother, Lily (and Harry himself), and their importance to Severus Snape, especially at his death. As mentioned earlier, Frances Hodgson Burnett's books *A Little Princess* and *The Secret Garden* feature characters whose eyes are green, "just like their mother's," and whose vision or way of seeing things is magical, even what saves them. But these green eyes are not Burnett's invention. The emphasis on green eyes may well be a reference to Dante's *Divine Comedy*.

Green eyes, belonging here to Dante's love, Beatrice, appear at perhaps the most critical moment of Dante's journey when he has come to the gates of Paradise after being guided through Hell and Purgatory by Virgil. The nymphs there draw him through the River Lethe to wash away his memories and he is granted a vision through the green eyes of his beloved Beatrice, who appears in a chariot drawn by a giant red and gold Griffin (the source of Hogwarts's "golden Griffin," or in French "Griffin d'or").

The Griffin is half eagle (king of heaven) and half lion (king of earth) and is, consequently, a traditional symbol of Christ, the King of Heaven and Earth. Dante has a vision of Christ in Beatrice's eyes, a vision he experiences as sacramental, after which he enters Paradise. He travels from sphere to sphere there by looking each time again into his beloved's green eyes for transcendence.

As a result of his devotion to Lily, Snape's experience with Harry's eyes—eyes inherited from his mother—carries the same level of spiritual importance. Severus Snape, you recall, had a long-standing love for Lily Evans (later Potter). Once friends, Severus's fascination with the Dark Arts and his companionship with potential Death Eaters led to a break in their relationship. He continued to love her, and, perversely, even hoped that he could win her affections after the Dark Lord killed James Potter and Lily's son, Harry. But Snape pledged his life to Dumbledore to protect her from Voldemort and later makes a pledge to protect Harry once Dumbledore tells him that the boy has his mother's eyes (*Deathly Hallows*, chapter thirty-three). The shape and color of Harry's eyes trigger remorse or grief in Severus, "what Dumbledore would call love," the agony that makes him a great Occlumens and double agent, and the love that moves him to sacrifice his public life to protect Lily's son, the prophesied vanquisher of Lord Voldemort. We see what value these eyes have to Snape in the many times he locks eyes with Harry and most especially in his final request at his death that Harry "Look . . . at . . . me . . . ." (*Deathly Hallows*, chapter thirty-two).

Cleansed of his memories, having sacrificed his all in love and fidelity, Snape's final vision is of Lily's green eyes; and we are led to believe that through those eyes, like Dante, he transcends his failings and enters Paradise.[3]

Dumbledore's Eye in the Mirror: The Seeing Eye and I

Harry's green eyes and their similarity to his mother's are mentioned in each book, often more than once, as setups for this giant payoff in the Shrieking Shack at Snape's demise. As important as Harry's green eyes is the single eye of Dumbledore that Harry sees twice in *Deathly Hallows* in the shard of the mirror given him by his godfather. This eye acts as both a story frame and a key to what Rowling says is the meaning of the entire series of books.[4]

The first time Harry sees Dumbledore in the mirror is after he reads the interview with Rita Skeeter in the *Daily Prophet* featuring nasty bits of misinformation about Dumbledore and Harry. He is outraged and sees "a flash of brightest blue" on the mirror shard he is holding. The second time he sees the "brightest blue" of Dumbledore's gaze, he is trying to escape the cellar of Malfoy Manor and save Hermione from Bellatrix's torture. He asks Dumbledore for help and Dobby appears to help them escape. Though Dobby is killed in the process, this vision leads to Harry's renewed faith in Dumbledore. In both instances, Harry's glimpse of the eye is connected with his faith or loyalty to Dumbledore. But this "eye" in the mirror holds even greater meaning in terms of Harry's identity and his victory over the Dark Lord.

Of Course It's All in Your Head, Harry: *Harry Potter* and *Logos*

As discussed in chapter eight, Christians believe that reality is the creation of God's Word or *Logos*. Jesus of Nazareth was the historical incarnation of this *Logos* as perfect humanity. Christians believe it is through him and the sacraments of his Church that human beings consciously commune with the fabric and substance of reality, the *Logos*.

The prologue of the gospel according to John describes this *Logos* this way:

> *In the beginning was the Word, and the Word was with God, and the Word was God.*
>
> *The same was in the beginning with God.*

All things were made by him; and without him was not any thing made that was made.

In him was life; and the life was the light of men.

And the light shineth in darkness; and the darkness comprehended it not . . .

That was the true Light, which lighteth every man that cometh into the world. (John 1:1–5, 9, KJV)

This last verse cuts right to the heart of Harry's story and our experience of it. Jesus explains to the Pharisees that as *Logos* and God, "I am the light of the world: he that followeth me shall not walk in darkness, but shall have the light of life." The *Logos* principle that creates all things is light, life, and, most important for this discussion, the "true Light which lighteth every man that cometh into the world." Every person has a *Logos* within them that is their light. Jesus calls this light our "eye" in the Sermon on the Mount verses immediately after the verse on Ariana Dumbledore's tombstone:

The light of the body is the eye: if therefore thine eye be single, thy whole body shall be full of light.

But if thine eye be evil, thy whole body shall be full of darkness. If therefore the light that is in thee be darkness, how great is that darkness! (Matthew 6:22–23, KJV)

When Harry Potter looks into his godfather's mirror, consequently, and sees an "eye" where his "I" (his own image) should be, we shouldn't be surprised. As a story symbol for the *Logos* quality in us all, Harry is the seeing eye. As we increasingly identify with Harry as the story continues, and as we are sucked into his perspective, we begin to read and experience the story through the luminous eye of the heart in each of us. Our spiritual faculty, in other words, is awakened, engaged, and to some degree illumined or cleansed by Harry's inner victory and cathartic defeat of the Dark Lord.

This *Logos,* which "lighteth every man that cometh into the world," is our mind and conscience as well as our spiritual faculty. The *Logos* recognizes itself in each created thing. In other words, it is both the knowing subject and the known object—our minds are the place where they meet. To know the fabric of reality and the substance of all existence, to commune with what is real beyond the surface, in the Christian view, then, means fostering the light, life, and love within us that is this *Logos*. Believe it or not, that is largely the message of Ms. Rowling's *Harry Potter* stories.

Think about Harry's conversation with Dumbledore at King's Cross, especially their final exchange (*Deathly Hallows,* chapter thirty-five). The author has admitted quite openly that this exchange is perhaps *the* critical part of the book for understanding her work:

Q: *There's this dialogue between Harry and Professor Dumbledore: "Is this real? Or has this been happening inside my head?"*

A: *And Dumbledore says: "Of course it is happening inside your head, but why on earth would that mean that it is not real?" That dialogue is the key; I've waited seventeen years to use those lines. Yes, that's right. All this time I've worked to be able to write those two phrases; writing Harry entering the forest and Harry having that dialog [sic].*[5]

According to Dumbledore, the entire conversation at King's Cross "happens inside [Harry's] head." He also insists via a rhetorical question that this experience has been "real." Ms. Rowling's putting her finger on this exchange as essential brings up the questions of how this is possible and what Dumbledore means by "real."

When Harry asks, "Is this real?" the word "real" means something we have understood from information we have acquired via our physical senses or pictured and abstracted out of that information. Harry asks the question "is this real?" because his experience at what he thinks of as King's Cross Station (but which looks nothing like it!) has been in several important ways *unreal*. From the cloudy vapor becoming his surroundings and items he wants to his having a lively chat with a radiant, certifiably solid, and brilliant dead man aren't the stuff of energy and matter quantities or even the magical curriculum at Hogwarts. The trick is, if it's not "real" the way both Muggles and Magical folk think things can be real, what else can it be? Given Harry's track record at Hogwarts in being stunned by how little he understood of what was really going on, it's little wonder he asks the equivalent of "Did this really happen or have I mistaken what's only happening in my thinking for reality *again*?"

Dumbledore's response reveals that he thinks Harry has created a false dichotomy. There is *another* option to account for his experience rather than just either scientific knowledge or delusional opinion, either objective or subjective thinking. Harry, like the rest of us, is a de facto materialist. If he cannot touch, see, smell, taste, or hear it, he thinks it is less real than something he can know by sense perception. Because abstraction, thinking, feeling, fancy, imaginings, and dreams—the things that "happen in our heads"—are immaterial by definition, they are not dependable ways of knowing the hard and therefore "real" facts.

Prejudices, limited views, unfounded speculation, and private animosity can distort our thinking, so, like Harry, we don't count "inside our head" experience as *real*. Harry asks Dumbledore the skeptic's question and gives Dumbledore the empiricist's only two options: namely, objective "real" knowledge and subjective "unreal" knowledge. Dumbledore's answer asserts there is another answer—a union or conjunction between "what is real" and "what is happening in our heads" beyond sense perception.

Ron Weasley asks Harry incredulously when he pulls Harry out of the pool in the Forest of Dean—and again when he is disappointed that Harry decides to forsake the Elder Wand—"Are—you—*mental*?" But if we understand that Dumbledore is telling Harry that what happens inside your head is, indeed, *real, then* yes, we must concur that Harry is *mental.* The unity of existence as *Logos* means we all—Muggles, wizards, all created things—are *mental.*

C. S. Lewis said this was one of the most important things he learned from his friend Owen Barfield, that "the whole universe was, in the last resort, mental; that our logic was participation in a cosmic *Logos.*"[6] Lewis discusses this idea most directly in his essay "The Seeing Eye," which argues that conscience is "continuous with" the unity of existence.[7] His story version of the *Logos* reality beneath the surface, the "inside that is bigger than the outside," is much more well known because it appears at the climax of the Narnia novel *The Last Battle.* There King Tirian has been driven into a stable by the wicked Calormenes. Once there, he is surprised to find himself in Paradise:

He looked round again and could hardly believe his eyes. There was the blue sky overhead, and grassy country spreading as far as he could see in every direction, and his new friends all round him laughing.

"It seems, then," said Tirian, smiling himself, "that the stable

*seen from within and the stable seen from without are two dif-
ferent places."*

*"Yes," said the Lord Digory, "Its inside is bigger than its
outside."*

*"Yes," said Queen Lucy. "In our world too, a stable once had
something inside it that was bigger than our whole world." It
was the first time she had spoken, and from the thrill in her voice,
Tirian now knew why. She was drinking everything in even
more deeply than the others.[8]*

The not especially opaque reference Queen Lucy makes
here is to the stable in Bethlehem in which Jesus the incarnate
Logos lived as a newborn. Lewis is explaining in his story that
the "inside greater than the outside" is the *Logos* within and
beneath everything existent and the substance of minds; the
universe as *Logos* is mental.

Hence Dumbledore's response to Harry at King's Cross.
"Of course this is happening inside your head, Harry, but
why on earth should that mean it is not real?" Harry's Kings
Cross is the *Logos* reality inside his head that is the substance
of the lesser reality outside his head. Harry, as a symbol of
Logos mind or our spiritual faculty, creates his robes and the
palace of King's Cross just by thinking of them and is able
to answer every one of Dumbledore's and his own questions
there because he is in *Logos*-land and relatively omniscient.

Ms. Rowling prepared her readers for this meaning both

in locating her Wizarding world within and behind Muggle reality, invisible for the most part, and the several times the "inside" of magical things is much "bigger than their outside." Think of the magic cars, the Knight Bus, the Sorting Hat (with a Sword-in-Hat!), the tent that is a cabin, Hermione's beaded bag holding more than a U-Haul truck, the veiled archway in the Department of Mysteries, and the Room of Requirement, which expands indefinitely as necessary. The Room of Hidden Things seems even larger than Hogwarts in the search for the Ravenclaw Diadem and consequent firestorm. That the palace of King's Cross is inside Harry's head *and* real is only confirmation of the hidden, greater reality we have been living in for seven books.

Ms. Rowling, in her commencement address at Harvard in June 2008, told the graduating class and their families (quoting Plutarch) that imagination is important because "what we achieve inwardly will change outward reality." In the anagogical level, this refers to our experience of our spirit's purification via our identification with Harry and love's victory over death. By choosing to suspend disbelief and change our inner reality by identifying with the light within us, we are changed inside and out.

The use of a mirror and eye to see something beyond reality—onto a spiritual level—and to know our higher selves or *Logos* within isn't something that begins with Ms. Rowling and *Deathly Hallows*. In *The Little White Horse* Maria twice sees her perfected image in a mirror, first in Loveday's burnished silver glass where she has a halo and her hair is "silvery gold," the color resolving all contraries (*Horse,* chapter seven, part four), and then in the well where she finds the pearls of the Moon Maiden (chapter ten, part five). When readers of fantasy literature read about Harry's magic mirror and its connection to something more than just reflecting appearance, they are most likely reminded of Lewis's *Narnia* and, most especially, of Tolkien's magisterial *Lord of the Rings.* For mirrors, light, and seeing eyes, Galadriel alone is a virtual warehouse of magical objects; Tolkien lovers reading about the Mirror of Erised that reveals the heart's desire, the Pensieve, and Sirius's mirror fragment showing Dumbledore's eye think of Galadriel's reflecting pond that shows what might be and contains the light of the Evening Star. That is just the beginning of the Lewis and Tolkien correspondences and the echoes within Ms. Rowling's *Harry Potter.* Her relationship to them, though, is a fitting place to close this discussion of her books' anagogical meanings and her place in the pantheon of great English writers.

Lewis and Tolkien vs. Rowling: Traditional and Subversive Symbolists

When reporters ask the author about novels influencing her work, the only books and authors they routinely ask about by name are Lewis and his *Chronicles of Narnia* and Tolkien's *Lord of the Rings*. It should be said that Ms. Rowling, however, embraces neither Tolkien nor Lewis as an influence. But because of Rowling's place in the canon of great and widely read fantasy series as well as pop culture, the ties with her fantasy predecessors are unavoidable.

Both Lewis and Tolkien were enthusiastic Christians whose faith permeates their work, both are best known for the seven-part series of edifying fantasy each wrote,[9] and both are beloved if not worshipped by their loyal readers. Ms. Rowling's series, as different from *Narnia* and *Lord of the Rings* as those series are from each other, also comes in seven parts, contains Christian parallels and symbolism that she has described as "obvious,"[10] and has a fan base at least as fervent and worshipful as any among Lewis and Tolkien idolaters.

If the similarities weren't enough of a connection, Ms. Rowling has included significant echoes and direct allusions to Narnia and Middle Earth. Harry's journeys are "portal-quest fantasies,"[11] like those of Tolkien's and Lewis's heroes. The books sometimes even seem stocked with Lewis's taste in food and Tolkien's Hall of Monsters and characters. This goes beyond Butterbur/Butterbeer and Wormtongue/Wormtail assonances. The mere presence of Ms. Rowling's dementors has the same effect on people as Tolkien's Ring Wraiths. The effect of the One Ring on the Ring

Bearer is much like that of the locket Horcrux on the trio in *Deathly Hallows*. Sauron cannot be killed, in fact, because so much of his power is invested in the One Ring, which is reflected in Voldemort's faux immortality achieved by investing parts of his soul into Horcrux objects. Not to mention that many readers visualized Tolkien's Gandalf the White when they first met Albus Dumbledore, whose name means "white."

And there are more connections: Old Man Willow and the Whomping Willow, the Mirror of Galadriel's reflection in both the Mirror of Erised and the Pensieve, and the great spiders Shelob and Aragog the Acromantula.[12] Tolkien scholar Dr. Amy H. Sturgis of Belmont University notes that the similarities between *The Lord of the Rings* were more than superficial plot points; they touched on the core meaning of each series of books—that Harry Potter is Tolkienesque fantasy, pure and simple.[13]

Ms. Rowling, though, over the years, despite the testimony of those who knew her in college and when she began writing *Harry Potter* that she was a serious reader of *Lord of the Rings*, has increasingly distanced herself from Tolkien. Each individual report of Ms. Rowling's thoughts on Tolkien and the progression of her memory about the importance of *Lord of the Rings* in understanding Harry only becomes louder and clearer with time; this author is not a Tolkien reader or fan and thinks it would be best to shelve the Shire as a place of great influence on her creative imagination. Dumbledore is no Gandalf shadow, etc. As Maureen Lamson has explained, given the obvious story echoes in *Potter* that strike any Tolkien reader, these denials are mind-boggling.[14]

The situation with Lewis is, if anything, even more bizarre. Ms. Rowling before the year 2000 confesses only unbridled admiration of Lewis and his *Chronicles of Narnia*. In 1997, she said she "reveled in Narnia" as a child.[15] He is a "genius" to whom she is flattered to be compared;[16] she cannot be in the same room with a *Chronicles* novel and not rush over and pick it up;[17] she loves the series, especially Eustace Scrubb.[18] *Voyage of the Dawn Treader* is her favorite *Chronicle*.[19]

But in 2005 she said that she never read the *Chronicles'* last book.[20] That same year, Lev Grossman, of *Time* magazine, reported:

> *There's something about Lewis's sentimentality about children that gets on [Rowling's] nerves. "There comes a point where Susan, who was the older girl, is lost to Narnia because she becomes interested in lipstick. She's become irreligious basically because she found sex," Rowling says. "I have a big problem with that."[21]*

Lewis readers scratch their heads over these comments. Beyond the contradiction with Ms. Rowling's previously stated admiration for Lewis, it would be difficult for her to take issue with this particular plot point because it is only mentioned in the end pages of *The Last Battle*, the series finale, a book she has said she has not read.

Why does she embrace the hermetic writing of Burnett and Nesbit and exalt in the "direct influence" of Goudge but balk at acknowledging the popular fantasies of Lewis and Tolkien that are obvious influences on her writing? For me, the way to come to some understanding of Ms. Rowling's simultaneous discomfort with and admiration for Lewis and Tolkien is in Colin Manlove's essay "Parent or Associate? George MacDonald and the Inklings."[22] Manlove distinguishes between two types of fantasy or symbolist writers: the subversive and the conservative. The subversive writer "aims to undermine his reader's assumptions and ways of seeing the world" either "for the sake of broadening our perspective on life" or "for the purpose of leading us toward God. His or her fantasies are full of paradoxes, riddles, and other reverses to point us to a new and transcendent level of discourse."

Speaking about MacDonald as a subversive, Manlove says his fantasies "are founded on words, scenes, and events that continually reverse one another, pushing a deeper knowledge beneath a shallower one; and characters frequently change shape, according to their inner natures, or the spiritual nature of the person looking at them." He could, of course, be describing Ms. Rowling's work here.

Conservative fantasy writers, in contrast, "seek to preserve something, to keep things as they are." Manlove says this is especially true of Lewis's Space Trilogy and *Narnia*. Rowling and the Inklings Lewis and Tolkien are all Christian symbolist writers, but as "subversive" and "conservative" authors, their works differ in tone and posture. Perhaps Rowling is hesitant to claim a connection to Tolkien and Lewis because she sees those books as being so fundamentally different from hers.

All of the writers that we've discussed share a worldview and an argument against the empiricism and materialist perspective of our times. A group including Swift, Shakespeare, Austen, Sayers, Shelley, Nesbit, Stoker, Goudge, Dante, Homer, Dickens, Burnett, Hughes, Lewis, and Tolkien couldn't be much different from one another. They wrote in different ages in genres and styles as diverse as epic poetry, alchemical drama, ribald satire, and detective fiction. Many of them are Christians, certainly, but, more to the point, all of them who write on an allegorical and anagogical level share an understanding of the human person as essentially spiritual, or, as Barfield, Lewis, and Ron Weasley would have it, "mental."

Whether on the subversive or conservative bank of this symbolist stream of writing, all these writers, like Austen and Shelley, are arguing against the scientists and secularists that would restrict reality to the world we know and measure. Each points to a greater, invisible reality, beneath, behind, and within the surfaces of things known by us via that same metaphysical reality that is in us, our *Logos* spirit.

Ms. Rowling writes in a tradition that works to Apparate readers out of the cavernous Shadowlands for an experience of the sunlight and the light that is in them and all things. Her special accomplishment is not her popularity so much as it is in the artistry of anagogical alchemy and allegory that created *Potter* mania. She has sewn a seamless garment of ten genres on four levels of meaning combining the best of hero's journey, mystery, schoolboy fiction, gothic settings, postmodern morality, and Christian fantasy her readers wrap themselves in as we would Harry's Invisibility Cloak. Transcending ourselves and having an imaginative experience of what is most real, we are transformed, the greater "inner reality" changing the outer. Her books serve as a gateway to the great books, certainly, but, more important, to the world outside our egotistic selves and Plato's Cave that these books all call us to. Pepperdine professor and *Repotting Harry Potter* author James Thomas says Ms. Rowling's books seem "too juvenile, too current, and too popular" to many academics for them to qualify as works of art that will be read and savored for generations. In addressing and offering some experience of truly human life, however, I have no doubt of her inclusion among the greats. Whatever the judgments of academics or literati, however, Harry has won his sure place in that divine part of the hearts of Rowling's readers that is the still point of King's Cross and the origin and center of all that is.

Notes

Introduction
1. Renton, Jennie. "Wild About Harry." *Candis Magazine*, November 2001. See http://www.accio-quote.org/articles/2001/1101-candis-renton.html.

2. Renton, Jennie. "The Story Behind the Potter Legend: J. K. Rowling Talks About How She Created the *Harry Potter* Books and the Magic of *Harry Potter*'s World." *Sydney Morning Herald*, October 28, 2001. See http://www.accio-quote.org/articles/2001/1001-sydney-renton.htm.

3. "Magic, Mystery, and Mayhem: An Interview with J. K. Rowling." Amazon.com, early spring 1999.

4. Crawford, Brad. "J. K. Rowling: On Setting Priorities—J. K. Rowling Discusses Her Influences, Secrets About Harry Potter, and How She Makes Writing a Priority." *Writer's Digest*, February 2000.

5. "Magic, Mystery, Mayhem."

Chapter One: Narrative Drive and Genre: Why We Keep Turning the Pages
1. Anelli, Melissa, and Emerson Spartz. "The Leaky Cauldron and MuggleNet interview Joanne Kathleen Rowling: Part Two,"

The Leaky Cauldron, July 16, 2005. See http://www.accio-quote .org/articles/2005/0705-tlc_mugglenet-anelli-2.htm.

2. Gerritsen, Tess. "No romance, please. We're mystery readers." February 24, 2007. See http://tessgerritsen.com/blog/2007/02/.

3. I am indebted in this discussion to John G. Cawelti's *Adventure, Mystery, and Romance: Formula Stories as Art and Popular Culture* (University of Chicago Press, 1977). I urge the reader to read his brilliant exposition of the cultural and psychological factors that fostered the formula and success of detection fiction in the nineteenth and twentieth centuries (chapter four, pp. 80–105) as well as his exploration of Christie and Sayers.

4. On detective fiction as moral literature, see W. H. Auden, "The Guilty Vicarage," in *The Dyer's Hand* (Vintage, 1948), pp. 146–158.

5. Wright, Willard Huntington. "Twenty Rules for Writing Detective Fiction," first published in the *American Magazine*, September 1928, and subsequently incorporated in the omnibus *Philo Vance Murder Cases* (1936). See http://www.sfu.ca/english/ Gillies/Engl38301/rules.htm; cited by David Stroud at http:// hogwartsprofessor.com/?p=457#comment-37190.

6. Ibid.

7. Sayers, Dorothy. "Gaudy Night," originally published in *Titles to Fame* (1937, ed. Denys Roberts), reprinted in *The Art of the Mystery Story* (New York: Carroll & Graf, 1992), pp. 208–209. See http:// www.sfu.ca/english/Gillies/Engl38301/sayquotes.htm; cited by David Stroud at http://hogwartsprofessor.com/?p=457#comment -37210.

8. Wright, "Twenty Rules for Writing Detective Fiction."

9. Sayers, "Gaudy Night."

10. Sayers, Dorothy. *Busman's Honeymoon*, cited in Barbara Reynolds's *Dorothy Sayers: Her Life and Soul* (St. Martin's, 1993), p. 270; thanks to Robert Trexler, editor of *CSL*, for this find.

11. Sayers, Dorothy. Private letter, cited in Barbara Reynolds's *Dorothy Sayers: Her Life and Soul*, p. 188.

12. Renton, "The Story Behind the Potter Legend."

13. Coleridge, Samuel Taylor. *Biographia Literaria* (New York: Harper & Brothers, 1868), Chapter 13.

Chapter Two: *Pride and Prejudice* with Wands

1. Rowling, J. K. "From Mr Darcy to Harry Potter by Way of Lolita." *Sunday Herald*, May 21, 2000; the transcript of JKR's statements for a BBC Radio4 show about famous people and their favorite books. See http://www.accio-quote.org/articles/2000/0500 -heraldsun-rowling.html.

2. Boquet, Tim. "J. K. Rowling: The Wizard Behind Harry Potter," *Reader's Digest*, December 2000. See http://www.accio-quote.org/ articles/2000/1200-readersdigest-boquet.htm.

3. Cf. Delasanta, Rodney, "Hume, Austen, and First Impressions," *First Things*, June/July 2003, pp. 24–29, http://www.firstthings .com/article.php3?id_article=502.

Chapter Three: Setting: The Familiar Stage and Scenery Props of the Drama

1. *Wikipedia: The Free Encyclopedia*, "*Enid Blyton.*" See http://en .wikipedia.org/wiki/Enid_blyton#Statistics.

2. Byatt, A. S. "Harry Potter and the Childish Adult." *The New York Times*, July 11, 2003. See http://www.accio-quote.org/ articles/2003/0711-nyt-byatt.html.

3. My discussion of the formula and specific elements of the school-boy novel and *Harry Potter* as an example of same is largely taken from my understanding of Karen Manners Smith's "Harry Potter's Schooldays: J. K. Rowling and the British Boarding School Novel," in *Reading Harry Potter: Critical Essays,* ed. Giselle Lisa Anatols (Greenwood Publishing/Praeger, 2003), pp. 69–88, and David K. Steege's "Harry Potter, Tom Brown, and the British School Story: Lost in Transit?" in *The Ivory Tower and Harry Potter,* ed. Lana A. Whited (University of Missouri Press, 2004), pp. 140–156.

4. Hattenstone, Simon. "Harry, Jessica and me," *The Guardian*, July 8, 2000. See http://www.accio-quote.org/articles/2000/0700-guardian -hattenstone.htm.

5. Renton, "Wild About Harry."

6. Mack, Edward C. (1941), quoted in John Reed, *Old School Ties: The Public School in British Literature* (New York: Syracuse University Press, 1964), p. 18; cited in Steege, "Harry Potter," p. 156.

7. Steege, "Harry Potter," pp. 143–145.

8. Smith, K., "Harry Potter's Schooldays," p. 74.

9. Ibid., p. 77.

10. Ibid., p. 78.

11. Ibid., p. 82.

12. Steege, "Harry Potter," p. 151.

13. Hughes, Thomas. *Tom Brown's Schooldays* (New York: Oxford University Press, World Classics, 1989), pp. 374–376.

14. Steege, "Harry Potter," p. 150.

15. Smith, K., "Harry Potter's Schooldays," pp. 69–88.

16. Ibid., p. 76.

17. Ibid., p. 77.

18. Hughes, from the preface to *Tom Brown's Schooldays.*

19. Simpson, Anne. "Face to Face with J. K. Rowling: Casting a Spell over Young Minds," *The Herald*, December 7, 1998. See http://www.accio-quote.org/articles/1998/1298-herald-simpson.html.

20. Grossman, Lev. "J. K. Rowling Hogwarts and All," *Time*, July 17, 2005. See http://www.accio-quote.org/articles/2005/0705-time-grossman.htm.

21. J. K. Rowling Official Site, FAQ section, "What Exactly Happened When Voldemort Used the Avada Kedavra Curse on Harry in the Forest?" See http://www.jkrowling.com/textonly/en/faq_view.cfm?id=122.

22. Edinburgh "cub reporter" press conference, ITV, July 16, 2005. See http://www.accio-quote.org/articles/2005/0705-edinburgh-ITVcubreporters.htm.

23. J. K. Rowling on "The Diane Rehm Show," WAMU Radio, Washington, D.C., October 20, 1999 (rebroadcast December 24, 1999). See http://www.accio-quote.org/articles/1999/1299-wamu-rehm.htm.

24. Lewis, C. S. *A Preface to Paradise Lost* (London: Oxford University Press, 1962), p. 55.

25. This was excerpted from an ITV press conference on July 6, 2005. The entire press conference can be seen at www.accio-quote.org/articles/2005/0705-edinburgh-ITVcubreporters.htm.

26. Bloom, Harold. "Can 35 Million Book Buyers Be Wrong? Yes,"

The Wall Street Journal, July 11, 2000. See http://www.accio-quote .org/articles/2000/0711-wsj-bloom.html.

Chapter Four: Gothic Romance: The Spooky Atmosphere Formula from Transylvania

1. My thanks to Dr. Amy H. Sturgis, Belmont University, for the distinction between real and late gothic preferred in the academy.

2. Tracy, Ann B. *Patterns of Fear in the Gothic Novel, 1790–1830* (New York: Ayer Company, 1980), pp. 8–16, 328.

3. Tracy, Ann B. "Gothic Romance," in *The Handbook to Gothic Literature,* ed. Marie Mulvey-Roberts (New York: New York University Press, 1998), p. 104.

4. Tracy, *Patterns of Fear in the Gothic Novel,* p. 316.

5. Ibid., pp. 315, 327.

6. Ibid., p. 315.

7. Ibid., p. 328.

8. Ibid., p. 326.

9. Sage, Victor. "Gothic Novel," in *The Handbook to Gothic Literature,* ed. by Marie Mulvey-Roberts (New York: New York University Press, 1998), p. 82.

10. "Living with Harry Potter." Interviewer: Stephen Fry from BBC Radio4 Broadcast, December 10, 2005. See http://www.accio -quote.org/articles/2005/1205-bbc-fry.html.

11. Correspondence with Dr. Amy H. Sturgis. "Ann Radcliffe, in her discussion of 'The Supernatural in Poetry': 'Terror and horror are so far opposite, that the first expands the soul, and awakens the faculties to a high degree of life; the other contracts, freezes, and nearly annihilates them. I apprehend, that neither Shakespeare nor

Milton by their fictions, nor Mr. Burke by his reasoning, anywhere looked to positive horror as a source of the sublime, though they all agree that terror is a very high one . . .'"

12. MacDonald, George. Preface to *The Letters from Hell* by Valdemar Adolph Thisted (New York: Funk and Wagnall's, 1887), pp. vi–vii, viii–ix. (Thanks to Robert Trexler.)

13. Sturgis, Dr. Amy H., ed. *The Magic Ring* by Baron de la Motte Fouque (Chicago: Valancourt Books, 2006), pp. 343–344.

Chapter Five: *Harry Potter* as Postmodern Epic

1. Goldschmidt, Rick. "Rudolph: Behind the Scenes." See http://www.tvparty.com/xmasrudolph.html.

2. See http://www.filespie.com/rudolph-the-red-nosed-reindeer/.

3. Grossman, "J. K. Rowling Hogwarts and All."

4. "Living with Harry Potter." sections of the following postmodern discussion are taken from *The Deathly Hallows Lectures* (Zossima Press, 2009) and used with permission.

5. Gibbs, Nancy. "Person of the Year 2007 . . . Runners-Up." *Time* 2008. See http://www.time.com/time/specials/2007/personof theyear/article/0,28804,1690753_1695388_1695436,00.html.

6. Vieira, Meredith. "Harry Potter: The Final Chapter." *Dateline* (NBC), July 29, 2007. See http://www.accio-quote.org/articles/2007/0729-dateline-vieira.html.

7. Grossman, "J. K. Rowling Hogwarts and All."

Chapter Six: The Satirical *Harry Potter*

1. Bloom, Allan, trans. *The Republic of Plato* (New York: Basic Books, 1965), p. 189.

2. Bloom, Allan, trans. *Plato's Republic* (New York: Basic Books, 1968), VII, 514a–520a, pp. 193–197; VI, 508e, p. 189.

3. Eliade, Mircea. *The Sacred and the Profane* (New York: Harvest Books: 1968), p. 205.

4. Johnston, Ian. "Lecture on Swift's *Gulliver's Travels*," (Nanaimo, B.C.: Malaspina University College, 1994). See http://records.viu .ca/~johnstoi/introser/swift.htm.

5. Ibid.

6. Lepore, Jill. "The Lion and the Mouse: The Battle That Reshaped Children's Literature," *The New Yorker*, "Lives and Letters," July 21, 2008. See http://www.newyorker.com/reporting/2008/07/21/ 080721fa_fact_lepore/?currentPage=all.

7. "Living with Harry Potter."

8. Gibbs, "Person of the Year."

9. Vieira, "Harry Potter."

10. "*Harry Potter* and Me." (BBC Christmas Special, British version), BBC, December 28, 2001. See http://www.accio-quote.org/ articles/2001/1201-bbc-hpandme.htm.

11. Solomon, Evan, moderator. "J. K. Rowling Interview," *CBCNews-World: Hot Type*, July 13, 2000. See http://www.accio-quote.org/ articles/2000/0700-hottype-solomon.htm.

12. UPI. "Rowling Donates $1.8 Million to Labor Party," September, 20, 2008. See http://www.upi.com/Entertainment _News/2008/09/20/Rowling_donates_18M_to_Labor_Party/ UPI-53161221945425/.

13. Olbermann, Keith. "Countdown with Keith Olbermann," October

22, 2007, updated October 24, 2007. See online transcript: http://
www.msnbc.msn.com/id/21456011/.

14. Cruz, Juan. "Ser invisible...eso sería lo más," *Edimburgo,* August 2,
2008. See http://www.elpais.com/articulo/cultura/Ser/invisible/
seria/elpepicul/20080208elpepicul_1/Tes; and see also http://www
.the-leaky-cauldron.org/2008/2/9/jkr-discusses-dursley-family
-religion-us-presidential-election-and-more-in-new-interview.

15. Solomon, "J. K. Rowling Interview."

16. *Telegraph,* U.K. "Harry Potter Lives in Thatcher's Britain," October
19, 2007. See http://www.telegraph.co.uk/news/worldnews/1567536/
%27Harry-Potter-lives-in-Thatcher%27s-Britain%27.html.

17. CNN. *"Harry Potter* Author: I Considered Suicide," March 23,
2008. See http://edition.cnn.com/2008/SHOWBIZ/03/23/rowling
.depressed/index.html. Jerry Bowyer notes (private correspondence, December 15, 2008): "Rowling is a deeply hurt lady. There's
a great deal of therapeutic material in her books: light to dispel devil's snare, humor to resist boggarts, happy images to dispel dementors, chocolate to recover. Clearly, she's had counseling. She's been
hurt, and she associates that hurt with the political right, I think."

18. Wyman, Max. "'You can lead a fool to a book but you can't make
them think': Author has frank words for the religious right," *The Van-
couver Sun* (British Columbia), October 26, 2000. See http://
www.accio-quote.org/articles/2000/1000-vancouversun-wyman
.htm.

19. Lumley, James. "J .K. Rowling Wins Appeal in Lawsuit Over
Child Photos," Bloomberg, May 7, 2008. See http://www
.bloomberg.com/apps/news?pid=20601102&sid=aFg6lRR9kmuw
&refer=uk.

20. J. K. Rowling at Carnegie Hall Reveals Dumbledore Is Gay; Neville Marries Hannah Abbott, and Much More, "Edward," *The Leaky Cauldron* (fan website transcript), October 20, 2007. See http://www.the-leaky-cauldron.org/2007/10/20/j-k-rowling-at-carnegie-hall-reveals-dumbledore-is-gay-neville-marries-hannah-abbott-and-scores-more/page/6.

21. Cf. Marjorie Hope Nicholson and Nora M. Mohler, "The Scientific Background of Swift's Voyage to Laputa," in *Science and Imagination*, ed. Marjorie Hope Nicholson (Cornell University Press), cited in *Gulliver's Travels*, ed. John Chalker (New York: Penguin Classics, 1985), p. 356 n. 25.

22. Claude Rawson. *Introduction to Gulliver's Travels* by Jonathan Swift (New York: Oxford University Press, 2005), p. xliv.

23. I neglect here the positive solutions Ms. Rowling offers within her satire of schools, media, and government in the Cave. I can do this because it is covered so well in Travis Prinzi's *Harry Potter and Imagination* (Zossima, 2008), especially the chapters on education and on the members of the Order of the Phoenix as Fabian Socialists, Ms. Rowling's proper political designation.

Chapter Seven: *Harry Potter* as an Everyman Allegory

1. Lewis, C. S. Letter to Ms. Hook, December 29, 1958, and *The Allegory of Love* (II), quoted in Walter Hooper's *C. S. Lewis: Companion and Guide* (New York: HarperSanFrancisco, 1996), p. 551.

2. Lepore, "The Lion and the Mouse."

3. Robertson, D. W., Jr. *A Preface to Chaucer: Studies in Medieval Perspective* (New Jersey: Princeton University Press, 1962), pp. 366–367.

4. Robertson, D. W., Jr. *Essays in Medieval Culture,* "The Allegorist and the Aesthetician" (New Jersey: Princeton University Press, 1980), pp. 99–100.

5. The allegorical meaning of the Chamber scene is explained in detail in "Harry Potter and the Inklings: The Christian Meaning of *The Chamber of Secrets,*" which I wrote in 2002. The article in its entirety is posted at http://www.george-macdonald.com/harry _potter_granger.htm.

6. The allegorical meaning of Harry's walk into the forest is given in step-by-step detail in chapter three of *The Deathly Hallows Lectures* (Zossima, 2008).

7. Bunyan, John. *The Pilgrim's Progress* (Chicago: Donohue, Henneberry, 1907), pp. 80–82.

8. Robertson, *Preface,* pp. 315–316.

9. See Bloomsbury.com. "J. K. Rowling and the Live Chat," July 30, 2007 (2:00–3:00P.M., BST).

10. See "Hagrid's Tale" (*Order of the Phoenix,* chapter twenty), "Elf Tails" (*Half-Blood Prince,* chapter nineteen), and "Kreacher's Tale" and "The Prince's Tale" (*Deathly Hallows,* chapter ten and chapter thirty-three), not to mention "The Tale of the Three Brothers" (*Deathly Hallows,* chapter twenty-one).

11. "The Tale of the Three Brothers" and the fates of Voldemort, Dumbledore, and Harry are obviously meant to be read in parallel. Voldemort dies as does the older brother because he is unworthy of the Death Stick, Dumbledore dies in a story echo of the second brother after he rashly tries to use the Resurrection Stone to see his late sister, and Harry's story is largely about his becoming the Unseen All Seeing-Eye/I beneath the Invisibility Cloak (about which, see chapter ten).

12. Robertson, *Preface*, p. 334.

13. Ibid.

14. From *The Idiot* (1868) the character speaking is Prince Myshkin the hero of the piece, who is, however, overexcited, naïve, and prone to epileptic fits, not unlike Dostoevsky: "Roman Catholicism is even worse than Atheism itself, in my opinion! Yes, that's my opinion! Atheism only preaches a negation, but Catholicism goes further: it preaches a distorted Christ, a Christ calumniated and defamed by themselves, the opposite of Christ! It preaches the Antichrist, I declare it does, I assure you it does!"

15. Not unlike the "emblems" and images in the "House of the Interpreter" Bunyan's Christian understands before being freed of his backpack loaded with sins in *Pilgrim's Progress*'s "Place of Deliverance."

16. Landow, George P. "Closing the Frame: Having Faith and Keeping Faith in Tennyson's 'The Passing of Arthur,'" *Bulletin of the John Rylands University Library of Manchester* 56 (1974), 423–442. Cited in "The Passing of Arthur" and "In Memoriam."

17. See http://bulfinch.englishatheist.org/idylls/chapter12.html.

18. Vieira, "Harry Potter."

19. Ruskin, John. *The Queen of the Air* (New York: John Wiley and Sons, 1873), pp. 15–18.

Chapter Eight: The Magical Center of the Circle

1. Ruskin, *The Queen of the Air*, pp. 15–18.

2. Cited at http://en.wikiquote.org/wiki/Mark_Twain#Education.

3. Lewis, C. S. *The Literary Impact of the Authorised Version*. The Ethel

M. Wood Lecture delivered before the University of London on March 20, 1950 (London: The Athlone Press, 1950), p. 26.

4. Lings, Martin. *Shakespeare's Window into the Soul: The Mystical Wisdom in Shakespeare's Characters* (New York: Inner Traditions, 2006), pp. 193–195.

5. Gilson, Nancy. "A Fantastic Success for J. K. Rowling," *Columbus Dispatch* (Ohio), October 28, 1999. See http://www.accio-quote.org/articles/1999/1099-columbusdisp-gilson.html.

6. Fraser, Lindsay. "Harry Potter—Harry and Me," *The Scotsman*, November 2002. See http://www.accio-quote.org/articles/2002/1102-fraser-scotsman.html.

7. America Online chat transcript. AOL.com, October 19, 2000. See http://www.accio-quote.org/articles/2000/1000-aol-chat.htm.

8. J. K. Rowling at the Edinburgh Book Festival, Sunday, August 15, 2004. See http://www.accio-quote.org/articles/2004/0804-ebf.htm.

9. Prinzi, Travis. "Dumbledore, the Order of the Phoenix, and the Fabian Society," June 2006; Prinzi credits David Colbert (*Magical Worlds of Harry Potter*) for spotting the Fabian Society/Order of the Phoenix name and garb connection. See http://thehogshead.org/fabian-society-post/.

10. Quoted in Cutsinger, James. *That Man Might Become God: Lectures on Christian Theology.* Unpublished, p. 48: available at www.cutsinger.net.

11. Adler, Shawn. "*Harry Potter* Author J. K. Rowling Opens Up About Books' Christian Imagery," MTV.com, October, 17, 2007. See http://www.mtv.com/news/articles/1572107/20071017/index.jhtml. See also: http://hogwartsprofessor.com/?p=196.

12. Burnett, Frances Hodgson. "Mrs. Burnett Not a Christian Scientist,"

Chicago Post, April 10, 1909; cited in Gerzina, *Frances Hodgson Burnett*, p. xxvii. This 1909 article is a statement by Burnett; it is cited in *The Annotated Secret Garden*, ed. Gretchen Holbrook Gerzina (New York: W. W. Norton, 2007), and printed in full in *The Secret Garden: A Norton Critical Edition*, ed. Gretchen Holbrook Gerzia (New York: W. W. Norton, 2006) pp. 249–250.

Chapter Nine: *Harry Potter* as Alchemical Reading Magic

1. Simpson, Anne. "Face-to-Face with J. K. Rowling: Casting a Spell Over Young Minds," *The Herald*, December 7, 1991. See http://www.accio-quote.org/articles/1998/1298-herald-simpson.html.

2. Much of what follows is based on the three chapters of *Unlocking Harry Potter* (Zossima, 2007) that explore literary alchemy in depth and from the chapter in *The Deathly Hollows Lectures* (Zossima, 2008) devoted to that book's intricate and involved alchemical artistry. Readers wanting to lean more about the subject should go to these books first.

3. Cf. Stanton J. Linden's *Darke Hieroglyphicks: Alchemy in English Literature from Chaucer to the Restoration* (University of Kentucky Press, 1998); Lyndy Abraham's *A Dictionary of Alchemical Imagery* (Cambridge University Press, 1998); *Cauda Pavonis*, an academic journal devoted to literary alchemy; and an alchemical website: See http://www.levity.com/alchemy/index.html.

4. Eliade, *The Sacred and the Profune*, p. 149.

5. See Jean Paris's "The Alchemistic Theatre" in her *Shakespeare* (Grove Press, 1960) pp. 87–116, and Martin Lings, *The Secret of Shakespeare* (Inner Traditions, 1984).

6. Abraham, *Dictionary of Alchemical Imagery*, p. 135.

7. Ibid., p. 5.

8. Ibid., p. 174.

9. Haeffner, Mark. *Dictionary of Alchemy* (Inner Traditions, 1994), p. 147.

10. Cowell, Alan. "All Aboard the Potter Express," *New York Times*, July 10, 2000. See http://www.accio-quote.org/articles/2000/0700 -nyt-cowell.htm.

11. Smith, Sean. *J. K. Rowling: A Biography* (London: Michael O'Meara Books, 2003), pp. 87–88. Similarly, Mcginty, Stephen. "The J. K. Rowling Story," *The Scotsman*, June 16, 17, 18, 2003. See http://www.accio-quote.org/articles/2003/0616-scotsman -mcginty.html. See also John Granger's "Tale of Two Cities: Why We Should Expect a Beheading in *Deathly Hallows*." See http:// hogwartsprofessor.com/?p=89.

Chapter Ten: The Secret of the Mirror and the Seeing Eye

1. Renton, "The Story Behind the Potter Legend."

2. Fraser, "Harry Potter—Harry and Me."

3. This is a much-abridged version of *The Deathly Hallows Lectures*, chapter four, "Snape's Green-Eyed Girl," used with permission of Zossima Press.

4. The following discussion of the Eye in the Mirror is a much-abridged version of chapter five, "The Seeing Eye," in *The Deathly Hallows Lectures* and used with permission of Zossima Press.

5. From an interview in *El País* from February 2008. See http://www .the-leaky-cauldron.org/2008/2/9/jkr-discusses-dursley-family -religion-us-presidential-election-and-more-in-new-interview.

6. Lewis, C. S. *Surprised by Joy: The Shape of My Early Life* (New York: Harcourt, Brace, Jovanovich, 1955), pp. 208–209.

7. Lewis, C. S. "The Seeing Eye," in *Essay Collection* (Toronto: Harper-Collins, 2003), chapter 8, pp. 58–65.

8. Lewis, C. S. *The Last Battle* (New York: HarperCollins, 2002), chapter 13, pp. 176–77.

9. The *Chronicles of Narnia* and *The Lord of the Rings*; the latter is often described as a "trilogy," though it is six books, often published as three. With *The Hobbit* as prequel, it is a seven-book epic.

10. Adler, "*Harry Potter* Author J. K. Rowling Opens Up."

11. Mendelsohn, Farah. "The Portal-Quest Fantasy," in *Rhetorics of Fantasy* (Middletown, Connecticut: Wesleyan, 2008), chapter 1, p. 1.

12. All Tolkien/Rowling echoes courtesy of Maureen Lamson in comments at Hogwarts Professor, my weblog: http://hogwartsprofessor .com/?p=462#comment-37322.

13. CSL: The Bulletin of the New York C. S. Lewis Society, "Harry Potter Is a Hobbit." May/June, 2004, Vol. 35, No. 3, pp. 1–12. See http://www.prpc-stl.org/auto_images/1183926416harry_is_a _hobbit.pdf.

14. All Tolkien/Rowling echoes courtesy of Maureen Lamson in comments at Hogwarts Professor, my weblog: http://hogwartsprofessor .com/?p=462#comment-37322.

15. Electronic Telegraph, August 2, 1997. See http://www.accio-quote. org/articles/1997/0897-telegraph-dunn.html. All Rowling quotations and sources about Narnia and C. S. Lewis that follow are taken from Maureen Lamson's response to a post at HogwartsProfessor .com: http://hogwartsprofessor.com/?p=462#comment-37322.

16. Williams, Rhys. "The Spotty Schoolboy and Single Mother Tak-

ing the Mantle from Roald Dahl," *The Independent* (London), January 29, 1999. See http://www.accio-quote.org/articles/1999/0199-independent-williams.html.

17. Electronic Telegraph, July 25, 1998. See http://www.accio-quote.org/articles/1998/0798-telegraph-bertodano.html.

18. Barnes and Noble interview, March 19, 1999. See http://www.accio-quote.org/articles/1999/0399-barnesandnoble.html.

19. Blakeney, Sally. "The Golden Fairytale," *The Australian*, November 7, 1998. See http://www.accio-quote.org/articles/1998/1198-australian-blakeney.html.

20. ITV, July 16, 2005. See http://www.accio-quote.org/articles/2005/0705-edinburgh-ITVcubreporters.htm.

21. Grossman, "J. K. Rowling Hogwarts and All."

22. As seen in McGillis, Roderick (ed.). *George MacDonald: Literary Heritage and Heirs* (Wayne, Pennsylvania: Zossima Press, 2008), pp. 235–236.

Bibliography

Abraham, Lyndy. *A Dictionary of Alchemical Imagery*. Cambridge: Cambridge University Press, 1998.

Aeschylus. *The Oresteian Trilogy*. Translated by Philip Vellacott. Baltimore: Penguin, 1974.

Anatols, Giselle Lisa, ed. *Reading Harry Potter: Critical Essays*. Westport, Connecticut: Greenwood Publishing (Praeger), 2003.

Anelli, Melissa, and Emerson Spartz. "The Leaky Cauldron and MuggleNet interview Joanne Kathleen Rowling: Part Two," *The Leaky Cauldron*, July 16, 2005, http://www.accio-quote.org/articles/2005/0705-tlc_mugglenet-anelli-2.htm.

Ariosto, Ludovico. *Orlando Furioso*. Translated by Guido Waldman. New York: Oxford University Press, 1991.

Auden, W. H. *The Dyer's Hand*. New York: Vintage, 1948 (especially "The Guilty Vicarage," pp. 146–158).

Austen, Jane. *Emma*. Vol. IV: *The Oxford Illustrated Jane Austen*. New York: Oxford University Press, 1988.

Baird Hardy, Elizabeth. *Milton, Spenser, and The Chronicles of Narnia: Literary Sources for the C. S. Lewis Novels*. Jefferson, North Carolina: McFarland, 2007.

Barfield, Owen. *What Coleridge Thought*. Middletown, Connecticut: Wesleyan University Press, 1971.

Battistini, Matilde. *Astrology, Magic, and Alchemy in Art*. Translated by Rosanna M. Giammanco Frongia. Los Angeles: Getty Publications, 2007.

Bloom, Allan (trans.). *Plato's Republic*. New York: Basic Books, 1968.

————. *The Republic of Plato*. New York: Basic Books, 1965.

Bloom, Harold. *The Western Canon: The Books and Schools of the Ages*. Orlando, Florida: Harcourt Brace, 1994.

Booth, Wayne C. *The Rhetoric of Fiction* (Second Edition). Chicago: University of Chicago Press, 1983.

Borella, Jean. *The Secret of the Christian Way: A Contemplative Ascent Through the Writings of Jean Borella*. Translated and edited by G. John Champoux. Albany: State University of New York Press, 2001.

Brontë, Charlotte. *Jane Eyre*. New York: Penguin Classics, 2006.

Brontë, Emily. *Wuthering Heights*. New York: Puffin Classics, 1990.

Bunyan, John. *The Pilgrim's Progress*. Chicago: Donohue, Henneberry, 1907.

Burckhardt, Titus. *Alchemy: Science of the Cosmos, Science of the Soul*. Translated by William Stoddart. Baltimore: Penguin, 1972.

————. *Mirror of the Intellect: Essays on Traditional Science and Sacred Art*. Translated and edited by William Stoddart. Cambridge: Quinta Essentia, 1982.

————. *The Annotated Secret Garden*. Edited by Gretchen Holbrook Gerzia. New York: W. W. Norton, 2007.

Burnett, Frances Hodgson. *A Little Princess*. New York: Platt & Munk, 1981.

————. *The Secret Garden*. Stamford, Connecticut: Longmeadow Press, 1987.

————. *The Secret Garden: A Norton Critical Edition*. Edited by Gretchen Holbrook Gerzia. New York: W. W. Norton, 2006.

Byatt, A. S. "Harry Potter and the Childish Adult." *The New York Times*, July 11, 2003. http://www.accio-quote.org/articles/2003/0711-nyt-byatt.html.

Cahoone, Lawrence (ed.). *From Modernism to Postmodernism: An Anthology*. Malden, Massachusetts: Blackwell, 2001.

Carroll, Lewis. *Alice's Adventures in Wonderland* and *Through the Looking-Glass*. New York: Barnes & Noble, 2004.

_____. *The Annotated Alice: The Definitive Edition*. Introduction and Notes by Martin Gardner. New York: W. W. Norton, 2000.

Cawelti, John G. *Adventure, Mystery, and Romance: Formula Stories as Art and Popular Culture*. Chicago: University of Chicago Press, 1977.

Chaucer, Geoffrey. *The Riverside Chaucer*. Edited by Larry D. Benson. Boston: Houghton Mifflin, 1987.

Chesterton, G. K. "A Defence of Penny Dreadfuls" (From *The Defendant*), published in *The Wayfarer's Library*. London: J. M. Dent and Sons, Ltd., 1901.

Christie, Agatha. *Murder at the Vicarage*. New York: Black Dog and Leventhal, 2006.

_____. *The Mysterious Affair at Styles*. New York: Black Dog and Leventhal, 2006.

Coleridge, Samuel Taylor. *Aids to Reflection*. New York: Chelsea House, 1983.

_____. *Biographia Literaria*. Vol. III: *The Complete Works of Samuel Taylor Coleridge*. New York: Harper & Brothers, 1868.

Cutsinger, James. *The Form of the Transformed Vision: Coleridge and the Knowledge of God*. Macon, Georgia: Mercer, 1987.

_____. *That Man Might Become God: Lectures on Christian Theology*. Unpublished: available at www.cutsinger.net.

Dante, Alighieri. *The Divine Comedy*. Translated by Henry Cary and edited by Ralph Pite. Rutland, Vermont: Everyman, 1994.

_____. *The Divine Comedy 1: Hell*. Translated by Dorothy Sayers. Baltimore: Penguin, 1975.

_____. *The Divine Comedy 2: Purgatorio*. Translated with commentary by John D. Sinclair. New York: Oxford University Press, 1967.

_____. *The Divine Comedy 2: Purgatory*. Translated by Dorothy Sayers. Baltimore: Penguin, 1975.

_____. *The Divine Comedy 3: Paradise*. Translated by Dorothy Sayers. Baltimore: Penguin, 1975.

Delasanta, Rodney. "Hume, Austen, and First Impressions." *First Things*, June/July 2003; available online at http://www.firstthings.com/article.php3?id_article=502.

Dickens, Charles. *A Tale of Two Cities*. Garden City, New York: Nelson Doubleday, 1978.

_____. *A Tale of Two Cities*. London: The Folio Society, 1985.

Dostoevsky, Fyodor. *The Brothers Karamazov*. Translated by Constance Garnett. New York: Barnes & Noble, 2004.

Duriez, Colin. *Field Guide to Harry Potter*. Downer's Grove, Illinois: Inter-Varsity Books, 2007.

Eliade, Mircea. *The Forge and the Crucible: The Origins and Structures of Alchemy* (Second Edition). Translated by Stephen Corrin. Chicago: University of Chicago Press, 1978.

_____. *Myth of the Eternal Return*. Princeton: Princeton University Press, 1971.

_____. *The Sacred and the Profane*. New York: Harvest Books, 1968.

Forde, Jasper. *The Eyre Affair*. New York: Penguin, 2003.

Foster, Thomas C. *How to Read Literature Like a Professor*. New York: Quill/HarperCollins, 2003.

Fraser, George MacDonald. *Flashman: A Novel*. New York: Plume, 1984.

Freud, Clement. *Grimble*. London: Puffin Books, 1974.

Frye, Northrop. *Anatomy of Criticism: Four Essays*. Princeton: Princeton University Press, 1957.

_____. *The Double Vision: Language and Meaning in Religion*. Toronto: University of Toronto Press, 1991.

Gager, Valerie L. *Shakespeare and Dickens: The Dynamics of Influence*. New York: Cambridge University Press, 1996.

Gallico, Paul. *Manxmouse*. New York: G. P. Putnam's Sons, 1968.

Gerzina, Gretchen Holbrook. *Frances Hodgson Burnett: The Unexpected Life of the Author of The Secret Garden*. Piscataway, New Jersey: Rutgers University Press, 2004.

Goldschmidt, Rick. *Rudolph the Red-Nosed Reindeer: The Making of the Rankin-Bass Holiday Classic*. Bridgeview, Illinois: Miser Bros. Press, 2001.

Goudge, Elizabeth. *The Little White Horse*. New York: Puffin Books, 2001.

Granger, John. *The Deathly Hallows Lectures: The Hogwarts Professor Explains Harry's Final Adventure*. Allentown, Pennsylvania: Zossima Press, 2008.

_____. *How Harry Cast His Spell: The Meaning Behind the Mania for J. K. Rowling's Bestselling Books* (Third Edition). Carol Stream, Illinois: Tyndale, 2008.

_____. *Unlocking Harry Potter: Five Keys for the Serious Reader*. Wayne, Pennsylvania: Zossima Press, 2007.

Guenon, Rene. *The Esoterism of Dante*. Translated by C. D. Bethell. Ghent, New York: Sophia Perennis, 1996.

_____. *Fundamental Symbols: The Universal Language of Sacred Science*. Compiled and edited by Michel Valsan, translated by Alvin Moore, Jr., revised and edited by Martin Lings. Cambridge: Quinta Essentia, 1995.

_____. *Symbolism of the Cross*. Translated by Angus McNab. London: Luzac, 1975.

Haeffner, Mark. *Dictionary of Alchemy: From Maria Prophetissa to Isaac Newton*. San Francisco: Aquarian Harper, 1991.

Hamilton, Edith, and Huntington Cairns (eds.). *The Collected Dialogues of Plato*. Princeton: Princeton University Press, 1978.

Hogle, Jerrold E., ed. *The Cambridge Companion to Gothic Fiction*. New York: Cambridge University Press, 2002.

Honan, Park. *Jane Austen: Her Life*. New York: St. Martin's, 1987.

Hooper, Walter. *C. S. Lewis: Companion and Guide*. New York: Harper, 1996.

Hughes, Thomas. *Tom Brown's Schooldays*. New York: Oxford University Press, 1989.

Jacobs, Alan. *The Narnian: The Life and Imagination of C. S. Lewis*. New York: Harper, 2005.

Johnston, Ian. "Lecture on Swift's *Gulliver's Travels*" (unpublished), Malaspina University-College, Nanaimo, B.C., 1994. Available online at http://records.viu.ca/~johnstoi/introser/swift.htm.

Klossoswki de Rola, Stanislas. *The Golden Game: Alchemical Engravings of the Seventeenth Century*. New York: Thames & Hudson, 1997.

Lattimore, Richmond (trans.). *The Iliad of Homer*. Chicago: University of Chicago Press, 1961.

_____. *The Odyssey of Homer*. New York: Harper Colophon, 1967.

Lewis, C. S. *The Discarded Image: An Introduction to Medieval and Renaissance Literature*. Cambridge: Canto, 1994.

_____. *English Literature in the Sixteenth Century Excluding Drama*. New York: Oxford University Press, 1954.

_____. *Essay Collection*. Toronto: Harper Collins, 2003.

_____. *An Experiment in Criticism*. Cambridge: Cambridge University Press, 1961.

_____. *The Last Battle: Book 7 of the Chronicles of Narnia*. New York: HarperCollins, 2002.

_____. *Literary Impact of the Authorized Version*. London: The Athlone Press, 1950.

_____. *Perelandra: A Novel*. New York: Collier Books, 1965.

_____. *A Preface to Paradise Lost*. London: Oxford University Press, 1962.

_____. *The Problem of Pain*. New York: Macmillan, 1970. p. 162

_____. *Surprised by Joy: The Shape of My Early Life*. New York: Harcourt, Brace, Jovanovich, 1955.

_____. *That Hideous Strength*. New York: Collier Books, 1946.

Linden, Stanton J. *Darke Hieroglyphicks: Alchemy in English Literature from Chaucer to the Restoration*. Lexington: University of Kentucky Press, 1996.

Lings, Martin. *The Secret of Shakespeare*. New York: Inner Traditions, 1984.

————. *Shakespeare's Window into the Soul: The Mystical Wisdom in Shakespeare's Characters*. New York: Inner Traditions, 2006.

MacDonald, George. Preface to *The Letters from Hell*, Valdemar Adolph Thisted. New York: Funk and Wagnalls, 1887.

Maguire, Gregory. *Wicked: The Life and Times of the Wicked Witch of the West*. New York: Harper Fiction, 2007.

McGillis, Roderick (ed.). *George MacDonald: Literary Heritage and Heirs*. Wayne, Pennsylvania: Zossima Press, 2008.

Mendelsohn, Farah. *Rhetorics of Fantasy*. Middletown, Connecticut: Wesleyan University Press, 2008.

Meyer, Stephenie. *Twilight*. New York: Little, Brown, 2005.

Mulvey-Roberts, Marie (ed.). *The Handbook of Gothic Literature*. New York: New York University Press, 1998.

Nel, Philip. "Harry's Language: The Transfiguration of Words." In *The Ivory Tower and Harry Potter*, ed. Lana A. Whited, pp. 261–285. St. Louis: University of Missouri Press, 2004.

Nesbit, E. *E. Nesbit: 7 Books in 1*. London: Shoes and Ships and Sealing Wax, Ltd., 2004.

Paris, Jean. *Shakespeare*. New York: Grove Press, 1960.

Penn, William. *Some Fruits of Solitude/More Fruits of Solitude*. Rockville, Maryland: Wildside Press, 2007.

Poe, Edgar Allan. *The Tell-Tale Heart and Other Writings*. New York: Bantam Classics, 1983.

Prinzi, Travis. *Harry Potter and Imagination: The Way Between Two Worlds*. Allentown, Pennsylvania: Zossima Press, 2008.

Rankin, Arthur (producer), & Larry Roemer (director), 1964. *Rudolph the Red-Nosed Reindeer* (VHS). Available from Amazon.com at http://www.amazon.com/Rudolph-Red-Nosed-Reindeer-Burl-Ives/dp/B00005M2FD/ref=sr_1_12?ie=UTF8&s=video&qid=12354071 31&sr=8-12.

Reed, John. *Old School Ties: The Public School in British Literature.* Syracuse, New York: Syracuse University Press, 1964.

Reynolds, Barbara. *Dorothy Sayers: Her Life and Soul.* New York: St. Martin's, 1993.

Rhys, Jean. *Wide Sargasso Sea.* New York: Popular Library, 1966.

Robertson, D. W., Jr. *Essays in Medieval Culture.* Princeton: Princeton University Press, 1980.

————. *A Preface to Chaucer: Studies in Medieval Perspectives.* Princeton: Princeton University Press, 1962.

Rowling, J. K. "From Mr Darcy to Harry Potter by Way of Lolita." *Sunday Herald,* May 21, 2000. http://www.accio-quote.org/articles/2000/0500-heraldsun-rowling.html.

————. *Harry Potter and the Chamber of Secrets.* New York: Arthur Levine Books, 1998.

————. *Harry Potter and the Deathly Hallows.* New York: Arthur Levine Books, 2007.

————. *Harry Potter and the Goblet of Fire.* New York: Arthur Levine Books, 2000.

————. *Harry Potter and the Half-Blood Prince.* New York: Arthur Levine Books, 2005.

————. *Harry Potter and the Order of the Phoenix.* New York: Arthur Levine Books, 2003.

————. *Harry Potter and the Prisoner of Azkaban.* New York: Arthur Levine Books, 1999.

————. *Harry Potter and the Sorcerer's Stone.* New York: Arthur Levine Books, 1998.

Ruskin, John. *The Queen of the Air.* New York: John Wiley and Sons, 1873.

Sage, Victor. "Gothic Novel." In *The Handbook to Gothic Literature,* ed. Marie Mulvey-Roberts. New York: New York University Press, 1998, p. 82.

Sayers, Dorothy. "Busman's Honeymoon," cited in Barbara Reynolds's *Dorothy Sayers: Her Life and Soul*, p. 270. New York: St. Martin's, 1993.

_____. "Gaudy Night." Originally published in *Titles to Fame* (1937, ed. Denys Roberts), reprinted in *The Art of the Mystery Story*, New York: Carroll & Graf, 1992 (pp.208–209), cf. http://www.sfu.ca/english/Gillies/Engl38301/sayquotes.htm; cited by David Stroud at http://hogwartsprofessor.com/?p=457#comment-37210.

_____. *Introductory Papers on Dante*. Vol. I: *The Poet Alive in His Writings*. Eugene, Oregon: Wipf & Stock, 2006.

_____. *Lord Peter*. New York: Avon, 1972.

_____. "The Omnibus of Crime." Originally published in *Great Short Stories of Detection, Mystery, and Horror* (1928), reprinted in *The Art of the Mystery Story*, New York: Carroll & Graf, 1992 (p. 104).

_____. Private letter, cited in Barbara Reynolds's *Dorothy Sayers: Her Life and Soul*, p.188 New York: St. Martin's, 1993.

Schlike, Paul. "Dickens and Shakespeare" (unpublished), Aberdeen, Scotland: University of Aberdeen. Available online at http://wwwsoc.nii.ac.jp/dickens/archive/general/g-schlicke.pdf.

Schuon, Frithjof. *The Eye of the Heart: Metaphysics, Cosmology, Spiritual Life*. Bloomington, Indiana: World Wisdom Books, 1997.

_____. *Logic and Transcendence*. Edited and translated by James Cutsinger. Bloomington, Indiana: World Wisdom, 2008.

Shakespeare. *The Riverside Shakespeare*. Edited by G. Blakemore Evans. Boston: Houghton Mifflin, 1974.

_____. *Romeo and Juliet: The Pelican Shakespeare*. Edited by John Hankins. New York: Penguin, 1985.

Shelley, Mary W. *Frankenstein*. New York: Penguin Classics, 2003.

Smith, Frederik N. *The Genres of Gulliver's Travels*. Wilmington: University of Delaware Press, 1990.

Smith, Karen Manners. "Harry Potter's Schooldays: J. K. Rowling and the British Boarding School Novel." In *Reading Harry Potter: Critical*

Essays, ed. Giselle Lisa Anatols, pp. 69–88. (Westport, Connecticut: Greenwood Publishing (Praeger), 2003.

Smith, Sean. *J. K. Rowling: A Biography.* London: Michael O'Meara Books, 2003.

Steege, David K. "Harry Potter, Tom Brown, and the British School Story: Lost in Transit?" In *The Ivory Tower and Harry Potter,* ed. Lana A. Whited, pp. 140–156. St. Louis: University of Missouri Press, 2004.

Stevenson, Robert Louis. *The Strange Case of Dr. Jekyll and Mr. Hyde: And Other Tales of Terror.* New York: Penguin Classics, 2003.

Stoker, Bram. *Dracula.* New York: Barnes & Noble Classics, 1998.

————. *The Essential Dracula.* Edited by Leonard Wolf. New York: Plume/Penguin, 1993.

Strauss, Leo. *Persecution and the Art of Writing.* Chicago: University of Chicago Press, 1988.

Streatfield, Noel. *Ballet Shoes.* New York: Random House, 1937.

Sturgis, Dr. Amy H., ed. *The Magic Ring* by Baron de la Motte Fouque. Chicago: Valancourt Books, 2006.

Swift, Jonathan. *Gulliver's Travels.* Edited by John Chalker. New York: Penguin Classics, 1985.

————. *Gulliver's Travels.* Introduction by Claude Rawson. New York: Oxford World's Classics (Oxford University Press), 2005.

————. *Gulliver's Travels: A Norton Critical Edition.* Edited by Albert J. Rivero. New York: W. W. Norton, 2002.

Symonds, John. *The Lady with the Magic Eyes: Madame Blavatsky, Medium and Magician.* Whitefish, Montana: Kessinger Publishing, 2006.

Thomas, James. *Repotting Harry Potter: A Professor's Book-by-Book Guide for the Serious Re-Reader.* Allentown, Pennsylvania: Zossima Press, 2008.

Thwait, Ann. *Waiting for the Party: The Life of Frances Hodgson Burnett, 1849–1924.* New York: Charles Scribner's Sons, 1974.

Tillyard, E. M. W. *The Elizabethan World Picture: A Study of the Idea of*

Order in the Age of Shakespeare, Donne, and Milton. New York: Vintage, 1959.

Todorov, Tzvetan. *The Fantastic: A Structural Approach to a Literary Genre*. Translated from the French by Richard Howard. Ithaca, New York: Cornell University Press, 1993.

Tracy, Ann Blaisdell. "Gothic Romance." In *The Handbook to Gothic Literature,* ed. Marie Mulvey-Roberts, p. 104. New York: New York University Press, 1998.

_____. *Patterns of Fear in the Gothic Novel, 1790–1830*. New York: Ayer Publishing, 1980.

Virgil. *Aeneid*. Translated by Robert Fitzgerald. New York: Random House, 1983.

Ward, Michael. *Planet Narnia: The Seven Heavens in the Imagination of C. S. Lewis*. Oxford: Oxford University Press, 2007.

Whited, Lana A., ed. *The Ivory Tower and Harry Potter*. St. Louis: University of Missouri Press, 2004.

Williams, Anne. *Art of Darkness: A Poetics of Gothic*. Chicago: University of Chicago Press, 1995.

Williams, Charles. *The Figure of Beatrice: A Study in Dante*. Berkeley, California: Apocryphile Press, 2005.

Wright, Willard Huntington. "Twenty Rules for Writing Detective Fiction." First published in the *American Magazine* for September 1928 and was subsequently incorporated in the omnibus *Philo Vance Murder Cases* (1936). http://www.sfu.ca/english/Gillies/Engl38301/rules.htm; cited by David Stroud at http://hogwartsprofessor.com/?p=457#comment-37190.

Yates, Frances A. *The Art of Memory*. Chicago: University of Chicago Press, 1974.

_____. *Giordano Bruno and the Hermetic Tradition*. Chicago: University of Chicago Press, 1979.

Thank you for joining me on this fire-hose tour of English literature and *Harry Potter*. Please write to me at my e-mail address john@Hog wartsProfessor.com. Or you can just jump into the conversation at www.HogwartsProfessor.com. Either way, I look forward to hearing from you and continuing the conversation we started here.